Lucky 73

NEW PERSPECTIVES ON MARITIME HISTORY AND NAUTICAL ARCHAEOLOGY

UNIVERSITY PRESS OF FLORIDA

Florida A&M University, Tallahassee
Florida Atlantic University, Boca Raton
Florida Gulf Coast University, Ft. Myers
Florida International University, Miami
Florida State University, Tallahassee
New College of Florida, Sarasota
University of Central Florida, Orlando
University of Florida, Gainesville
University of North Florida, Jacksonville
University of South Florida, Tampa
University of West Florida, Pensacola

Eight Thousand Years of Maltese Maritime History: Trade, Piracy, and Naval Warfare in the Central Mediterranean, by Ayşe Devrim Atauz (2007)

Merchant Mariners at War: An Oral History of World War II, by George J. Billy and Christine M. Billy (2008)

The Steamboat Montana and the Opening of the West: History, Excavation, and Architecture, by Annalies Corbin and Bradley A. Rodgers (2008)

Attack Transport: USS Charles Carroll *in World War II*, by Kenneth H. Goldman (2008)

Diplomats in Blue: U.S. Naval Officers in China, 1922–1933, by William Reynolds Braisted (2009)

Sir Samuel Hood and the Battle of the Chesapeake, by Colin Pengelly (2009)

Voyages, The Age of Sail: Documents in Maritime History, Volume I, 1492–1865; Volume II: The Age of Engines, 1865–Present, edited by Joshua M. Smith and the National Maritime Historical Society (2009)

Voyages, The Age of Engines: Documents in Maritime History, Volume II, 1865–Present edited by Joshua M. Smith and the National Maritime Historical Society (2009)

H.M.S. Fowey *Lost . . . and Found!*, by Russell K. Skowronek and George R. Fischer (2009)

American Coastal Rescue Craft: A Design History of Coastal Rescue Craft Used by the United States Life-Saving Service and the United States Coast Guard, by William D. Wilkinson and Commander Timothy R. Dring, USNR (Retired) (2009)

The Spanish Convoy of 1750: Heaven's Hammer and International Diplomacy, by James A. Lewis (2009)

The Development of Mobile Logistic Support in Anglo-American Naval Policy 1900–1953, by Peter V. Nash (2009)

Captain "Hell Roaring" Mike Healy: From American Slave to Arctic Hero, by Dennis L. Noble and Truman R. Strobridge (2009)

Sovereignty at Sea: U.S. Merchant Ships and America's Entry into World War I, by Rodney Carlisle (2009)

Commodore Abraham Whipple of the Continental Navy: Privateer, Patriot, Pioneer, by Sheldon S. Cohen (2010)

Lucky 73: USS Pampanito's *Unlikely Rescue of Allied POWs in WWII*, by Aldona Sendzikas (2010)

Aldona Sendzikas

Foreword by James C. Bradford and Gene Allen Smith

University Press of Florida

Gainesville

Tallahassee

Tampa

Boca Raton

Pensacola

Orlando

Miami

Jacksonville

Ft. Myers

Sarasota

Lucky 73

USS *Pampanito*'s Unlikely Rescue
of Allied POWs in WWII

Copyright 2010 by Aldona Sendzikas
Printed in the United States of America. This book is printed on Glatfelter Natures Book, a paper
certified under the standards of the Forestry Stewardship Council (FSC). It is a recycled stock that
contains 30 percent post-consumer waste and is acid-free.

15 14 13 12 11 10   6 5 4 3 2 1

Library of Congress Cataloging-in-Publication Data
Sendzikas, Aldona.
Lucky 73: USS Pampanito's unlikely rescue of Allied POWs in WWII / Aldona Sendzikas; foreword
by James C. Bradford and Gene Allen Smith.
p. cm.—(New perspectives on maritime history and nautical archaeology)
Includes bibliographical references and index.
ISBN 978–0-8130-3427-0 (alk. paper)
1. Pampanito (Submarine) 2. World War, 1939–1945—Naval operations, American. 3. World
War, 1939–1945—Naval operations—Submarine. 4. World War, 1939–1945—Search and rescue
operations—Pacific Ocean. 5. United States. Navy—Search and rescue operations—Pacific Ocean—
History—20th century. 6. World War, 1939–1945—Prisoners and prisons, Japanese. 7. Prisoners
of war—Great Britain—History—20th century. 8. Prisoners of war—Australia—History—20th
century. 9. Prisoners of war—Japan—History—20th century. I. Title. II. Title: Lucky seventy three.
D783.5.P4S46 2010
940.54'72529–dc22   2009036026

Frontispiece: Australian War Memorial Negative Number 088958

The University Press of Florida is the scholarly publishing agency for the State University System
of Florida, comprising Florida A&M University, Florida Atlantic University, Florida Gulf Coast
University, Florida International University, Florida State University, New College of Florida,
University of Central Florida, University of Florida, University of North Florida, University
of South Florida, and University of West Florida.

University Press of Florida
15 Northwest 15th Street
Gainesville, FL 32611-2079
http://www.upf.com

Contents

Series Foreword ix

Preface xiii

Chronology of Key Events xxi

List of Abbreviations xxiii

1. The Sighting 1

2. USS *Pampanito* 16

3. The Fall of Singapore 34

4. The Burma-Thai Railroad 47

5. The Hellships 74

6. The Rescue 97

7. The POWs aboard the Subs 130

8. Saipan 158

9. Home 176

10. Looking Back 198

Epilogue 213

Notes 223

Bibliography 239

Index 251

Series Foreword

Water is unquestionably the most important natural feature on earth. By volume the world's oceans compose 99 percent of the planet's living space; in fact, the surface of the Pacific Ocean alone is larger than that of the total land bodies. Water is as vital to life as air. Indeed, to test whether the moon or other planets can sustain life, NASA looks for signs of water. The story of human development is inextricably linked to the oceans, seas, lakes, and rivers that dominate the earth's surface. The University Press of Florida's series "New Perspectives on Maritime History and Nautical Archaeology" is devoted to exploring the significance of the earth's water while providing lively and important books that cover the spectrum of maritime history and nautical archaeology broadly defined. The series includes works that focus on the role of canals, rivers, lakes, and oceans in history; on the economic, military, and political use of those waters; and upon the people, communities, and industries that support maritime endeavors. Limited by neither geography nor time, volumes in the series contribute to the overall understanding of maritime history and can be read with profit by both general readers and specialists.

The sea rarely reveals its secrets. Ships sink, to be lost forever; sailors perish, leaving family and friends to wonder about their fate. Even during the twentieth century, ships and sailors, like history, fall between the cracks of time, to be forgotten by all except those who participated. In this case, historian Aldona Sendzikas rediscovered a treasure trove of World War II documents, memoirs, and records that conveyed the little-known but heart-wrenching saga of the submarine USS *Pampanito* (SS-383), a vessel whose actions ultimately bound together Americans, Australians, and Britons in three days of terror.

Constructed at the Portsmouth Naval Shipyard, Portsmouth, New Hampshire, *Pampanito* appeared to be an ordinary vessel. One of 256 *Balao*-class submarines ordered during World War II—the largest class of submarines in U.S. history—she was laid down in March, launched in July, and commissioned in early November 1943. Crewed by approximately eighty officers and enlisted men, the submarine completed six war patrols in 1944 and 1945 and sunk six enemy ships.[1] In fact, *Pampanito* earned six battle stars for her distinctive World War II service.

During her third and most significant cruise, *Pampanito* operated in a wolf pack with two other submarines, *Sealion* (SS-215) and *Growler* (SS-315), in the South China Sea. On 12 September 1944 the three encountered a slow-moving column of Japanese ships. *Pampanito* torpedoed and sank two ships, the 10,509-ton transport *Kachidoki Maru* and 5,135-ton tanker *Zuiho Maru*, and damaged a third ship. Returning from pursuit of the Japanese column to the site of the original attack on 15 September, *Pampanito* discovered survivors clinging to anything that would float. As the submarine moved in closer, the American sailors heard the survivors yelling in

English—the survivors were Australian and British POWs being transported from Singapore to Japan to serve as slave labor for the Axis war effort. During the frantic rescue that followed, *Pampanito* saved 73 of the 2,218 Allied prisoners, while three other submarines picked up an additional 86 survivors, all of whom were taken to Saipan. *Pampanito* proceeded on to Pearl Harbor, and Sendzikas shifts her focus to describing the reception of the survivors in Saipan, their transfer to Australia, treatment there, and subsequent lives, including their connection to *Pampanito*.

Sendzikas's account documents more than an emotional story of the rescue of Australian and British POWs in the South China Sea during September 1944. It highlights Japanese brutality toward these prisoners—a brutality that was based in part on racial and nationalistic stereotypes. The survivors who boarded *Pampanito* recorded their experiences, and those preserved stories form the foundation of this account. Historians had not previously used these stories to describe this episode or to highlight the role of submarines in the South Pacific.

More important, this account represents a significant firsthand perspective that fleshes out the danger and emotion of this colorful story of the war in the South Pacific. It details *Pampanito*'s daring attack and rescue in the South China Sea, yet it also conveys the extent of human endurance and the compassion of the human spirit for those involved. The story reveals the overwhelming desire of British and Australian soldiers to survive and highlights the fortitude that kept some men alive. Ultimately, the *Pampanito*'s attack and subsequent rescue represents a story of wartime redemption in which U.S. submarines sunk POW ships and then saved a significant number of those ships' captives from almost certain death in prison work camps, thereby later becoming their savior, illustrating that seldom during wartime can events be described in stark black-and-white terms.

James C. Bradford and Gene Allen Smith
Series Editors

Preface

She looks very peaceful and quiet as she lies at her berth and very few who see her can imagine how different it was in her more active days. The name "*Pampanito*" means little to most people but to me it means the life I have now, and which she gave to me. The name will be remembered by me as long as that life lasts.

Bill McKittrick, POW rescued by *Pampanito*

My [first] impression of *Pampanito* was that this is a beautiful boat, this is going to be a great experience. . . . It could dive deep, it could run fast, it could carry a lot of torpedoes, it seemed like a great craft to be on. The men, it took a little while to become acquainted with them, but the more we got to know them the more we respected them and actually liked them. It became a very close bonding situation very early on and continued that way.

Gordon Hopper, *Pampanito* crew member

Floating peacefully in the waters of San Francisco Bay, at Pier 45 in the busy tourist district of Fisherman's Wharf, a World War II American submarine serves as one of the few reminders that the Bay Area was once a busy military center. USS *Pampanito*, restored to her 1945 appearance, now serves not as a warship but as a tourist attraction, a museum of history and technology, and a memorial to the men who served aboard her as well as the more than 3,500 American submariners who lost their lives during the course of the war. Serving on submarines was a dangerous business. Of the 288 American submarines that patrolled during the war, 52 were lost, victims of enemy fire or depth charges, of mines strategically laid by the enemy, and a couple even lost through a tragic "circular run" of one of their own torpedoes. One in five submariners did not return. Their shipmates refer to them as being "on eternal patrol." Most remain in the watery graves where they went down during the war, and have no tombstone or cemetery plot to mark their passing. For their family members, submarine memorials such as *Pampanito* must fulfill that function.

Ironically, *Pampanito* serves also as a reminder of the men that she, and other submarines, sent to their deaths. The main role of the U.S. submarine fleet during World War II was to attack and destroy enemy shipping. Indeed, the submarines, although comprising just 1.9 percent of U.S. naval strength, by war's end were responsible for 55 percent of Japanese shipping sunk—over five million tons. The crewmen of these torpedoed vessels also have no graves, just memorials such as *Pampanito* to mark their deaths.

The diesel-electric submarines of World War II, the precursors of nuclear submarines, were, technically speaking, submersibles rather than true submarines: designed for surface operation, they could submerge for limited periods of time, and traveled at a slower speed underwater. Even with a limited underwater capacity, these submarines proved to be versatile and useful vessels. While seeking and sinking enemy shipping was their main task, they also performed reconnaissance, transported troops and supplies, and laid mines.

Undoubtedly, one of their most rewarding tasks was lifeguard duty, in which a sub would be dispatched to a location where an Allied air raid was to take place, and ordered to stand by to rescue any downed aviators. More than five hundred American aviators owe their lives to submarines. And some submarines, including *Pampanito*, had the opportunity to rescue other survivors of the war as well.

Pampanito's battle flag tells her story. (The tradition of the submarine's crew designing and sewing a battle flag to "show off" their exploits and achievements began during World War II and has been continued up to the present by nuclear submarines returning from service in Afghanistan and Iraq.) The flags were made from whatever materials were available on board, then flown from the periscope or radar mast while returning to port. *Pampanito*'s battle flag (see p. xvi) features a caricature of the fish after which she was named; six red hash marks, representing the six war patrols she completed; and Japanese flags indicating her battle tally: six ships destroyed, an additional four damaged. The fish logo, the hash marks, the Japanese "kill flags": these were all fairly standard symbols found on the battle flags of the submarine fleet. But what distinguishes *Pampanito*'s flag is a large number "73," superimposed on a red cross. This symbol recalls *Pampanito*'s most famous, and her crew's proudest, achievement: the rescue of 73 Australian and British POWs from the South China Sea in September 1944. These men had been taken prisoner by the Japanese when Singapore fell in February 1942. After enduring two and a half years of imprisonment, including being forced to work on the construction of the Burma-Thai Railroad, in the fall of 1944 they were loaded onto transport ships and sent to Japan for further labor. The transports never reached Japan, however: en route to their destination they were torpedoed by a wolf pack of American

Pampanito's battle flag. Flown from the periscope shears when the sub returned from patrol, it boasted of the sub's achievements: six war patrols completed, six Japanese ships destroyed, four Japanese ships damaged, and 73 Allied POWs rescued. USS *Pampanito* (SS-383) Collection, San Francisco Maritime National Park Association.

submarines. Three days later, two of those subs returned and picked up survivors. *Pampanito* was one of those submarines that pulled men out of the water; ironically, however, she was also one of the submarines responsible for putting them there. It is a bittersweet story, but one that reflects the many ironies of war.

While working as the curator of USS *Pampanito*, cataloging the collection of artifacts and documents associated with the submarine, many of them donated by her former crew members, I came across two thick folders that had been tucked away in a filing cabinet drawer. They turned out to be full of firsthand accounts written by the Australian and British POWs who were rescued by *Pampanito* on that fateful day in 1944. Many of the accounts appeared to have been written immediately after the rescue, while the ex-POWs were still aboard the submarine. As soon as the rescued men started to recover, *Pampanito* crewmen apparently wasted no time in handing them paper and pens. The survivors scribbled their names and contact information on scraps of paper and in journals and diaries, along with words of heartfelt gratitude to their rescuers. Some wrote lengthy accounts of their experiences, describing in harrowing detail the fall of Singapore, the horrors endured in POW camps, and the experience of being aboard a transport ship that was hit by a submarine torpedo. In some cases the POWs were too weak to write, so they dictated their accounts to the submariners, who recorded them on paper.

The accounts collected in these folders are astounding. They offer a glimpse of the human side of the war. They reveal details that are at times shocking, horrifying, almost unbelievable, exposing the horrors of which humans are capable. Yet at the same time, these accounts by survivors of some of the most brutal circumstances imaginable reaffirm the amazing capacity and will of human beings to endure and survive. My co-workers and I realized that these important stories needed to be shared, to be published. So began an effort to research and document these accounts and the rescue, a process that has involved interviews and correspondence with the ex-POWs, their families, and the former crew members of *Pampanito*. In addition to the oral histories and personal accounts collected from these individuals, official military documents, patrol reports, and newspaper articles have been consulted in order to piece together the narrative of events as completely as possible. Although the story has been told before, this book attempts to tell it a little bit differently: through the eyes of those who lived it, based largely on their own accounts, and supplemented by the official documents and other supporting sources.[1]

A few notes on the methodology used are in order. Most of the spelling and grammatical errors found in the firsthand accounts cited have been corrected for the sake of readability. In addition, in order to preserve the integrity of the original POW accounts, wherever possible the version cited is the original version written by the POW himself, or the copy that is closest to the original version. In some cases, a single account has been transcribed numerous times. I have chosen to use, in order of preference: (1) the version handwritten by a POW aboard the sub; (2) the version dictated by a POW aboard the sub and written down by a *Pampanito* crew member; (3) the typed transcription of a POW's original handwritten account; and (4) the typed transcription of a transcription done by a *Pampanito* crewman. Often, official U.S. Navy reports of the incident include a transcription of the final sort: one could call them "cleaned-up" versions of the original. From features such as spelling or choice of terminology it is often apparent where in the hierarchy a written account lies. For example, original accounts written by the POWs themselves employ British-style spelling and terminology (e.g., "Burma-Thai Railway"), while in their transcriptions, *Pampanito* crewmen tended to revert to U.S.-style spelling and terminology ("Burma-Thai Railroad"). In addition, terms that the modern reader may find offensive or inappropriate, such as "Jap" and "Nip," have been left as found in the material cited. Readers may also notice that the stories of Australian survivors are more numerous than those of British survivors in this account; this is largely because more Australians were picked up by *Pampanito* during the rescue—47 out of 73 men rescued by this sub were Australian.

Pampanito torpedoman Woodrow Weaver, who had been keeping a careful record of his experiences in a personal journal aboard the sub, recognized immediately when the rescue took place that it was a historical moment and needed to be included in his journal. He decided to go to the source. He asked one of the rescued POWs, K. C. Renton, to write a firsthand description of the events and circumstances that had landed him in this unlikeliest of places, an American submarine under way on a war patrol in the middle of the South China Sea. Renton began his account with the following stipulation: "I shall try to explain facts as clearly as possible, and won't write anything unless I seen it with my own eyes."[2] This book is an attempt to retell an amazing rescue story of World War II based on the accounts and memories of the individuals who "saw it with their own eyes."

It has been my good fortune and great honor to have been able to meet many of *Pampanito*'s wartime crew, including many of those who played a part in the events described in this book. I thank them for participating in oral history interviews and sharing their memories of the rescue. Over the years, many have also donated various artifacts, photographs, and documents to the *Pampanito* museum, items that have helped to piece together this story.

I am also indebted to the former POWs for their willingness to tell of their experiences, either in written accounts or in oral history interviews that are now in the *Pampanito* museum archives. I have had the great pleasure of meeting a number of the relatives of the rescued POWs. For the information and memories they have shared so generously, I would particularly like to thank Neryl Quilty and the rest of the McKittrick family; Tim Farmer, son of the very first POW pulled out of the sea by *Pampanito*'s crew; and Scott Thiele, grandson of Ken Williams.

Although one of the key players in this story, *Pampanito* pharmacist's mate "Doc" Demers, has passed away, I am grateful to his sons, Larry and Kevin, for their kindness in sharing their father's story and related artifacts with me and the *Pampanito* museum.

Thanks to the quick thinking of *Pampanito* volunteer Bob Taylor, I was put in touch with Andrew Hart, former medic at the Saipan Army Hospital, after Mr. Hart visited San Francisco and toured *Pampanito*. I thank Mr. Hart for sharing his memoirs with me. Thanks are also owed to Thomas Richardson, former assistant ship's manager, for pointing me to the primary documents in the *Pampanito* collection and suggesting that I undertake this project; to former ship's manager Christian Bach, current ship's manager Aaron Washington, and the San Francisco Maritime National Park Association, for their encouragement and cooperation in this project; and to my former co-worker Robin Deley, for everything from helping with oral history interviews to endless photocopying to moral support. I am also indebted to the late Russell Booth, former ship's manager of *Pampanito*, who began the museum's efforts to contact the former POWs and collect their stories. Karen Hansen of Hansen Designs in London, Ontario, skillfully transformed a three-and-a-half-foot-long World War II tracking chart into a compact and readable version for this book. And finally, my thanks to the readers of the manuscript, Michael Gannon and William Thiesen, for their very helpful comments and suggestions, and to Meredith Morris-Babb, the director of University Press of Florida, whose interest in and enthusiasm for this project made it happen.

USS *Pampanito* is open to the public daily at Pier 45 in Fisherman's Wharf, San Francisco, California.

Chronology of Key Events

February 15, 1942: fall of Singapore

June 1942: construction of the Burma-Thai Railroad begins

July 12, 1943: USS *Pampanito* (SS-383) launched at Portsmouth, New Hampshire

October 25, 1943: construction of the Burma-Thai Railroad completed

November 6, 1943: *Pampanito* commissioned

January 15, 1944: *Pampanito* sails from New London, Connecticut, en route to Panama Canal Zone and Pearl Harbor

March 15, 1944: *Pampanito* departs Pearl Harbor to begin first war patrol

August 12, 1944: *Pampanito* departs Midway to begin third war patrol

September 6, 1944: The POWs board the hellships *Rakuyo Maru* and *Kachidoki Maru*, bound for Japan

September 12, 1944: USS *Growler* (SS-215) sinks *Shikinami* and *Hirado*; USS *Sealion* (SS-315) sinks *Nankai Maru* and *Rakuyo Maru* (approximately 1,300 POWs on board); *Pampanito* sinks *Zuiho Maru* and *Kachidoki Maru* (ex-*President Harrison*) (approximately 900 POWs on board)

September 15, 1944: *Pampanito* sights and picks up 73 POWs.
Sealion picks up 54 POWs

September 16, 1944: POW John Campbell dies on board
Pampanito and is buried at sea

September 17: USS *Queenfish* (SS-393) picks up 18 POWs; USS
Barb (SS-220) picks up 14 POWs

September 18, 1944: *Pampanito* and USS *Case* (DD-370)
rendezvous at sea to transfer supplies to *Pampanito*

September 20, 1944: *Pampanito* arrives at Saipan; 72 remaining
POWs transferred to U.S. Army 148th General Hospital

October 18, 1944: rescued Australian ex-POWs arrive at New Farm
Wharf, Queensland

December 15, 1945: *Pampanito* decommissioned

March 15, 1982: *Pampanito* opened to the public as a museum ship
at Fisherman's Wharf, San Francisco

January 14, 1986: *Pampanito* designated a National Historic
Landmark by the U.S. secretary of the interior.

Abbreviations

AIF	Australian Imperial Force
CO	commanding officer
COMSUBPAC	Commander, Submarine Force, U.S. Pacific Fleet
NCO	non-commissioned officer
OC	officer in command
OOD	officer of the deck
POW	prisoner of war
XO	executive officer

hit and *Hirado* began to sink—so close to *Growler* that the sailors standing on her bridge could feel the heat from the burning ship.[1] The wolf pack continued tracking the convoy, and three and a half hours later a tremendous explosion shattered the night as *Sealion* got in an attack. The rest of the day was spent in pursuit of the remaining Japanese ships. Aboard *Pampanito*, skipper Pete Summers's frustration mounted as the sub lost track of the convoy once, then again. Finally, late that night, *Pampanito* had a promising contact: a cargo ship and a large transport appeared in firing range. At 10:40 p.m., Captain Summers ordered five torpedoes launched from her forward tubes, then rapidly swung the boat around and sent forth four more of the deadly "fish" from the stern tubes. Seven of the torpedoes hit targets; two hit the transport *Kachidoki Maru*.

Three days later, on September 15, *Pampanito* was patrolling on the surface near the island of Hainan. It was late afternoon, and the waters of the South China Sea were calm as the submarine sailed along in an easterly direction. The port and starboard lookouts watched the horizon from their usual perches on the periscope shears, while a third lookout covered the stern from his station on the cigarette deck. Frank Fives was officer of the deck; he and the assistant deck officer, Richard Sherlock, had just taken over the watch at around 4 p.m. when the port lookout reported seeing an object in the water just under the horizon. Fives and Sherlock immediately moved to the port side of the bridge and, along with the lookouts, began scanning the horizon. Suddenly more objects floated into view, as if out of nowhere: large clumps of debris and floating wreckage. Captain Summers was notified and called on deck. After taking a quick look through binoculars, he gave orders to alter course and the ship began to steer toward the objects in the water for closer

The Sighting

By the start of USS *Pampanito*'s third war patrol, in the late s
of 1944, the submarine had experienced severe and prolonge
charging, but as of yet she had no sinkings to add to her ba
and her reports to COMSUBPAC. And her bad luck see
hold: as she headed out from Midway Island toward her a
patrol area for this third run, the crew dealt with perplexing
ment problems, faced Japanese air patrols, spotted no poten
gets, and even had to handle some extensive and difficult re
sea after the sub sprang a leak. At last, in the early mornin
of September 12, *Pampanito*'s radioman picked up a blip
radar: a Japanese convoy. *Pampanito* was operating as part c
pack of three subs during this patrol, and the three subm
Growler, *Sealion*, and *Pampanito*—closed in on the slow
ing columns of enemy ships. Just before 2 a.m., *Growler* d
blood. As she moved in for the attack, one of the convoy's
the freighter *Hirado*, had detected the sub and began char
ward her. *Growler* did not back down and, in a daring bow
surface attack, launched three torpedoes at the escort; the

investigation. Soon one large piece of floating debris began to take identifiable shape: it was a lifeboat. Aware that they were only a little to the north of where the wolf pack had attacked the enemy convoy on the night of September 12, Summers realized that the lifeboat may very likely have occupants—survivors of some of the convoy's sunken ships. As the sub carefully moved in alongside the lifeboat, Summers observed that the boat was empty. However, at that moment a lookout reported seeing two more rafts on the horizon, these clearly with men aboard. "It was naturally believed that these would be Japanese, so small arms were broken out and preparations made for taking prisoners," Summers recorded later in his written report of the incident. As the submarine drew closer to one of the lifeboats, her crew could see that it was actually nothing but a makeshift raft, made of hatch covers and timbers laced together. Aboard this crude vessel were over a dozen men. They were clothed scantily, if at all; some had makeshift headgear to protect them from the sun, others appeared to be wearing regulation Japanese soldiers' caps—yet all were so thoroughly coated in thick, black oil that it was hard to identify them by either their scraps of clothing or their physical appearance. Many of them were shouting and waving frantically at the submarine. Summers later described this initial sighting in his patrol report: "1634: The men were covered with oil and filth and we could not make them out—black curly hair didn't look like Japs. They were shouting but we didn't understand what they were saying, except made out the words 'Pick us up *please*.'"[2]

The thick oil coating the men's bodies had probably kept them alive by protecting them from the harsh rays of the sun each day while they floated at sea, but now it concealed their identities from the submarine's captain and crew, who could only assume that the miserable beings they saw waving desperately at them from the water were Japanese sailors who had somehow survived the sinking of the convoy three days earlier.

Gordon Hopper was the 20-millimeter gunner; he and the rest of the gun crew members were ordered topside. Hopper loaded the 20-millimeter deck gun and awaited further orders from the captain. Some other crewmen grabbed shotguns or submachine guns and came up on deck as well. Soon a small crowd had gathered topside.[3]

Tony Hauptman had been down below when he received orders from the skipper to arm himself and come on deck. Hauptman grabbed a Tommy gun and was making his way topside when one of the torpedomen approached him: "Hey, let me help you." Hauptman handed him the machine gun and went back to the small-arms locker. This time he took a shotgun and a box of buckshot. Topside, he took a position on the bow of the submarine, shotgun poised, ready to fire as the first raft neared the submarine. Before he could get a shot out at the darkened figures on the raft, he heard one of them shout "Yank!" Hauptman turned to the skipper. "These ain't Japs," he said.[4]

When they first spotted the rafts in the area of the convoy attack, the submariners had had no reason to assume that the men they saw in the water clinging to bits of ship wreckage were anything other than Japanese. But a tiny vessel like *Pampanito* hardly had enough room for her own crew, much less space to take prisoners aboard. Still, if one of the men in the water knew some English, it might prove useful to take him aboard for interrogation. Using a sound-powered megaphone, the skipper ordered one, and only one, of the men to be taken aboard. "Get the one who speaks English," he ordered. "You dumb bastards," came the exasperated reply from the raft, clearly audible to all the crewmen forward of the conning tower, "we *all* speak English." As the sub pulled closer they could hear additional voices yelling, also in English. One of the shouts provided a clue as to who these men were: "You bloody Yanks," one of the men yelled up at the submariners, "First you sink us, now you want to shoot us! I thought we were allies!"[5]

The first man taken aboard was Australian Frank Farmer. He explained that he and the other oil-soaked, scarecrow-thin men on the raft had been aboard *Rakuyo Maru*, the ship sunk by *Sealion* on September 12. What the submariners had not known when they launched their torpedoes at *Rakuyo Maru* was that her cargo included more than thirteen hundred Allied prisoners of war—British and Australian soldiers who had been taken prisoner by the Japanese at the surrender of Singapore in February 1942. Held captive for two and a half years, many had been worked nearly to death in the construction of the infamous Burma-Thai Railroad. Those POWs who survived the railroad were loaded aboard transport ships and were en route to labor camps in Japan when they found themselves victims of an American submarine attack.

Summers realized that many more of these men might still be alive in the waters nearby, grasping for life aboard a raft or clinging to debris. He ordered a full-out rescue operation. "All hands went into action immediately," he recorded later that day. "Those below decks sent up bales of rags and began preparing hot soup and tea in quantities; the Pharmacist's Mate assembled his gear for immediate treatment, and the rescue party commenced bringing the survivors aboard. The poor fellows were so frantic with joy at this unbelievable piece of good fortune that they began jumping from the raft and trying to clamber up the sides of the ship. Members of the rescue party dived over the side to make the raft fast, herded the survivors back onto the raft and aided them up to the ship's deck. The weakened condition of these men, as well as their covering of slippery crude oil, made the actual recovery quite difficult. Some of them could help themselves, but the majority had to be lifted and dragged aboard bodily."[6]

The skipper had asked for volunteers—the men who were the strongest swimmers—to form the "rescue party." These men swam out to the rafts with ropes; then, grabbing a raft with one hand, they held onto the rope with the other while crewmen on the sub towed them in. Other crew members waited on deck or climbed out onto the saddle tanks that bulged out from the sub's main hull to help haul the weak and emaciated men aboard. Pharmacist's Mate Maurice Demers, who functioned as the ship's sole medic, performed triage on deck and, with the meager supplies on hand, began first aid. The crude oil coating the men's bodies was sponged off using the submarine's supply of diesel oil. Those suffering from extreme shock were given morphine and then carefully lowered through the hatches into the submarine.

Torpedoman Bob Bennett was off duty in the forward torpedo room when word was passed around that the skipper wanted available crewmen to come topside. Bennett went up through the gun hatch and was amazed to see men floating in the water, clinging to boards and pieces of shoring. When he realized who the men were, Bennett, a good swimmer, joined the rescue party, swimming out to the rafts and hauling their occupants to the submarine. Gordon Hopper, who minutes before had been poised on the deck, ready to fire at the men on the rafts as soon as the captain gave the order, now dove into the water and began hauling in the rafts. Meanwhile, other crew members climbed down to the saddle tanks to assist. They included Tony Hauptman, who had put down the shotgun and, with the help of a fire controlman, was doing his best to grab hold of the slippery men and heave them onto the deck.[7]

As the survivors were being pulled on board, more and more debris appeared, floating in the distance. Realizing the immensity of the task ahead, Summers called down to the radiomen to contact the other two members of the wolf pack and request their assistance. USS *Sealion* received the message and immediately headed to the location; USS *Barb* and USS *Queenfish*, operating nearby, headed to the area as well. In the meantime, *Pampanito* reached a second raft full of survivors, and bearings were taken of three more rafts that were in sight. The second raft contained nine men who were quickly brought aboard. While heading toward the next group of survivors, the submariners passed a grim sight: a small raft bearing a single dead body, with part of the head missing—probably the work of a shark, thought Summers. *Pampanito*'s crewmen managed to pull eleven more men from the third and fourth rafts. Then, a small raft was sighted with just one man aboard. He was lying on his back, motionless, but appeared to be alive. When one of the swimmers dived into the water with a line and headed toward him, the figure sat up suddenly, as if startled, and began to go over the side of the raft. The swimmer managed to persuade him to remain seated on the raft until he could be helped aboard the sub. When he was finally brought aboard, the man was almost blind and in a semiconscious state.[8]

Clarence Williams, who had been manning the phones down below, came topside to relieve the after lookouts. As the survivors were being helped off the third and fourth rafts, Williams spotted danger coming from above and shouted, "Three planes in formation astern!" He later recalled: "It was pretty hairy up topside at that time, a lot of excitement . . . and it looked like [the airplanes] were turning and fixing to dive on us—and I really jumped; I was excited, and I started hollering and yelling, 'C'mon, get on board, let's go, we gotta get down.'"[9]

By now there were close to fifty men on *Pampanito*'s deck: the captain, the bridge personnel, the rescue team, the pharmacist's mate, and some of the survivors. Under normal operating conditions, only five people needed to clear the deck in the thirty seconds it took the submarine to submerge: the OOD, the assistant OOD, and the three lookouts. But diving the boat at this moment would have left much of the crew and most of the survivors in the water to drown. Luck intervened. As Summers explained in his task force report, "Fortunately one of the planes was seen to flap its wings proving the formation to be large birds gliding in perfect order." The relief on board was palpable, and so was Williams's mortification: "The captain was right beside me, and he just looked up at me about as hard as I've ever been stared at, but I just melted, it just cooled me down, calmed me down." Lieutenant McMillan Johnson, who was standing between the skipper and Williams, helped to ease the tension: "Better safe than sorry!" he pointed out. Williams's potentially tragic error was not mentioned again.[10]

As afternoon turned into evening, *Pampanito*'s search became more and more frantic as her crew spotted more and more objects floating in the sea. Summers ordered Sherlock to climb the periscope shears to get as high a view as possible and to look for more rafts on the horizon. Shortly after 6 p.m., two more rafts were sighted, with thirteen more survivors aboard. While the rescue party worked to get them onto the submarine, the high periscope watch reported sighting yet another raft, but also the masts of a ship in the distance. The ship was identified as a submarine; it appeared to have a gun aft, and Summers was immediately wary, as one of the survivors now aboard *Pampanito* had reported seeing a German U-boat in the vicinity. When the submarine did not reply to a surface search radar challenge, *Pampanito* dove to periscope depth to investigate. After several minutes of periscope observation, and realizing that the other sub had stopped in one spot and was hardly moving at all, it was determined that the sub was none other than *Sealion*, joining in the rescue. *Pampanito* resurfaced and resumed her search. For the next four or five hours she steamed from raft to raft, picking up every survivor her crew could find.

By now it was almost completely dark. In the distance a lone man on a small raft was seen, frantically waving what appeared to be a white hat; it turned out to be his hand, bleached white by the elements. He was pulled aboard the sub. Despite the onset of darkness, *Pampanito* managed to locate the last raft that had been sighted before she had submerged, and twelve more men were rescued.[11] "I guess we flailed around from raft to raft and from one piece of junk to another," remembered Sherlock, "and sometimes we would find somebody and other times we wouldn't and I guess it was about, oh, 2200 by the time the captain decided to stop for the night. So we spent the night circling and zigzagging and just trying to stay out of harm's way because we thought there could be some Japanese submarines roaming around, waiting for some likely targets like us, when we were dead in the water." By the time darkness fell, *Pampanito*'s crew had plucked seventy-three men out of the sea.[12]

At first light on September 16, *Pampanito* resumed the search. The submariners tried to calculate, based on the location and track of the submarine and the tide and the winds, where any remaining rafts might have drifted, "but the sea was just perfectly blank," noted Sherlock. "There wasn't anybody around." Not a single raft or piece of debris could be seen, but the submariners stubbornly refused to give up. For hours *Pampanito* kept moving through the area, her crew desperately looking for signs of life in the water. Finally, at 11 a.m., Summers received orders from Pearl Harbor to break off the search and head directly to Saipan with the survivors. The crew was disappointed at the possibility of abandoning other survivors who were still afloat somewhere, but also realized that the seventy-three who had been lucky enough to be pulled on board during the night needed serious medical attention if they were to survive—more attention than the submarine could provide. According to Sherlock, the captain of one of the other submarines that joined the rescue operation "broke off the search when he had far less than we had because he was afraid there was too many for the boat, but Captain Summers, I think, would have stayed there for five days and picked up every man he could have found—I mean if COMSUB-PAC hadn't ordered us back to Saipan. And for that I'll always think highly of Pete Summers."[13]

USS *Pampanito* Track Chart Narrative

11 September 1944

2130: *Pampanito* makes rendezvous with *Growler* and *Sealion* (A) and proceeds to search for reported convoy.

12 September 1944

0155: *Growler* attacks convoy (B).

0527: *Sealion* attacks convoy (C).

0706: *Pampanito* dives and tracks convoy by periscope
observations of smoke until able to surface undetected.

1122: *Pampanito* surfaces; convoy not in sight.

1200: *Pampanito* picks up smoke with high periscope and
resumes tracking convoy.

1508: *Pampanito* dives as convoy makes a radical "zig" to the north.

1542: *Pampanito* surfaces and observes convoy.

1839: Plane sighted from bridge; *Pampanito* dives to avoid
detection.

1909: *Pampanito* surfaces.

1936: Plane sighted again from bridge; *Pampanito* dives.

1955: *Pampanito* surfaces, only to find she has lost sight of the
convoy.

2106: Radar contact made with the convoy; *Pampanito* closes in
for attack.

2240: *Pampanito* launches five torpedoes from her forward tubes,
then swings hard right and launches four torpedoes from
her stern tubes (D). Seven of the torpedoes hit targets. From
the bridge, Captain Summers watches three ships sink. The
convoy's escorts begin dropping depth charges at random.

2253: One depth charge lands near *Pampanito*, shaking the
entire ship. *Pampanito* pulls clear to get rid of a "hot run"
torpedo that has activated prematurely in her number 4 tube
and to reload her torpedoes.

2339: Reload completed; *Pampanito* resumes pursuit of convoy.

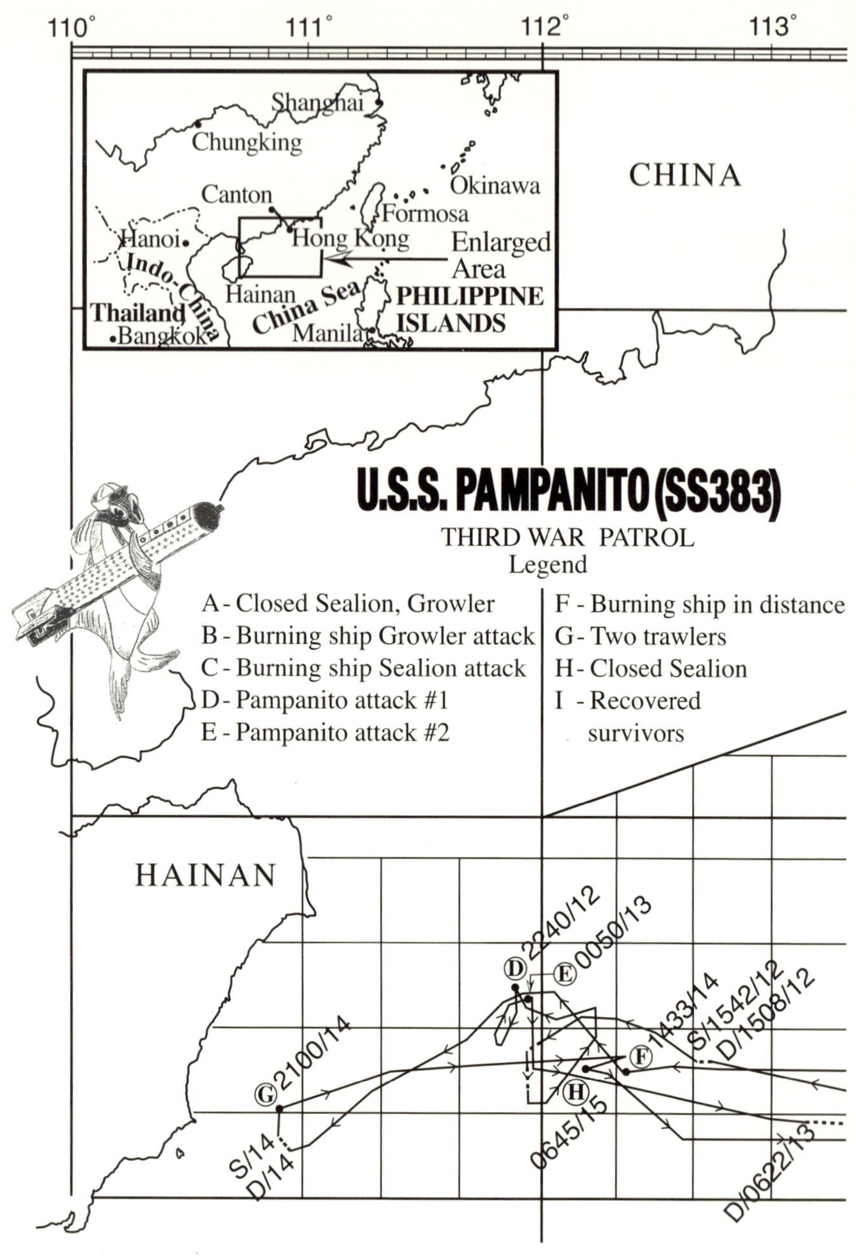

Map. Detail of USS *Pampanito* track chart, showing the submarine's route during the attack on convoy HI-72 on September 12, 1944, and the subsequent rescue of the POWs. Captain Summers submitted the original chart to COMSUBPAC as part of his report documenting the submarine's third war patrol. Dives are indicated by the letter "D" and a dotted line in the submarine's route; "S" represents surfacing. Numbers signify the time and date. Thus, "D/0706/12" indicates the

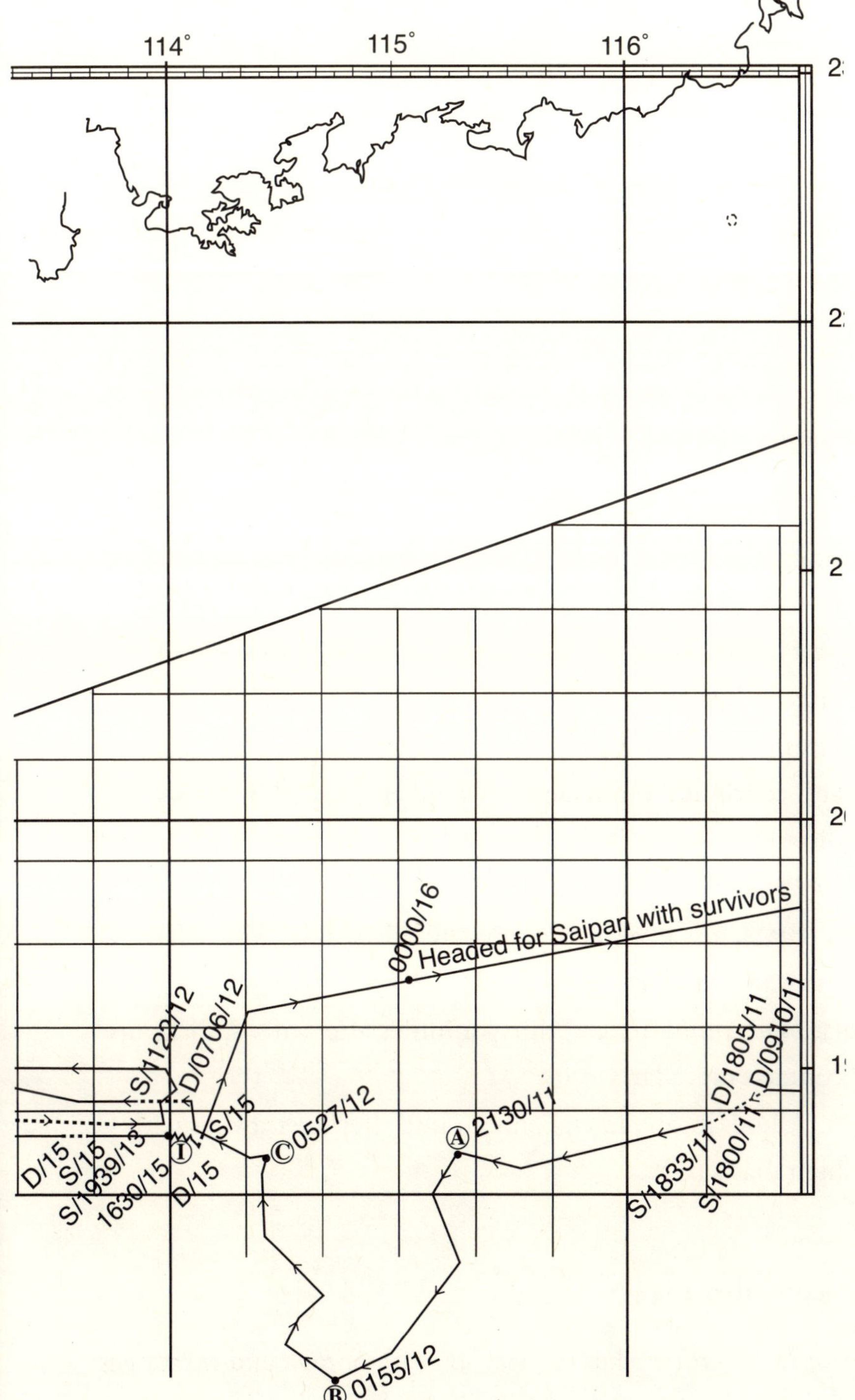

spot on the route where *Pampanito* submerged at 7:06 a.m. on September 12. P. E. Summers, Commanding Officer, USS *Pampanito* (SS-383), Report of War Patrol Number Three, SS383/A16, 28 September 1944. U.S. Navy.

13 September 1944

0050: *Pampanito* launches three torpedoes at the convoy (E); no hits.

0622: *Pampanito* dives for submerged patrol.

1939: *Pampanito* surfaces.

14 September 1944

0632: *Pampanito* dives.

1433: *Pampanito* surfaces to investigate source of observed smoke; sees it is from a burning ship (F).

1630: Heading toward Hainan, *Pampanito* sights several life rafts and lifeboats; most appear to be empty. CO Summers assumes they are probably Japanese sailors from the convoy and continues to pursue two "smokes" sighted in the distance.

1839: *Pampanito* sights Hainan coast.

1915: *Pampanito* dives approximately thirty miles from Hainan to await darkness.

2013: *Pampanito* surfaces, thirty minutes after sunset. Picks up contacts on radar.

2100: Closes in on targets, only to find they are trawlers with high masts (G).

15 September 1944

0630: *Pampanito* makes rendezvous with *Sealion* and exchanges information about the attack (H).

1340: *Pampanito* sights plane from bridge; dives.

1420: *Pampanito* surfaces; all clear.

1555: Various debris and wreckage sighted floating in the water.

1605: Bridge lookout sights some men on a raft, "so stood by small arms, and closed to investigate."

1634: *Pampanito* approaches men on rafts. Begins rescue operations (I).

1710: *Pampanito* radios *Sealion* for assistance.

1905: *Pampanito* dives after a submarine is sighted which fails to answer *Pampanito*'s challenge.

1940: *Pampanito* surfaces; decides other submarine is *Sealion*.

2005: *Pampanito* recovers final group of survivors, now in complete darkness.

2015: *Pampanito* makes final search of area, then sets course for Saipan at four engine speed.

Source: P. E. Summers, USS *Pampanito* (SS-383), Report of War Patrol Number Three. 28 September 1944.

USS Pampanito

Most of the men assembling in Portsmouth, New Hampshire, in 1943 who were assigned to the new submarines under construction at the shipyard there had chosen to serve on submarines, rather than in the surface fleet, for many of the same reasons. There was, of course, the extra pay that submarine sailors received—50 percent more than a surface sailor made—an incentive that was particularly important to young men who had grown up during the Great Depression. Many of them had been unable to afford college, so joining the military had seemed the only viable career option. What was not appealing was the idea of being a foot soldier in the Army— something that conjured up images of crawling through mud and sleeping in trenches. At least on a ship, they figured, one was always assured of having a bunk to sleep in and meals served on a regular basis. Even more unappealing was the possibility of coming back from the war wounded or disabled. At least, more than one potential submariner reasoned, if I went to war on a submarine I'd come back in one piece, or not at all.

By 1943 submarine construction had increased to meet the grow- ing demands of war, and it was not uncommon for two submarines to be launched at the same time. USS *Pampanito* (SS-383) was launched in a double ceremony, sharing the occasion with USS *Picuda* (SS-382) on July 12 at the Portsmouth Navy Yard. *Pampanito* and *Picuda* were fleet submarines—a type of submarine developed in the years after World War I that was designed to be able to keep up with the surface fleet. This meant the subs had to be able to reach and maintain the speed of a battleship, or twenty-one knots, while on the surface. Submerged, they traveled much more slowly, closer to ten knots, and were less easily maneuvered. Indeed, they were more accurately "submersibles" rather than true "submarines"—surface vessels that had the capacity to submerge for limited periods of time. Underwater, these submarines switched from their diesel-electric engines to battery power; it was the lifespan of the batteries, along with the need to admit breathing air for the crew, that limited the submergence time of the fleet boat. *Pampanito* was a *Balao*-class submarine, the product of years of submarine development. The *Balaos* were known as "thick-skinned" boats: their slightly thicker hull, made of high-tensile steel seven-eighths of an inch thick, gave them the capacity to submerge one hundred feet deeper than their predecessor class, the *Gatos*, were able to. *Pampanito*'s safe operating depth was four hundred feet; six hundred feet was considered crush depth.

Roger Walters, who had trained aboard a primitive S-class boat, USS *S-16*, off Coco Solo, Panama, before being assigned to *Pampanito*, was thrilled when he came aboard the much more modern vessel: "Oh, it was just a beautiful experience. You know, here's a million dollar boat that is brand new, brand spanking new." Not only was *Pampanito* significantly roomier than the old *S-16*, but *Pampanito* even had showers for the crew. "The size of the boat, the bunks, the air-conditioning, the showers, everything about it was just magnificent for a newcomer." Woodrow Weaver had served on a destroyer before volunteering for submarine service, and he too was thrilled by the fact that *Pampanito* had air-conditioning. Aboard the destroyer, he had slept many nights topside, on the deck, where at least it was a little bit cooler than down below.[1]

Not everyone would agree that serving on a fleet submarine, even one as modern as *Pampanito* was in 1943, could be considered exactly comfortable. For one thing, a surface sailor would very likely find life aboard a submarine exceptionally cramped and crowded. The small vessel, measuring 311 feet, 9 inches in length and 27 feet, 3 inches in the beam, carried a crew of seventy to eighty men plus a complement of ten officers. Privacy was a little-known commodity aboard submarines, so for the sixty days that a war patrol normally lasted, the crew lived in close quarters, got to know each other well, and had to learn to work together well. Given these conditions, it is not surprising that the submarine force only took volunteers, and even these were not accepted into the submarine service until they had passed a series of physical and psychological tests. It was, however, largely these same trying conditions that built an outstanding spirit of camaraderie among the crew. Every man knew every job on a submarine, every man relied on every other man. And so, even after spending two months in close and cramped quarters, underwater, living and working together, sub crews also tended to stick together on shore leave during the two short weeks they had between patrols for rest and recreation while their submarine was repaired, refitted, and readied for the next sixty-day patrol.

Portsmouth

In the fall of 1943, the crew members of the new submarine *Pampanito* had begun to assemble in Portsmouth. Gordon Hopper had spent the summer training aboard USS *R-10* out of Key West. In September he arrived in Portsmouth and got his first look at *Pampanito*, which was then in the final stages of construction. In addition to learning the ship and all of her systems as preparation for earning his submarine qualification that autumn, he took part in softball games that pitted *Pampanito*'s crew against that of her sister ship, USS *Parche* (SS-384). "Don't recall who won but remember that *Parche* skipper, Red Ramage, attended to cheer his crew while our captain, C. B. Jackson, was nowhere to be seen." William Grady, who had just come off two years' service aboard USS *Plunger* (SS-179), thought the crew that had assembled to man the new submarine on her first patrol were "a great bunch of guys," but he was a little bit apprehensive upon discovering that there were few combat-experienced submarine sailors among them. He struggled to push aside his concerns: "So we had a lot of guys who hadn't been there as of yet. But, they were submarine school graduates and they liked submarines and they learned real quick and I knew they'd be fine once we got in the war zone. Of course, the first depth charging they got real scared. Everybody does in the first one, real scared. But they survived and everyone was fine after the first depth charging."[2]

On November 6, *Pampanito* was commissioned and officially became part of the United States Navy. Lieutenant Commander Charles B. Jackson Jr. was the boat's first commanding officer. Jackson had served previously on USS *Spearfish* (SS-190); his XO on

Pampanito, Lieutenant Commander Paul E. Summers, had served seven patrols on USS *Stingray* (SS-186). Gordon Hopper was excited as *Pampanito* drew closer to action: "Commissioning, November 6, 1943, was a turning point. We were soon to take the *Pampanito* out for a shakedown. Things were getting real. We'd be heading for the war before long."[3]

The next couple of months were spent training the crew and conducting test trials between Portsmouth and the New London naval base near Groton, Connecticut. *Pampanito* underwent practice approaches, fired her guns and launched exercise torpedoes, and went out to sea on a six-day practice patrol. She also spent eleven days in dry dock for some last-minute repairs.

After enlisting in the Navy in Chicago, Robert Bennett had completed torpedo school in Great Lakes, Illinois, then attended an advanced training school in Keyport, Washington, before choosing submarines. He then was sent to submarine school in New London. Before leaving New London he got married; then his new bride went home to Chicago, and Bennett, assigned to *Pampanito*, headed to Portsmouth. He was struck by how cold it was that winter in New Hampshire—so cold that he would remember it as the most uncomfortable part of the entire war for him. He hated the shakedown runs in the cold waters of the Atlantic, the combination of freezing weather and rough seas, the ice everywhere. The worst part, however, soon proved to be standing lookout on the sub's periscope shears. Some days it was so cold that Bennett would ball his hands into fists in an attempt to keep them warm while he clutched the binoculars. Even worse was the fear of not hearing the diving alarm sound and being left topside when the submarine submerged into the frigid waters. "So I told the captain on duty down below or the officer on duty that when they sound the diving alarm, grab my pant leg and give it a jerk, and he would do that and then I was sure I wouldn't be left outside." Bennett's worst fear was never realized, and as it turned out, he would remain aboard *Pampanito* for all six of her war patrols.[4]

Another commissioning crew member, Motor Machinist's Mate William Grady, also remembered above all the biting cold that winter in Portsmouth. "The coldest, coldest, coldest place in the world to be is in a submarine engine room in the North Atlantic in wintertime. Believe me. We'd have heavy fall-weather gear while the engines were running because the main induction was open, then we'd dive and immediately the temperature in the engine room goes to about 130 degrees, 120 minimum. So off comes the fall-weather gear. Then they'd surface. And in come the frigid North Atlantic winds and then we'd put the clothes back on. And of course in the shakedown cruises such as it was in those days, it was a lot of surfacing and diving, so it was clothes on, clothes off, freeze and sweat."[5]

Finally, in early 1944, the new submarine was ready to head into action. *Pampanito* departed New London on January 15, transiting the Panama Canal on the twenty-fourth. Torpedoman Woodrow Weaver kept a list in his journal of each deck watch and topside watch he stood aboard *Pampanito* as the submarine traversed the Panama Canal and until she reached Pearl Harbor on Valentine's Day of 1944. Electrician Duncan Brown kept a log of "miles travelled by sea" in his journal: New London to Panama, 2,808 miles; Panama to Pearl Harbor, 4,910 miles. Gordon Hopper, who had also found the winter operating off of Portsmouth and New London to be almost unbearably cold and utterly miserable, felt a sense of relief as the submarine steamed toward the tropical climate of

Panama. As he reported to the bridge for lookout duty, he noted that the weather felt a little bit warmer each day.[6]

In the Panama Canal Zone, *Pampanito* stopped for four days in the port city of Balboa for some minor tests and repairs. Crew member Paul Pappas, a professional photographer in civilian life, took advantage of the opportunity to stock up on Kodak film for his camera. Due to wartime rationing, film was almost impossible to purchase in the United States at the time, but in Panama it was readily available.[7]

Pearl Harbor

And then, it was on to Hawai'i. The voyage across the Pacific provided more opportunities for pre-combat training for the less experienced members of the crew. On one occasion, when Summers decided to let two men who needed to qualify man the bow and stern planes on a dive, the two inadvertently let the boat get away from them and *Pampanito* suddenly began to descend rapidly at an alarmingly steep angle. Gordon Hopper recalled that it was only because of the quick thinking and reaction of another crew member on the air manifold, who managed to stay on his feet and blow the bow buoyancy tank without waiting for orders from the diving officer, that disaster was averted. (Unfortunately for him, the diving officer at the time was Summers!) But the crewman's quick thinking brought the boat up from the dangerous dive, and very likely saved the boat and crew. *Pampanito*'s bow swung upward, "And where we had been going down at a very steep down angle very rapidly, then the bow came up and we made an equally steep ascent. And I remember vividly that dinner was being put on the tables downstairs and it was all, splashed all over the forward bulkhead as we came back up again." One of the crew, Tony Hauptman, who was a talented artist, later made a sketch to commemorate the event: an illustration of *Pampanito* proceeding from Panama to Pearl Harbor, sounding and broaching like a porpoise.[8]

Hopper was excited as *Pampanito* finally neared the Hawaiian Islands and the Pearl Harbor naval station came into sight. "As we entered the storied port, remains of the December 7, 1941, attack still everywhere, we became aware that we'd soon be seeing action. For many of us, this would be our first war patrol. Unaware of what to expect, we were eager to make that first 'kill.'" *Pampanito* arrived at the Pearl Harbor submarine base on Valentine's Day. After undergoing some additional repairs, on February 23 she commenced a short and intensive training period in preparation for her first war patrol. This final training session included the conducting of torpedo approaches, as well as nighttime and daytime radar runs. Four exercise torpedoes were launched, and *Pampanito* received "indoctrinational depth charging" to prepare her for what almost surely lay in store. Duncan Brown kept track in his journal of the number of "friendly" depth charges he endured during the month the sub was in Pearl: ninety-seven. Six weeks into the first patrol, and more than one hundred depth charges later—these from the enemy—he would confess, "The feeling of being depth-charged is unexplainable. I pray God I will never have to withstand another."[9]

At Pearl Harbor, before departing for the first patrol, Lieutenant Commander Jackson's duties as skipper were taken over by his XO, Paul Summers, on March 6. Summers went by the nickname "Pete." His crew had mixed feelings about him. Many felt uncomfortable around him. He seemed more formal, less friendly, than some other skippers that the men had served under. The crew noted, for example, that Summers always wore khakis—"pressed pants and starched shirts"—and never shorts while on board the sub, as did many other COs (or skivvies, as did Frank Fenno, who would take over command for *Pampanito*'s fourth patrol!). It also did not escape the crew's notice that Summers rarely went to some of the compartments of the sub unless he had to, avoiding any friendly contact with the crew. (Fenno, on the other hand, would stop by the crew's mess and have a bowl of soup with the crew.) One crew member recalled of Summers years later at a crew reunion, "I was scared of him and I wasn't even near him." Another remarked: "The first time he ever talked to me he had the grayest eyes. He could chew you out without ever saying a word."[10]

First War Patrol

Training was finally completed on March 14. The boat was loaded with torpedoes: sixteen in the forward torpedo room and eighteen aft. *Pampanito* was ready for war. The next day she departed Subase Pearl Harbor and headed for her assigned patrol area near the Marianas Islands, at the southwest approaches to Saipan and Guam. This patrol would include lifeguard duty south of Yap (a period described by Summers in the ship's war diary as follows: "No planes down but received 'Thank you for standing by' from birdmen overhead") as well as offensive patrol. On April 7 the sub sighted a small convoy and pursued it for four days. As *Pampanito* repeatedly tried to maneuver into attack position, the enemy vessels dropped depth charges on the submarine. Gordon Hopper was in the forward torpedo room, where "the sound of the exploding 'cans' defied description.

I watched, horrified, as the massive air manifold over the torpedo tubes bent to a horseshoe shape. Valves to the sea were spun open by the force of the charges and had to be re-seated." Later he was surprised to learn that only five depth charges had been dropped during this attack; for Hopper and others who were experiencing an enemy depth charge for the first time, it had felt like many more. Duncan Brown, also in the forward torpedo room while the boat was being depth-charged, wrote afterward: "I can honestly say that every man was scared and quiet. Thanks to God we were spared for another encounter with our foe."[11]

After some quick repairs, Summers resumed tracking the convoy. By April 10, *Pampanito* had finally caught up to her prey. She closed in and launched six torpedoes at a freighter and a destroyer in the convoy, and in return was pelted with a rain of depth charges from three destroyers. Upon surfacing the next day, the damage to the submarine was inspected. It had certainly been a "baptism by fire" for the new submarine and her crew.

Figure 1. USS *Pampanito* (SS-383) under way. U.S. Navy photo.

On May 3, *Pampanito* pulled in at Midway Island, where the submarine tender USS *Proteus* (AS-19) sent divers down to inspect the damage done by the depth charges. It was found to be substantial enough that *Pampanito* was ordered back to the Navy Yard at Pearl Harbor for dry-docking and overhaul.

Late in the afternoon of May 8, *Pampanito* arrived back at Subase Pearl Harbor. A refit crew took over the submarine for two weeks, while the boat's officers and crew headed to the Royal Hawaiian Hotel—the famous "pink palace" on Waikiki Beach—for R&R. The luxurious, rose-colored hotel had been closed to the public for the duration of the war, and was being used by the U.S. Navy as a rest center for submariners and aviators. *Pampanito*'s crew, now battle-experienced, stayed at the Royal Hawaiian until the twenty-fourth, then returned to the boat. Trial runs were made, torpedoes were loaded, and the sub was stocked with food and supplies for the next patrol.

Second War Patrol

As *Pampanito* pulled out of Pearl Harbor for Midway, most of her crew had no idea where they would be headed for the second patrol. It was only after they left Midway, where the sub had topped up with fuel on June 8, that they were told. This patrol would be "an Empire Run"—a patrol along the coast of Japan. *Pampanito* had been assigned to the area off Kyūshū, Shikoku, and Honshū, south of Japan. Gordon Hopper sensed no hesitation or fear on the part of the crew when they learned about this assignment: "Like all men who are convinced of their invulnerability, we were happy for the opportunity to make a killing along the coast of Japan." It was a patrol, however, that would later be classified as "unproductive" in the Ship's History. During this time *Pampanito* managed to damage only one enemy ship, a Japanese gunboat. And on two separate occasions during this run, the tables had been turned and torpedoes were launched at *Pampanito*.[12]

A submarine crew never wants to return from a war patrol with unlaunched torpedoes still aboard, but that was how *Pampanito* returned to Midway on July 23. Before turning the boat over to the relief crew, *Pampanito*'s men had to offload the unlaunched "fish." "This proved to be physically demanding," recalled Woodrow Weaver. "I did not realize how much the long days of submerged operations had taken out of us. We would unload one torpedo then pause for a rest." *Pampanito*'s crew then headed to the island's rest camp.[13]

Once the hard work was done, the submariners found that Midway was not nearly as exciting a port for R&R as Hawai'i had been. There was no fancy hotel here, just a camp composed of barracks. After a long submarine patrol with showers limited to one per week for most of the crew (cooks were exempted from this rule, which was intended to conserve water, and were permitted to shower more frequently), there was nothing Weaver was looking forward to more than a hot shower. He was appalled to find that the showers on Midway used salt water. Fresh water seemed almost as scarce here as it was aboard the submarine. Nor was there much on the island to occupy the submariners' time. Watching the island's gooney birds attempt their clumsy takeoffs and landings was a major activity on Midway—that, and drinking at the Gooney Bird Bar. The submariners made their own fun: "swimming, picnics, fighting and gambling," recalled Weaver. "The sailors on Midway were frustrated by their confined duty so they rigged up regular gambling casinos in the mess halls after working hours. Gambling consisted mostly of shooting dice and poker. There were card sharks who regularly relieved some of the more gullible sailors of their cash each pay day." *Pampanito*'s crew also played a high stakes volleyball match against their archrival *Sealion*'s team.[14]

Refit was completed by USS *Proteus* and the Submarine Division 202 relief crew during the first week of August, and repairs and modifications to the sub were made. On August 8, underway sound tests were conducted. The next five days were spent completing underway training exercises. On August 14 and 15 the sub was loaded with fuel, torpedoes, ammunition, and food in preparation for the upcoming run.

Joining the crew for this third patrol was a new pharmacist's mate, Maurice Demers. Demers had served on destroyers in the Atlantic, where he had seen, and been duly impressed by, the quick diving and surfacing capability of a German U-boat in the Atlantic. This made him think that submarines might actually be safer than surface vessels, and he decided to switch to submarines. Demers had served in the Army for a year as a medic before joining the Navy in October 1941, so it was only natural that he became a pharmacist's mate. By August 1943 he had passed the series of exams that earned him the rating of pharmacist's mate first class. In October he reported to Submarine Pharmacist's Mates' School at New London. After he was graduated on November 27, with an impressive average of 80.63 percent, he began Submarine Basic Training School at New London two days later, completing the course in January 1944.[15]

In the summer of 1944 Demers was assigned to USS *Pampanito*, and he joined the crew for the submarine's third run. It was on this patrol that he would experience his first depth charging. It was also on this patrol that he would undergo what would be the biggest professional challenge of his life.

Pampanito's third patrol would be conducted in what was known as "Convoy College"—the area of the South China Sea between the southern coast of China and Hainan Island. It was to be an eventful run, a patrol that Navy brass would later commend as "brief, spectacular and effective." For *Pampanito*'s crew, the events of this patrol would be astonishing, unexpected, and unforgettable.[16]

Third War Patrol

Pampanito departed Midway Island on August 17, 1944, along with USS *Growler* (SS-215) and USS *Sealion* (SS-315) via the newly captured island of Saipan. Whereas *Pampanito* had worked alone on her first two patrols, this time she was part of a wolf pack. The three subs were to operate as a coordinated attack group, off of Hainan Island, with Lieutenant Commander T. B. "Ben" Oakley Jr., *Growler*'s CO, as the pack's tactical leader. The group was nicknamed "Ben's Busters." It was *Sealion*'s second patrol and *Growler*'s tenth.

Pampanito steamed out to the patrol area. Summers marked August 18 with a note in his patrol report: "Crossed International Date Line and dropped this day from calendar." The journey was largely uneventful, beyond the usual dives during the day to avoid enemy planes whenever they were sighted. Every day, recalled Woodrow Weaver, two or three plane contacts on radar forced *Pampanito* to dive as a precaution. "Submerging a submarine had to be a well coordinated operation conducted with precise timing. We had many opportunities to perfect the technique."[17]

On August 30, Ben's Busters, operating with a second wolf pack, "Ed's Eradicators" (consisting of USS *Queenfish*, SS-393, and USS *Barb*, SS-220, with Captain Edwin Swinburne as tactical commander aboard *Barb*), attacked a convoy, sinking seven enemy ships. *Pampanito*, however, found herself largely left out of the action; Summers blamed communications problems for his inability to make contact with the convoy. The next day, *Pampanito*'s OOD and assistant OOD sighted the hit convoy: they reported a "big column of smoke and flames billowing many hundred feet in air—Moon was down and the sight something for those seeing first torpedoed ship."[18]

Pampanito arrived at her patrol station on August 30. It was soon afterward that a serious mechanical problem was discovered. The boat was getting heavy forward—apparently taking on extra water, and upsetting the trim of the boat; and a loud squealing noise was heard coming from the inside of the forward trim tank whenever the submarine submerged. The tank was leaking, and the leak seemed to be getting worse, but the crew was having trouble locating the source of the leak. Lieutenant Howard Fulton and Motor Machinist's Mate E. W. Stockslader volunteered to enter the tank and check for leaks as the boat dove. Summers described the incident in his patrol report for September 4: "This prospect was very risky but felt the results would be worth it." When darkness fell, the two volunteers went topside, entered the tank through the manhole cover, and were sealed in the tank. Then, slowly, cautiously, the submarine submerged. "A few very tense minutes while we waited for word from men in tank. Levelled off at 60 feet. Finally established voice communications; everything allright." The source of the problem was not found, however. *Pampanito* had to continue to dive, reaching a depth of two hundred feet before the two men sealed in the tank reported that they had located the leak. The next step was repairing the tank—another risky undertaking, as the repair had to be made from the outside. Again, a volunteer stepped forward, Gunner's Mate Tony Hauptman. Over the next forty-eight hours, the submarine surfaced several times, under the cover of night, while Hauptman, wearing shallow-water diving gear, submerged and worked on the repairs, using a special wrench that had been fashioned by some of the crewmen specifically for this task. On September 6 Summers was able to write in his report: "Dived. Found to our joy that Forward Trim Tank was tight. The whole ship owes a big debt to those taking the risks to fix it." The war patrol was resumed.[19]

September 6 was also Pete Summers's birthday—his thirty-first. It was also the day that an ill-fated Japanese convoy, designated HI-72, departed Singapore bound for Japan. Soon it would be crossing *Pampanito*'s path.

In the early morning hours of September 12, Ben's Busters made contact with a Japanese convoy consisting of nine ships and five escorts. The wolf pack closed in. *Pampanito* was still maneuvering for position when *Growler* struck, hitting and sinking one of the ships at 1:55 a.m. Summers continued tracking the convoy and trying to get into an optimum firing position, hoping to get in the next shot. At 5:27 a.m. he reported: "In position ahead almost on convoy's track and ready to dive when someone got in another attack. (Later found to be *Sealion*.) . . . It was a tremendous explosion and followed by hits in another ship which burned brightly, evidently a tanker. These were followed by depth charges and gun fire." *Pampanito*, further away from the ships, could not get within firing range. Throughout the rest of the day, Summers pursued the remaining ships in the convoy. Air cover forced *Pampanito* to submerge twice, and she lost contact with the convoy. Summers's frustration was high.[20]

Finally, late that evening, contact was reestablished. By 10:40 p.m., *Pampanito* had closed in on the remainder of the convoy and was within shooting distance. Summers ordered five torpedoes launched from the forward tubes—three at a large transport ship and two at large cargo ships sailing astern of a transport. Three minutes later, after swinging the submarine hard to the right, he ordered four torpedoes launched from the stern tubes, two at each of the cargo ships in the farthest column of the convoy. This time he hit his marks. "In all, seven hits out of nine torpedoes. From the bridge we watched both the largest AP [transport] and the large AK [cargo ship] (one with two hits) sink within the next ten minutes, and saw the after deck house of the third ship, on which we saw one hit, go up into the air with ship smoking heavily. . . . A short interval after the seven hits, the escorts started dropping depth charges at random, but for once we didn't mind."[21]

The next day *Pampanito*'s radarman detected two ships. Tracking showed that one of them had stopped moving. Summers assumed these were likely escort vessels, picking up survivors of the previous day's sinkings. He decided to attack the vessels, but scored no hits this time.

Still, it had been a highly successful operation for Ben's Busters— the wolf pack had decimated an enemy convoy—and it was already a successful patrol for *Pampanito*. She would be credited with sinking one large transport ship (*Kachidoki Maru*) and two large cargo ships, totaling 23,600 tons, and damaging a medium-size (4,000-ton) cargo ship. At patrol's end, each crew member would receive a Combat Insignia Award to pin to his uniform, and COMSUBPAC would praise the sub's skipper, officers, and crew: "This splendid patrol, as well as resulting in severe damage to the enemy, is marked with outstanding resourcefulness and ingenuity in the repair of a serious leak in the forward trim tank."[22]

But on September 12 the patrol was not yet over. The most remarkable events of all were yet to come.

3 The Fall of Singapore

Many of *Pampanito*'s crew had enlisted in the Navy out of a compelling sense of duty following the Japanese attack on Pearl Harbor on December 7, 1941. But for the British and the Australians, the war—and that pressing sense of duty—had begun much earlier. Bill Cunneen and Reg Stewart had enlisted together at a Melbourne recruiting office in June 1940. They were drafted to the same battery of an artillery unit, then underwent training together at Royal Park, Bendigo, and Puckapunyal. When they went home on leave, they returned to the same Melbourne suburb. In 1941 they sailed together to Malaya, along with the rest of the Australian 8th Division. And when Singapore fell in 1942, they would become prisoners of war together.[1]

Jack Wall of Hopetown, Victoria, left Australia for the war zone in September 1941. It was only after he was aboard a ship and under way, departing from Fremantle in a convoy of five vessels, that he learned of their destination. Four of the ships were headed to the Middle East; the fifth, the one that Wall was aboard, was going to Singaporc. "We were greatly disappointed as we believed we would not see action at Singapore and would only [have] garrison

Figure 2. Australian Frank Farmer on final leave before shipping out to the war zone, Christmas 1941. USS *Pampanito* (SS-383) Collection, San Francisco Maritime National Park Association.

duties. How little we knew what was in store for us." On October 3 the ship landed at Singapore, where they were welcomed by the native population, who, despite the welcome, seemed a little apprehensive about the Australians, "as the Tommies had given them a bad impression of us. However, it was not long before we were good friends, as the Aussie boys were more free and easy than the Tommies. The natives called us all 'Joe.'" The men were taken to a base camp in Malaya and drafted into their various units. Here they spent the next four months "training on road camps and aerodrome work before the Jap came over to have a look at us. I think he must have liked the look of the place, as it was not long before he was getting busy sinking the best part of our small Navy and then we had nothing on the sea to stop him, and had very few aircraft. These were very obsolete and never had a chance against the Nip as there would be anything up to 100 planes over at a time and only four or five of ours, which were hopeless against such odds." After the fall of Malaya at the end of January 1942, they were sent back to Singapore, only to find themselves hopelessly outnumbered again by Japanese forces. "We were shelled from the sea, bombed from the air, and then they closed in on us from all sides in their landing craft by hundreds and thousands. You can realise what chance we had against such odds."[2]

H. J. Barker, a private in the 4th Royal Norfolk Regiment of the British Army, departed Liverpool with the 18th Division on a foggy morning in late October 1941. The sense of sadness he felt at the thought of leaving home was overcome by the promise of adventure. Already within the course of the next few weeks he would see places he had never dreamed he would ever see. He and his fellow troops were shipped across the Atlantic to Halifax, Nova Scotia, where they were transferred to American vessels—the personnel transports *West Point* (AP-23), *Wakefield* (AP-21), *Mount Vernon* (AP-22) and *Leonard Wood* (AP-25)—for the journey to Trinidad, in the West Indies. From Trinidad they proceeded to Capetown, South Africa, arriving on December 8, 1941, and there they enjoyed a good four-day shore leave. From Capetown they sailed to Bombay, India, and then to Singapore, arriving in late January. By now the Japanese had already taken most of Malaya, and Barker and his comrades found themselves stationed in the first line of defense.

Barker recalled: "There was nothing much to do until the Nip troops landed on Singapore the night of February 5th, 1942. We were all ready for them. All through the night heavy guns pounded the coast, some falling 200 yards short of our positions. At dawn, they halted. It was reported thousands of Japanese troops had been killed, but they had gained enough coast on the west side to get their mortars into action against our defense lines. We were under mortar fire for a two-hour, continuous barrage. Ahead of our lines, Bren gun carriers were maneuvering for positions to attack these mortars; but had to return owing to aircraft machine-gunning and bombing of the roads and areas around."

Soon the barrage of the Japanese mortars was overwhelming. Their position appeared hopeless, but the orders were to stay on; reinforcements were on their way, they were told. "We stayed only to find the next morning no troops or patrols to be seen. Our support in the rear was all wiped out by the hell on earth from the Jap mortars all through the night." The Brits were ordered to withdraw to the main road to Singapore City. Hoping that their rear mortar platoons could hold back the Japanese, they started along Bukit Tinah Road, only to find that the entire battalion was leaving as well. "That was the start of our defense breaking up. What a hell of a mess it was. Japs broke through them everywhere; snipers, machine gunners, and dive bombers razed the area for miles. We lost a hell of a lot of men there in a few hours. Nothing could hold them back. Everywhere we turned, men were falling, killed and wounded by this awful barrage from all around."

Then suddenly, everything stopped. "All was deadly silence. Our ears were ringing, and eyes were smarting from the gas of explosives. Fellows could be heard groaning, and shouting way back for help. The stretcher bearers were running back and forth . . . carrying back smashed bodies that were still alive but could never be made whole again." The order came to run for cover, and Barker made a mad dash into the surrounding rubber forests, where he huddled in a dugout with a handful of other men. Surrounded by the ceaseless Japanese mortar fire and cut off from the other troops, they spent the next three days there, afraid to move.

On the night of February 13 they decided to try to reach Bukit Timah Road again under cover of darkness, fearful all the while that at any minute machine-gun fire would cut them down. Reaching the road, they threw themselves into the trenches running alongside it, then crawled on their bellies through the trenches for what seemed like miles. Suddenly, right ahead of them, "mortars suddenly started crashing all around us, shrapnel whining and cutting down the road above us. It was the worst experience I had in action. It was only God's mercy that I wasn't hit by it; these red hot jagged bits of steel. It ceased again, this crashing and shining; deadly silence hung over us, we heaved our bodies, cramped and shaken. The sight was terrible, ahead of us few that were together. On the road were smashed arms, bits of bodies and deep holes that reeked with fumes of explosives, choking us and smarting our eyes almost to blindness." The men lay down in the trenches again, dreading the daylight that was steadily creeping in to destroy their cover. Suddenly they heard the sound of vehicles on the road. Not daring to move, they waited until the source of the noise became visible: it was a Bren gun carrier. Despite the shrapnel holes that had torn its body, they recognized their division's sign on its gun covers. They waved and shouted at the driver to stop, then clambered out of the trench and onto the vehicle which then tore down the road, the Bren gunner returning the enemy gunfire all the way, until they reached the temporary safety of their unit headquarters.

Here, they were given food, while the section commander informed them just how grave the situation was on the front lines. Japanese mortar fire had killed hundreds, he said, and without any reinforcements available, the front line would not hold. There was nothing to do but wait in dugouts for further orders from division headquarters. When the orders finally came, they were to lay down arms.[3]

Prisoners of War

Andy Anderson had arrived at Singapore Harbor on January 29, 1942, aboard USS *West Point*, eager to fight and ready to play his part in the war. But it took only days until any illusions he held about the glory and nobility of battle were permanently shattered. "My battalion went up to the front lines on the 12th February and then we knew what Hell was. Fifth column was dead against us and we had no support at all. Friday the 13th was a day never to be forgotten by any of us. Bombs rained on us from everywhere, and men were being slaughtered left and right." Two days later the order came for unconditional surrender.[4]

The sudden halt of hostilities on February 15 left the Allied troops stunned. One of the defenders of Singapore remembered his confusion on that day: "At about 8 p.m. . . . . we were told by our O.C. that Singapore had fallen and that we were now prisoners of war. All firing stopped. After the continuous roar of planes, bombs and shells, for days and nights, the sudden silence was strange. It was days before we fully realised it had finished. That night I slept like a log, and next day we marched to the Tanglin barracks to hand over our arms and equipment to the Japs."[5]

The surrender of Singapore—along with approximately one hundred thousand Allied troops—on February 15 came as an immense shock not only to its defenders but to those back home as well. Singapore had been considered invincible. Anxiety was particularly acute in Australia, where the fall of Singapore was seen as a national calamity. Most Australians had believed that as long as Singapore was secure, Australia itself remained safe. Four days after the surrender, Australians' feelings of vulnerability were reinforced as the city of Darwin was bombed by Japanese planes—the first direct attack on Australian soil. The disaster at Singapore was followed by more Allied defeats in Asia, and within weeks, twenty-two thousand Australians had become prisoners of war in Japanese hands.[6]

When Private Barker was told of the surrender, his immediate feelings were of relief: "it was all over, I was safe, alive." This was soon followed, however, by a sense of disbelief. He was astonished to see tears stream down his commanding officer's face as he gave them the news that it was over, that they had been beaten. The CO turned his head away from his men in shame, and with his hand waved them over to the positions they were to take as they prepared to surrender themselves to the Japanese soldiers who stood nearby, guns poised. "They waited until we were all lined up. Then each man was searched by a Jap soldier. They took our watches, rings and anything of value and then the officers (Japanese) gave us orders to the effect that we would be treated as prisoners-of-war and told us to obey all orders, or we would be shot." All weapons and ammunition were collected from the POWs.[7]

Escape seemed impossible; the men were told that the Japanese forces had their artillery trained on them, ready to shoot any attempted escapees. They soon got a taste of what life as a prisoner of the Japanese would be like, as they were forced to march to Changi prisoner-of-war camp, a distance of more than fifteen miles to the north of Singapore, without a single stop for rest. Most of the men were weak from lack of food and sleep over the past few harrowing days, and were in no shape for the constant marching. Many fell out along the roadside as night came on, some due to injured feet, others from sheer exhaustion.

Changi

Changi prison was a huge POW camp on the northeastern tip of Singapore Island. Once assembled here, the prisoners were organized into their units. The officers among the POWs took charge of their men, and in fact most of the prisoners had no contact with the Japanese themselves while at Changi. Conditions at Changi, under the control of the POW officers, were considered tolerable at first. But soon food began running out. The Japanese had seized all Allied bulk stocks of rations, and began issuing the prisoners a ration that seemed woefully inadequate to the POWs. Andy Anderson recalled the food as consisting of broken rice supplemented by a very small ration of fish and meat. To many of the men, the sudden change from the European rations to which they had been accustomed to a diet of rice was the first sure sign of how conditions would from this point forward deteriorate. Recalled one Australian POW: "then came the never-to-be-forgotten rice. When they talked about rice I imagined the delicious boiled rice, milk and sugar that mother used to make, but it turned out to be just plain rice cooked so that it was always gluey. Boiled pawpaw and hibiscus hedge leaves made a stew about five days a week, and the other two days we had a tin of 'bully' between 12 men. Some men starved for days until they could bring themselves to eat this diet."[8]

For the next several months, the POWs at Changi were put to work doing construction and laboring in salvage dumps. The guards were relentless in making sure that they exacted as much work as possible from their prisoners. Anderson says the guards loomed over them "like slave drivers with a dozen whips": "Our pay was 25¢ a day and by the time we had finished a day's work we had earned $25." Still, the prisoners managed to sustain some optimism about their situation. Although they were prisoners, they knew that the Geneva Convention guaranteed them a certain standard of treatment. This included medical care, Red Cross parcels to supplement their rations and supplies, and of course letters from home. There was a pervasive belief among the POWs that their situation, although unpleasant, was only temporary: Singapore would be retaken by the Allies any day. Conditions only had to be tolerated until that time. So they made the best of it. To keep their spirits up, some of the prisoners even organized themselves into teams and played cricket matches, Australians versus Brits.[9]

News of the progress of the war, so essential to maintaining morale, was hard to obtain, especially from their captors. One of the Changi POWs recalled: "The Japs were always boasting about what they had occupied or bombed. I asked one, 'Luna Park, bomb bomb?' He said, 'Yes. Luna Park, bomb bomb.' If you asked them had they occupied Shirley Temple or bombed Charlie Chaplin, they would say, 'Yes,' too." When, in May, three thousand of the prisoners were ordered to move, a rumor quickly spread throughout the camp that these men were going to be exchanged for Japanese prisoners. Another rumor suggested that the men were going to be exchanged for Australian wool—a bale for each prisoner. "These are just a couple of the hundreds of yarns we heard—and believed. Such stories kept up our spirits and helped us through the tougher times later on." In actuality, however, these three thousand men were not going to be released, but were sent back to Singapore on work detail. George Ward was among them. He and the others were stationed at a camp called "River Valley," housed in huts he remembered as being "lousy."[10]

Eventually, over the course of several months, the rest of the POWs at Changi were transferred out, to camps in Burma, Borneo, or Japan. They were moved out in groups, each group including one or more officers, NCOs, and usually a medical officer. At this stage all the POWs still had their own clothing and kits. John Hocking of the Royal Artillery had been put to work building a shrine for the Japanese on Bukit Tinah Road. He wasn't sure what to believe when the guards now told him that the camp he was now being sent to in Thailand would have "plenty of rest and good food!"[11]

There turned out to be little work to do for George Ward and the men at River Valley Camp, so they found themselves amongst those being sent to Thailand to build a railway. The journey was difficult. "Thirty-two men were stacked in a cattle truck [railroad car], just like herring in a tin. The Japs had one wagon for five men. It took us four days to get to Thailand; at early morning we had to walk three miles to camp."[12]

Most of the men who would later survive the sinking of *Rakuyo Maru* were members of "A" Force of the Australian Imperial Force (AIF), a force of three thousand under the command of its senior officer, Brigadier Arthur L. Varley. On May 15, 1942, "A" Force was embarked at Singapore in two ships, headed for Burma. They quickly learned why these transports were often referred to as "hellships": conditions on board were almost unbearable. "The PW [prisoners of war] were crammed below deck into holds horizontally subdivided so that they occupied floors only 3 to 4 feet high. The men had hardly space to move and had to sleep on one another. The conditions in the hold were appalling, owing to the heat, the foetid atmosphere and the insufficiency of the food, which consisted almost entirely of 3 small meals daily, rice, onion soup and a cup of tea occasionally. Water bottles were filled about every 3 days. Deck latrines were provided; but only a few men were allowed on deck at a time, and some had to wait for hours."[13]

Having endured this torturous journey, which lasted almost two full weeks, "A" Force was disembarked as three different units, each named after its most senior officer. Anderson Force disembarked at Tavoy, Burma, where they spent three months on the construction of an aerodrome before being transferred to Moulmein by barge, then from Moulmein to Thanbyuzayat. Green Force disembarked at Victoria Point, where they too spent three months on aerodrome construction, then moved overland via Ye to Thanbyuzayat. The third unit, christened Ramsay Force, was landed at Mergui and later transferred via Tavoy to Thanbyuzayat. While conditions at these locations where less than ideal, deaths up to this point did not exceed 1 percent of the strength of each force and were due mainly to bad cases of dysentery or to shootings by Japanese guards of POWs attempting escape. Some of the men who would later find themselves aboard *Rakuyo Maru* were not a part of the Singapore "A" Force but belonged to the Java Force of the AIF; they were sent by transport ship from Changi to Rangoon, then to Moulmein, then to Thanbyuzayat.[14]

The British POWs slated for work on the railroad were taken in October 1942 from Singapore through Malaya to Bampong in Thailand by train, and from Bampong they were marched to one end of the planned railway line, at Kanchanaburi. The Japanese plan called for the British POWs to begin construction of the line at Kanchanaburi and to continue working in a northerly direction until they met up with the Australian POWs, who were working down from Burma, at a distance of about eighty-five miles from Thanbyuzayat. The march from Bampong to Kanchanaburi was a labor in itself: the men walked a total of eighty miles, at first through relatively flat fields of rice, where they often had to wade through knee deep mud and slime, but before long the route began to get more and more difficult as it started to wind through dense jungle and up hills. "This march can best be imagined than described. Many without shoes, little clothing, through mud and wet, heat and rain, being beaten up by their guards for little or no offence greater than falling by the wayside from fatigue or sickness." John Hocking remembered the trek through the thick jungle as taking nearly a week, with "quite a few deaths" along the way before they reached their destination: a mosquito-infested swamp in the midst of the thick jungle. This site was to be their first camp.[15]

Although it was called a "camp" by the Japanese, there were no facilities at the site: the POWs had to build their own accommodations from bamboo, palm branches, and whatever other natural resources happened to be in the area. In the meantime, they slept anywhere they could find some sort of shelter from the weather. No mosquito nets were provided by the Japanese; the POWs tried to roll their blankets up over their heads to protect themselves from the swarms of mosquitoes in the jungle. Without any time to pause for rest after the harrowing journey, the POWs spent the next week building huts for themselves. Andy Anderson reflected on what was to come: "This place was called Wampo and it was here we found what living hell was."[16]

Sure enough, hell was only beginning. Once the camp facilities were built, the POWs were put to work on the construction of the Burma-Thai Railroad. It was a project that would cost so many lives that history would remember it as "The Railway of Death."

The Burma-Thai Railroad

As the Japanese Empire expanded rapidly after its initial successes in the Pacific, the need for supply lines increased. It proved particularly difficult for Japan to supply its army in Burma; the sea route required sailing south of Singapore—a lengthy route and one highly vulnerable to Allied attacks, particularly after the Battle of Midway in June 1942 had halted Japanese naval superiority in the Pacific. Thus, in order to reduce the cost of using its merchant marine to supply Burma, Japan began to consider an overland supply route: a railroad track connecting Bangkok to Rangoon. Such a railway would reduce a 2,000-mile sea route to a 350-mile overland route. The idea had not been seriously considered before, as it would require intensive labor through exceptionally harsh terrain. But now the Japanese had an available—and, in their view, expendable—labor force: it was to be drawn from the approximately 130,000 men who had surrendered to the Japanese when Singapore fell in February 1942. They included the 127,000 members of the British Commonwealth land forces, as well as survivors from Allied ships that had been sunk in the area, air crewmen whose planes had been shot down, Dutch and Commonwealth prisoners taken captive in erage number of men at each camp was usually around a thousand, and there were reportedly sixty camp locations along the length of the line. Most were temporary work camps, hastily erected by the POWs and then abandoned when that particular section of track was completed. The men lived in bamboo huts, with roofs thatched with palm leaves, and bamboo-tiered floors on which they slept. Sleeping on the bamboo poles, with the hard and rigid nodes that lined each stalk, was uncomfortable, but still preferable to lying on the ground, where one was exposed directly to lice and other insects.[5]

A few camps of a more permanent nature were also constructed by the POWs along the line. These were known as "base camps" and usually included a "base hospital"—in actuality a far cry from a serious medical facility. Some of these base camps were retained as maintenance camps when the line was completed. Most of the camps in Burma were named according to their distance, in kilometers, from Thanbyuzayat: for example, base camps in Burma included 18-Kilo Camp, 80-Kilo Camp, and 100-Kilo Camp. In Thailand, the camps were given names by the Japanese that sometimes, but not always, corresponded to nearby town names, such as Tarsoa, Ta Makan, and Kanchanaburi. At Kanchanaburi there were several camps designated as "rest camps" after the completion of the railroad, as well as one officers' camp.[6]

Australian Ray Burridge remembers the camp at Thanbyuzayat as being one of the better-organized camps. It included "rough hospital facilities" where a POW physician, Dr. Fisher, tended to sick and injured POWs. Occasionally, extremely ill POWs from work camps further down the line would be sent back to Thanbyuzayat for treatment. The Brits at the camp at Wampo, in the meanwhile, were not faring well. Andy Anderson recalled: "We lost 27 men within a month and things were very hard for us. Food consisted of plain rice and salt water for well over the first month and men were being ill-treated by the Japs in every shape and form working from dawn to dusk clearing virgin jungle and rocks for this thought impossible mad idea."[7]

The branch of the Japanese military charged with overall command of the construction of the Burma-Thai Railroad was Prisoner of War Branch no. 3, originally headed by Lieutenant Colonel Nagatoma, with headquarters based at Thanbyuzayat. Individual camp commanders—and this was the case at all Japanese POW camps, not just those along the railway—varied widely in rank, so that while one camp might be under the command of a captain, at another camp the officer in charge might be merely a private. Most were officers or non-commissioned officers. The camp commander, in turn, supervised a corps of guard personnel, which usually numbered around thirty men and was composed of Japanese enlisted men up to the rank of sergeant, along with large numbers of natives and Koreans. Korean guards were employed chiefly in the camps in Burma and Thailand, and so became very familiar to the POWs who worked on the railroad.[8]

Whatever the guards' rank or nationality, their cruelty toward the prisoners was a common trait shared by almost all of them. The intense and lasting disdain these guards earned from their charges was evident in the remarks gathered during interrogation of those POWs who survived the war. "The guards were illiterate and low-grade personnel. Their sudden rise to a position of command, directing the lives and labors of large groups of men[,] quickly developed a latent and infectious cruel streak in their characters. Domination over men of races which had, in their eyes, traditionally asserted a superiority over them was a new and wonderful thing; it led to an unrelieved display of arrogance, cruelty and hostility. They spoke no English, and made no apparent effort to learn it. Being largely treated as animals by their own superiors, they bettered their instructors, and showed an inspired skill in humiliating, degrading, and torturing those in their charge. Reports substantiating this analysis come from all sections of Southeast Asia without distinction."[9]

According to POW accounts, the camp commandants and guards varied in their attitudes toward and treatment of the prisoners. Some were even considered considerate, especially those who took steps to prevent excessive maltreatment of the prisoners. Others appeared to have no interest in making conditions better in the camps or in seeing to the fair treatment of the prisoners. Intelligence reports gathered from the *Rakuyo Maru* survivors included a list of names of Japanese officers who were considered to be "good," and others who were considered "very bad." Most postwar reports from former POWs claimed that the Korean guards were the worst, outdoing the Japanese in their cruelty, bashing the POWs "at the slightest pretext." "The Korean guards were bad to everyone. They do not rate any rank—they are just 'guards.'"[10]

Construction

The Burma-Thai Railroad was the biggest and, in terms of engineering, most complex project POWs would be assigned to, yet it was accomplished with minimal supplies and equipment, mainly picks, shovels, and blasting powder. As the construction began, work camps consisting of bamboo huts were built at intervals along the

Kwai Valley by advance parties of POWs, who lived in tents or bivouacs while completing this work. Next, main parties, consisting of several hundred men each, were brought in to clear paths through the jungle to join the camps. Clearing the land required pulling out huge clumps of bamboo; former POWs recall it as "back-breaking" work that took more then ten men per stalk of bamboo.[11] All work was done with crude, simple tools. Earth and rock were loosened using pick and shovel, chipping and blasting, and then moved by hand in small baskets. Boreholes for explosives were made with a crowbar and sledgehammer, a few millimeters at a time, until they were one meter deep. It took two men a full day to complete such a borehole.

Timber for bridges and culverts was cut in the nearby jungle or sent to the site by river. The POWs cut up the tree trunks using two-handed saws, then moved the logs to the construction sites, sometimes with the help of trained elephants. The actual construction of the railroad consisted of cutting through the virgin jungle and leveling a track, making embankments and cuttings, building bridges, and finally laying and ballasting the track. The northern section of track was particularly challenging, as the land was often hilly and mountainous; the track was kept to flatter land along water, but when this was not possible, the line ran along ledges cut out of the hillside by the labor of the POWs.

Former POW and British officer Basil Peacock, who had been one of those captured at the fall of Singapore and forced to work on the railroad, remarked that the construction and engineering of the railway were not so outstanding; what made the Burma-Thai Railroad exceptional was the fact that it was built by humans without machines. He wrote: "In fact, it was built as were the pyramids of old, with few tools but with enormous numbers of expendable laborers. No one who worked on the River Kwai now wonders how some of the mighty works of the ancients were completed without machines. They can guess the methods used even better than can some theorizing archaeologists."[12]

Living Conditions

The work itself was backbreaking, unthinkable, seemingly impossible. Surviving the work alone would be a challenge for any man. Yet making the POWs plight even more challenging, even more life threatening, were the living conditions, the meager diet, and the treatment they received at the hands of their captors. At first they had, not surprisingly, expected better. Unlike the status of POWs during World War I, this time there were international rules that had been established concerning the treatment of POWs. Certain minimum standards, designed to ensure the well-being and survival of prisoners, had been guaranteed by the Geneva Convention. Japanese representatives had signed the 1929 Geneva accords regarding the treatment of POWs, but the Japanese government had never formally ratified them. When pressed by the Imperial Prisoners of War Committee in February 1942 on this issue, the Japanese government indicated that while it did not feel bound by the conventions, it would still observe them. The Geneva terms included minimum standards for the care and treatment of POWs by the detaining power. According to these terms, prisoners were to receive the same rations as the troops of the captor nation were given. POWs could be used as labor, but not in dangerous or health-risking work or in labor projects connected with the war effort; POW officers were not to be used in labor at all. The prisoners must be lodged in buildings or barracks with all possible hygiene; canteens should be provided for the prisoners at camps, and tobacco permitted for the prisoners' use. "Intellectual diversions" and sports were to be encouraged whenever possible. Furthermore, according to the Geneva Convention, POWs had the right to have their persons and their honor respected: they must be at all times humanely treated and protected, including from acts of violence, insults, and "public curiosity." As for punishments, the only ones permitted were those provided by the holding power for the same acts of their own soldiers. Virtually all of these terms were soon abrogated by the Japanese.[13]

More than two years later, Stanley Costello would reveal to his stunned listeners aboard *Pampanito*: "We soon found out the Nips' true color. We worked long hours [with] small food and plenty of beating up. For three months we dug one square yard of soil per man with pick and shovel. By this time the lads were beginning to develop fever but this made no difference, they still had to work. We had one day a week rest, in which we were allowed to have a small concert but could not sing 'God Save the King.'" Work hours were long, and work continued in all weather conditions. The following work schedule was not uncommon for those who labored on the railway: they would leave camp at dawn, work for seven hours, eat lunch, and then continue to work until dark before walking back to camp, often an hour's walk. Often they were barefooted and wearing only a loincloth or G-string for clothes. The second meal of the day was not eaten until a full ten hours after lunch. As men became sick or died, from illness or malnutrition or sheer exhaustion, those who remained had to work harder and longer. Shifts increased from twelve to eighteen hours a day, and it was not unusual for the POWs along the railroad to sometimes work twenty-four hours in a row. At night they worked by the light of torches made of bamboo and filled with oil. Some former POWs recalled working from eight in the morning until five o'clock the following morning, with only three hours in the twenty-four to rest. "The only possible relief from the long working hours was a bad attack of fever." But even illness was no guarantee of a chance to rest. In Burma the normal routine seems to have required 80 percent of camp strength to be out on the work parties, with 10 percent left behind for housekeeping duties, and 10 percent considered too sick to work. However, at almost all times more than 10 percent of the camp population was sick—usually between 25 and 75 percent. Consequently, the housekeeping detail was usually comprised of sick men, and another large contingent of sick men had to go out in the working parties. All patients who were ambulatory were required to go to work. Even those who could not walk were not necessarily spared. Sick men with temperatures of up to 103 degrees Fahrenheit, or those suffering from other ailments, were carried to work on stretchers, given tools, and made to break stones and rock, or to drill holes for blasting. If they refused, they were beaten.[14]

This grinding work routine only resulted in more and more cases of illness, forcing the healthier men to do more work and keep longer hours as they desperately tried to meet the impossible quotas set by the overly optimistic Japanese for their ambitious railroad project. Recalled one POW: "It was impossible even to approach the quotas. The poor tools they gave us did not help. We had no drills, machinery or explosives—not even wheelbarrows; just a shovel, a pick and a rice bag for moving earth." Another POW remembered the increasing desperation of the project: "Because they were behind schedule, the Japs used to pull all the sick men out on parade, and guards would go along and feel their foreheads. Any man who had had a fever the day before and who had temporarily cooled down would be sent out. We called these 'Blitz Parades.' One night I had a temperature of 105.6, the second highest they recorded there, and the next morning I was blitzed out to the line. I just managed to struggle through a 14-hour shift."[15]

Although, per the terms of the Geneva Convention, POW officers were not supposed to be put to work, initially along the railroad the officers were organized into groups, along with the enlisted men, and often given the hardest and worst work to do. This was intended to demean them in front of the men and the native workers. Eventually this practice was discontinued, at least in the case of Australian officers. It was rumored that this change in policy occurred because after Japanese midget submarines attacked Sydney Harbor on May 31, 1942, the Australians respectfully sent back some remains of the sub crewmen to the Japanese. "This of course was considered the highest tribute, and as a reply to this gesture, Australian officers worked no more."[16]

Postwar reports from the former POWs generally concurred that the supervision of the work parties along the railroad seemed for the most part indifferent. It was fairly easy to leave a work party and casually walk off into the jungle. "There was some evidence that guarding on work parties was in fact of an extremely loose and slipshod variety; yet the security was adequate. The basis for this, of course, is the fact that in all of the areas under the scope of this report, internment was usually in isolated and jungle areas. . . . Thus, though it was often a relatively simple matter to get out of camp at night, or to walk off the job on a work party, the real question was what to do next." At Thanbyuzayat the Japanese had initially demanded that all men in each POW force sign an oath pledging that they would not attempt to escape. At first the men refused, until finally (and in the face of threats from the Japanese) the senior POW officers advised their men to sign, assuring them that the gesture was meaningless, since an agreement signed under duress could not be considered valid in any case. The officers, however, also advised the men not to attempt to escape, because escapees were almost invariably shot, and in addition any escape attempts, successful or not, would result in more severe treatment of those still in the camp. Reprisals against those remaining in the camp might include reduction of the already inadequate food rations, hourly roll call, and impromptu searches and extensive interrogations.[17]

While there were some attempts made to escape, particularly in the early months of 1943, escape was a much harder task in the Japanese camps than in a German POW camp. While there were no real physical barriers—no towers or sentries, at most there might be a bamboo fence and a ditch—the geography made escape virtually impossible. An escaped prisoner had nowhere to go. He could not hide by blending in with the locals. If caught, execution was certain. Even a successful escape held the horrifying prospect of the consequences that would be imposed on the other, remaining POWs, if one of their lot went missing. As one of the POWs later explained, there were no walls around the camps, and no need for them, either: "the Japs just said that's the line there. Cross that, and that's it, you're dead." The men were "geographical prisoners," guarded not by sentries in towers but by thick jungles, impenetrable swampland, and mountains; by a language barrier and incidents of treachery on the part of the natives in the local countryside; and by the knowledge of certain death upon recapture. The Japanese considered POWs who escaped to be on the level of soldiers who deserted, and the penalty for desertion was death.[18]

Though escape attempts were rare, the loose supervision of work parties gave POWs the occasional opportunity to make contact with the local population. Such contacts were also made near the camps by night. While it was never certain if a native could be trusted, many of the POWs sensed a feeling of sympathy from the natives they encountered, based on a realization that they were all in the same boat: under Japanese domination, and trying to cope with shortages of life's necessities. With their pay or by trading bits of clothing, or perhaps a blanket or some mosquito netting, if it could be spared, the POWs were sometimes able to obtain a few items of food, or some medicine or tobacco, from the natives, or—something also considered of great value to the POWs—some news of the progress of the war, in the form of newspapers or propaganda leaflets.[19]

The POW Diet

The rations provided to POWs consisted mainly of rice, sometimes, if the prisoners were lucky, with a little protein added—perhaps salted fish, buffalo, or pork. But meat was generally considered a luxury, and rarely seen by the POWs. More commonly the supplements added to the rice barely added any flavor, much less any nutrition. One of the POWs who was later rescued by *Pampanito* attested that his POW diet had consisted of two lots of rice a day and a pan of "radish stew": radishes boiled in water.[20] When possible, the prisoners would pool the meager pay they received from the Japanese to purchase things such as meat, eggs, or sugar. When this option was not available, they would try to supplement the rice with native foods and edible roots.

Two years later, aboard *Pampanito*, George Ward, writing an account of his experiences for *Pampanito* crewman Hubert Brown, included a list of the daily rations he received from the Japanese while a POW: "Breakfast—1 pint of rice. Dinner—1 pint of rice, vegetable water. Tea—1 pint of rice, tea." Bill Cunneen estimated after the war that during his two and a half years as a POW he must have eaten 672 pounds of rice. After the war, when reports were compiled based on information obtained from surviving POWs, it was concluded that the food situation had been the worst for the men who worked on the Burma-Thai Railroad. The rations were consistently inadequate, especially for men engaged in such strenuous and intensive daily labor. Sick men, who were seen as not pulling their weight, were given half rations—half of the already meager and substandard ration the rest received.[21]

In the jungle, all of the Japanese soldiers carried with them a small tube that functioned as a water filter. On one end of the tube was a box with chemicals for purifying water, and water found in the jungle could be safely consumed by drinking it through this straw. The POWs were not given any filters. They obtained their drinking water from nearby streams or other sources and were left to their own devices to make arrangements for boiling and purifying it. During the dry season, water became extremely scarce and difficult for the POWs to find at all.[22]

In interrogations by Allied intelligence officers after the war, former POWs indicated that the lack of food was, in many ways, the worst part of their situation. One interrogation officer commented in his report that "there was no single item in the long array of miseries imposed by the Japanese that rendered the internees more helpless. Living quarters could be and were given all possible attention and effort; even punishment and physical mistreatment was to some extent avoidable if the individual was willing to undergo the humiliations necessary to that end. But, save for the ceaseless watching for snakes and stray dogs, there was little that could be done to gain more food."[23]

Pay

Per the terms of the Geneva Convention, POWs were entitled to receive pay from their captors for any work they performed while in captivity. Pay to POWs was begun in June 1942. POWs on the railway initially received ten cents a day (fifteen cents for NCOs). As work became more arduous and hours longer, this was increased to twenty-five cents (thirty cents for NCOs). (George Ward, precise as always in his account to the crew of *Pampanito*, noted that twenty-five was equivalent to six and a half cents in American funds.) Sick POWs were not paid. Minimal as it was, the pay was crucial to the POWs, enabling them to purchase at least a small amount of supplementary native food or some tobacco. Sometimes the men's pay was collected by the POW officers and pooled to purchase some meat, the going price for a water buffalo being thirty-five dollars. Australian POW K. C. Renton, in an account he wrote aboard *Pampanito* for Torpedoman Woodrow Weaver in Weaver's journal, remarked that the pay was virtually worthless, as many natives refused to take it in exchange for goods. "[But] they would take clothes, and if you had them to spare you could get bananas and sugar and such like but very seldom we got an issue from the Japs because they were aware of our game."[24]

Illness

As the rations supplied to the POWs were reported to be consistently inadequate at every camp along the Burma-Thai Railroad, so were the living conditions at the camps. The bamboo huts with their palm leaf roofs were far from waterproof. Larger huts often had an unfloored and unroofed passage down the middle, which, during the wet season, became a knee-deep bog. The men sometimes slept directly on the bamboo floor of the huts. In some camps they built beds, bunks with four or five tiers. Each tiered unit was only allowed one and a half by six feet of space. Facilities for proper cooking or boiling of water were almost nonexistent. Open latrines were common, and during the rainy season flooding could be so intense that excrement from the latrines floated freely through the prisoners' huts. In one camp hospital, reported a prisoner after the war, the sick had to crawl, on all fours, a distance of fifty yards to reach an open-air latrine. "Drenched by the incessant monsoonal rain, they would return to bed, only to be drenched again an hour later. Shelters were old and never waterproof."[25]

Malnourishment and other factors soon led to a variety of ailments among the prisoners, from skin rashes to blindness and dementia. Mosquitoes brought malaria and dengue fever, and contaminated food and water—contamination that was spread further by the omnipresent flies—made dysentery a common ailment. Mites spread another fever, scrub typhus. The man in overall command of the railroad project—the commanding officer of Prisoner of War Branch no. 3—was repeatedly heard stating that is was his intention to let the sick prisoners die, as they were of no use to him. Consequently, even the hospitals provided for prisoners along the railroad line seemed more conducive to this end than to restoring the ill prisoners to any semblance of health. The Japanese provided "hospitals" but made no provisions for medical personnel to man them; care of the sick was left to the POWs themselves.[26] The doctors and surgeons at these hospital camps were drawn from the medical officers among the ranks of the POWs. And these POW medical officers were hardly prepared to deal with the conditions they faced in the camps. Matters were only made worse by the fact that the Japanese reduced, or sometimes stopped entirely, rations to the sick, demonstrating their disdain for a sick soldier as well as for any soldier who had surrendered.

The conditions the POW medical officers faced were challenging, to say the least. Medical supplies were sparse at best. The Japanese provided occasional stocks of bandages and cotton wool, at infrequent intervals, and in ridiculous amounts, such as half a pound of wool and six yards of bandages for fifteen hundred men. As for medicines, the Japanese issued mosquito cream, and plenty of quinine was made available, but little else. The doctors had to make do. POWs reported that ground charcoal was used extensively for dysentery and all other stomach complaints, while lime and sulphur were used for skin rashes, cuts, and scratches. Saline dressings were used for tropical sores, but the sores rarely healed, making many operations necessary. Surgical tools were not available; again, the doctors improvised, using razor blades, sawed-off spoons, table knives, shovel blades, and other crude implements fashioned by the prisoners.[27]

When surgery was required, only local anesthetics were available, even for major procedures such as amputations. Many of the patients had large tropical ulcers that had spread from the foot to the knee. Amputation was the only way to treat such an ulcer, and a large percentage of those undergoing amputation died in the process. One survivor later attested: "Once, at 105 Kilo, I saw one of the doctors do an amputation with a hacksaw borrowed from a camp workshop. He repeatedly asked the Japs for supplies and instruments, but could not get them."[28]

Under such conditions, it is not surprising that the death rate along the Burma-Thai Railroad was estimated at 25 percent. While the doctors struggled, they could not prevent the huge number of deaths—so many that usually there was not enough time for the prisoners to bury their dead comrades, and the bodies had to be burned. Cliff Farlow told his *Pampanito* rescuers that one of the hospital camps, at one stage, was burning twenty men per day, finally ending up with a total death tally of nine hundred dead out of a camp of twelve hundred.[29]

John Hocking survived the camps, but during his time on the railroad, like many of the POWs, he suffered from a host of ailments: yellow jaundice, dengue fever, beriberi, pellagra, dysentery, and recurring malaria. Still, he considered himself "one of the lucky ones, I didn't get cholera, of which very few survived." Another POW reported: "The Japs were meticulous about NOT burying patients when still alive. If a man was found to be still alive when thrown into a hole for burial, he would be pulled out, left near the hole and pushed in again when dead."[30]

Morale

Overall, the guards in the camps along the railway were reported to be particularly harsh and barbaric, often for no apparent reason except perhaps their own amusement. Jack Wall, having returned safely to his hometown of Hopetown, Victoria, in late 1944, told a local newspaper reporter about the cruelty he had encountered: "When a Jap smacked you across the face for a mere nothing, you simply had to stand and take it like a lamb. This annoyed the Jap as he loved to see us crack up and fall. He felt then that he had done something worth-while. He would then sometimes pick you up and give you a cigarette. It is hard to understand their mentality. Some of the boys got cunning at last, and as soon as they received a smack would purposely fall down and would perhaps score a cigarette. The Jap was evidently quite proud that he had knocked a white man down." Bill Cunneen of Victoria, after his rescue, made a list in a small notebook and titled it "Things that happened, but you won't believe it." The list included the time he had witnessed two American POWs at 105-Kilo Camp being made to stand at attention for ninety-seven hours for a very minor breach of camp rules.[31]

Somehow, in spite of the cruelty, the illnesses, the exhausting schedule, and the backbreaking work, the prisoners managed to maintain a surprisingly high level of morale. This was helped, in a few very rare instances, by the arrival of mail from home. The Red Cross sent packages to POW camps to supplement the men's meager supplies of necessities, but these packages rarely reached the POWs. Bill Cunneen reported that in two and a half years, one Red Cross parcel was received among seven men. The amount of correspondence allowed from the POWs to the outside world was also limited, and varied from camp to camp, at the discretion of the camp commander. Generally the POWs were only permitted to send correspondence in the form of postcards, with standard text phrases. Frank Farmer's wife, Mary, received this postcard: "I am interned at The War Prisoners Camp at Moulmein in Burma. My health is good. I have not had any illness. I am working for pay at 10 cents per day."[32]

In camp, to keep their spirits up, they sang, although the Japanese forbade the singing of patriotic songs such as "God Save the King" and "Rule Britannia" once they realized their significance. "Most camps possessed a bugle and at the sounding of 'Retreat' every man stood to attention. The spirit of Australians was unbroken." George Ward recalled the Japanese forbidding the prisoners to whistle or clap their hands during recreation periods. The prisoners were also

IMPERIAL JAPANESE ARMY.

I am interned at The War Prisoners Camp at
Moulmein in Burma.

My health is (good, ~~sound~~, ~~poor~~)

I have not had any illness.

~~I (am) (have been) in hospital.~~

I am (~~not~~) working (for pay at __10 cents__ per day).

My salary is __________ per month.

I am with friends __________

KEEP SMILING MARY RIP. THINK OF YOU ALL CONSTANTLY. TIM A BONNY CHAP? FONDEST LOVE.

From _Frank Farmer_

Figure 3. Postcard received by Mary Farmer from her husband, Frank, while he was a POW of the Japanese. USS *Pampanito* (SS-383) Collection, San Francisco Maritime National Park Association.

prohibited from holding religious services in the camps. Holidays were far from festive. At his first Christmas in a camp along the railway, Andy Anderson recalled, "the Japs opened their hearts and gave the camp of 1500 men two old sows and three chickens for their Christmas dinner."[33]

One POW related experiencing a different side of the Japanese character: "Toward the end of the construction of the railway, the Jap officer in charge took a sudden interest in the welfare of the POWs and initiated a system of calisthenics and recreation. Football was played—and singing (Japanese songs which the prisoners sang a bit half-heartedly!)" The prisoners kept up morale as best they could, and indeed, came home with a few good memories among the bad. Happier memories often centered on the camp concert parties that were held by the POWs in camps along the railroad. "Female impersonators in these parties used uniforms, rouge and lipstick left behind at Singapore by Australian nurses. Many of their songs hurled ridicule and insult at the Japanese, who, understanding only a few words of English, would howl with delight after every turn." The men gave their Japanese guards surreptitious nicknames such as "Fishface," "Blood Pressure," "Frankenstein," "Storm Trooper," and "Beefhead." Gambling was another form of recreation that the POWs often indulged in, despite a ban on gambling by the Japanese (and a potential penalty of "bashing"—punching or slapping in the face, or beating with a bamboo or rifle on the back or chest). "But, according to the rescued prisoners, it took more than a bashing to stop an Australian when he made up his mind to play poker, two-up or crown and anchor."[34]

Any news of life and the world outside the misery of their camps was a surefire morale booster, so at some camps, when letters arrived the officers would invite the men to submit any items of general interest to them. These tidbits were then written into a bulletin that was posted for all to read. Some of the home-front news items that the POWs learned about in this way included the name of the Melbourne Cup winner; football results; the growing number of women in the armed services; the arrival of American forces in Australia; and the introduction of clothes rationing. The Japanese sometimes circulated their own "bulletins" as well, for the benefit of the POWs. Usually about fifty of these newsletters were printed out and circulated among a thousand POWs. The POWs rushed to read them: "It was the only English reading matter they could get—and the only humour." The bulletins were filled with fantastic stories of the heroic exploits of the Japanese military, such as the tale of a Zero pilot who, upon noticing that the undercarriage of his plane was shot away, landed by putting his feet through the holes in the floor and running along until the plane stopped, undamaged, on the airfield. Many of the POWs felt that their guards actually believed these stories. Some POWs reported being told by their guards that Japan had overrun Darwin, occupied Sydney, taken Adelaide with a bayonet charge, and were now preparing for an invasion of the United States, having already shelled San Francisco.[35]

Two men who had worked on the railway at 105-Kilo Camp recalled an incident in which a Japanese cameraman arrived to photograph "happy prisoners" marching off cheerfully to work on the railway. The fittest-looking POWs were placed on the outside ranks, and the less-fit and less-clothed men were placed on the inside. They were ordered to sing as they marched. "When all was ready, the prisoners marched off singing loudly an unprintable version of 'Bless 'Em All.' The sound engineer's face lit up with pleasure, and he made it clear that he thought he had obtained a really great propaganda score." In another attempt at creating positive propaganda, on the Emperor's birthday in 1943, at a hospital in Burma, the Japanese selected one ward and cleaned it up. It was outfitted with pristine sheets, a full medical dispensary, and even white-coated Japanese orderlies. Next a movie camera and crew were brought in to film the orderlies assisting weak and disabled POW patients. The Japanese handed out blank sheets of paper to the prisoners and photographed them reading "letters from home." They filled bottles with cold tea, labeling them "pineapple juice" and "orange cordial," and filmed the POWs enjoying the beverages. "Other men were shown with Jap doctors 'operating' on them and immediately afterwards in a truckload of happy, singing men being driven out to work on the railway. This was the only occasion that prisoners were driven to work, and then the truck went only as far as the camp gate."[36]

The Rainy Season

From November through April the POWs worked under the intense tropical sun. As monsoon season began in May 1943, conditions on the railway turned even worse. For the next few months, torrential tropical rainstorms flooded many of the camps. The rain penetrated the palm-thatched roofs of the huts, turning the huts and the entire camps into swirling seas of mud. In such conditions, the POWs' flimsy blankets and scanty rags of clothing quickly deteriorated. They were not replaced, and soon many of the men were reduced to wearing only a loincloth. Incidents of malaria, beriberi, and other illnesses increased, as did the number of deaths. Rations had been decreased after March or April 1943, and as a result, cases of malnutrition became even more numerous and severe. Soon afterward, a cholera epidemic swept through the POW labor camps along the line; deaths multiplied, and with no time to haul away the bodies of the deceased, many were burned onsite. Still the work carried on.[37]

Aboard *Pampanito*, Harry Chivers would recount some of the miseries that accompanied the rainy season in the camps: "As the wet season progressed so did the ulcers. It was here that I first heard men asking the doctors to cut their legs off so as to get some relief." The tropical ulcers, he said, were one of the most terrible things he had ever seen. Another survivor aboard *Pampanito*, K. C. Renton, confirmed that an unprecedented number of men during this period lost legs and arms, having developed tropical ulcers for which the only option was amputation.[38]

During the cholera attacks, the patients would be segregated in tents well away from the rest of the camp. If the camp was ready to move to the next stage of railway construction and a man was too sick to be moved, it was not unusual for the Japanese guards to order that the ill man be left behind. Reported the POWs: "Our men would insist on taking them, a deal of controversy would take place, culminating in some instances in a Jap officer going up and shooting the man himself in his tent."[39]

The bodies of those who died from cholera were usually burned in order to prevent further spread of the disease. The disease was known to spread very quickly, and precautions had to be taken such as sterilizing eating utensils and not drinking any water that had not been boiled. This period—starting around May 1943—was perhaps the most harrowing time for the POWs in the construction of the railway, as conflicting stresses arose: the need to complete the railroad on schedule, complicated by the depletion of laborers by disease; and the extra work needed to boil all water, disinfect or burn contaminated clothes, and dispose of the numerous bodies. By June 1943 a new factor of stress was added: Allied bombers began hitting towns along the railway route, sometimes inadvertently killing POWs. One Australian POW later recalled, "There are few things so testing of morale as being bombed in a POW camp."[40]

Completion of the Railroad

And through it all, in spite of it all, work progressed. And, finally, in October 1943, the two ends of the railroad line met at the ninety-six-mile point. Just four months beyond the projected twelve months, the new railway was complete. On October 25 the last spikes were driven in at the ceremonial opening of the new railroad. A POW recalled the occasion with some well-justified bitterness: "A typical Japanese pantomime of propaganda took place. All POWs were cleared away from the precincts, Japanese engineers were brought up, and surrounded by cinema cameras, the ceremony of joining the last ties was photographed, in proof of the wonderful work done by them."[41]

Over the next few months following completion of the railway, batches of POWs were gradually taken back to camps in Thailand. The sick POWs and the amputation cases from the railroad camps were removed to a camp near Bangkok. However, many thousands were kept on the line to perform maintenance and repair, to cut wood for fuel, and for other tasks—including the repair of damage being caused to the track by Allied bombers. On January 1, 1944, some of these men were finally sent back to camps in Thailand. Amazingly, their spirits were not yet broken. "Some of these men left the railway about New Year's Day 1943/44, and at midnight during the train journey a great hullaballoo took place, the prisoners' band (they had been allowed to take band instruments with them) starting up all along the train, blowing the New Year in, with the zest of realising that they were travelling to a fair land of civilisation in POW camps in Thailand after 19 months in the jungles." K. C. Renton wrote in his account for Woodrow Weaver: "At last the line was finished and so was [*sic*] nearly all of us. On Christmas Day I had rice and radish water for dinner. Oh boy what a feed! Then on the first of January 1944 we were sent to Thailand for a rest, to a place that was much better. We could get a few eggs, fruit, and we were getting veggies in the stew. But the fittest of us still had to work."[42]

Indeed, their work was not finished. The Japanese had other plans for them. The POWs remained in various camps around Kanchanaburi for the next three to four months, until in March 1944 the Japanese selected from among them those who seemed the most physically fit. "They were told that they were going to the most beautiful country in the world where work would be lighter and far different from that which they had been doing—that they would be employed on more technical jobs in keeping with their trades." In fact, they were being readied to be sent to Japan, which was experiencing a labor shortage, particularly in heavy industries. Plans were made to transfer ten thousand of the POWs from Thailand to Japan. The challenge would be transporting them. The less-healthy POWs were sent back up the line to join the maintenance force, while those considered more fit and able to endure travel were chosen for the "Japan Force." Room was found for them aboard merchant vessels headed to Japan. The POWs were moved through Cambodia, where from Phnom Penh they traveled in river steamers down to Saigon, and from Saigon downriver again to the Cape St. Jacques area for embarkation in ships to Japan. The POWs were already loaded onto the ships to transport them to Japan when the trip was canceled, most likely due to some recent Allied air raids and sinkings in the area, and they were taken back upriver to Saigon. Here the POWs were put to work on the docks and on an airfield until early June. At that point it was decided that these men would be sent to Japan not from Saigon, but from Singapore. And so on June 23, 1944, the POWs began their journey to Singapore, via Phnom Penh and Bangkok, all the while traveling in the same rail trucks. Arriving in Singapore on July 4, the majority of the POWs were sent to the River Valley Camp to await embarkation aboard *Rakuyo Maru* in early September. While at Singapore, no chance to exploit their labor was wasted: the POWs were made to work up to the last moment in the dockyards. At last, in early September, they were loaded onto the transport ships that were to carry to Japan—ships that the POWs would learn to know and refer to as "hellships."[43]

The Hellships

After the Burma-Thai Railroad was completed, ten thousand of the most "fit" POWs were selected to be shipped to Japan, to meet a labor shortage in heavy industries. The less healthy were sent back up the line to do maintenance, including repairing damage caused to the track by Allied bomber attacks. Between December 1943 and March 1944, those POWs deemed healthy enough for travel were moved to Saigon in preparation for the sea journey to Japan. Roy Cornford was one of those selected for the latter group. He and his fellow POWs were lined up to listen to a speech by a Japanese commander. "All men should be honored to know that they are going to a land of peace and tranquility where even the birds can nestle on the hunter's hand and will not be harmed. Where the snow covers the land in winter and the warm sun of spring melts it, leaving the country clean. A land of milk and honey. In Japan it is a sin to eat and not work, so to prevent all the men from becoming sinners, we shall put you to work."[1]

Perhaps they would not become sinners, but they would again be slave laborers. The Japanese sorted out the POWs who had technical or trade qualifications, apparently for factory work; the others were told they would be working in Japan's coal mines. Mining, in Japan, was traditionally considered a low-status form of work, consigned to the lowest castes of society. It was extremely dangerous work, and death rates for miners in Japan were higher than in many other countries. Next, the POWs underwent a medical examination, although they found it hard to take very seriously. The "examination" consisted of being made to walk past a Japanese medical officer who was in fact a dentist, and who usually relied on the advice of an Australian POW doctor.[2]

As the POWs selected for Japan were gathered at Saigon, they were immediately put to work. At least the living conditions were better in Saigon. Food was more plentiful, and even the guards treated them more humanely. The POWs concluded that this was probably because the Japanese were trying to look good in front of the large numbers of Europeans who were in Saigon and who seemed generally sympathetic to the plight of the POWs. K. C. Renton recalled that in Saigon the "French was [sic] very good to us, supposed to be Vichy but only to the Japs, can't blame them." French civilians occasionally slipped small gifts of food, medicine, or cigarettes to the POWs, sometimes along with a furtive "V for victory" sign when the Japanese guards were not looking.[3]

American submarines' campaign against Japanese shipping was at a peak in 1944. Although the POWs chosen for shipment to Japan were now all assembled at Saigon, ready for transport, it was decided that it was not safe to ship the POWs to Japan from Saigon, because of heavy Allied submarine activity along the route. So, after about three months in Saigon, once again the POWs were moved, this time to Singapore—a fifteen-hundred-mile journey, mostly by train. As they were loaded into cattle trucks, the POWs braced themselves for what they knew would be an unpleasant ride. Between twenty-four and thirty men were crammed into each car. For seven or more days they rode in the cattle trucks, periodically receiving rations of rice and dried fish in portions even smaller than those they had become accustomed to while working on the railway. At Bangkok the train stopped and the cattle trucks holding the POWs were each half-filled with bags of rice. From that point for the rest of the journey, the POWs rode atop the bags of rice. To the POWs, it seemed like an unbearably long ride. "I think we were still rattling for a week after," recalled Harry Chivers. When they were finally released from the crowded cattle trucks, their first activity was a long march to the prison camp.[4]

At Singapore, the camp they were herded into consisted of two-tiered huts that seemed very rickety and were propped up with sticks. Indeed, one night a hut collapsed, injuring fifteen British POWs sleeping inside. Almost immediately upon their arrival, a thousand of the men were sent out to work on a new dry dock being constructed by the Japanese at Singapore, and the POWs began to wonder if they were ever going to be sent to Japan after all. Singapore was experiencing a food shortage, and even the civilian population was starving. POW rations at Singapore were reduced by half.[5]

After several long weeks in Singapore, Harry Chivers finally heard rumors that the journey to Japan was back on. "We did not feel too happy about it either. We knew that convoy after convoy had had a go at getting through and not too many had made the trip." Indeed, while selecting the POWs fit enough to be sent to Japan, the Japanese guards had taunted the prisoners, telling them they would most likely not make it to Japan and instead end up as fish food. The men were counted and marched to the wharf at Singapore Harbor, where they were made to wait for several hours while the convoy that would be carrying them was readied for sailing. The convoy, designated HI-72, included two oil tankers, two large transports (*Rakuyo Maru* and *Kachidoki Maru*), and several escort vessels. The POWs watched as native workers loaded the ships with rubber and tin. While they waited, the POWs could not help but wonder if indeed they would ever reach Japan. Bill McKittrick remembered that, while waiting at the harbor, "We were cheerily informed by the natives that our chances of getting there were nil because the U.S. Navy was busy sinking the convoys." Roy Cornford and some of his mates noticed a German sub in Singapore Harbor. One of its crew spoke with the POWs: "He asked us who we were, where we came from, where we were going. We told him and he told us we wouldn't get there."[6]

As the POWs waited in the hot Singapore sun, they watched trucks arrive dockside, delivering additional passengers for the Japan-bound transport ships: wounded Japanese soldiers, Japanese nurses, Japanese and Korean prostitutes, and some Japanese civilians, including a few children—residents of Singapore who were now returning to Japan. Most of them boarded the larger transport, *Kachidoki Maru*. Finally the POWs were lined up and marched aboard the transport ships. The date was September 6, 1944. As they boarded, each POW was given a block of rubber, approximately twelve inches square, having a rubber handle, and instructed to carry the block aboard. The guards informed them that the blocks were their life preservers. The POWs were dubious; these blocks, which seemed to weigh about fifty pounds each, hardly seemed capable of floating. "They were as useful as a block of concrete in the

East River," sneered Bill McKittrick. It was more likely, suspected the POWs, that this was simply a way for the Japanese to load raw rubber aboard the ship. As the men boarded the ships, they had to walk by some of the prostitutes: "These girls spat at us so you can imagine what language we used on them."[7]

Bill McKittrick and Roy Cornford were among the approximately seven hundred Australians, remnants of Anderson Force, who were herded up the gangway of *Rakuyo Maru*, on board and down a ladder into number 3 hold, located just forward of the ship's bridge. Following close behind was a group of about six hundred British POWs who were taken aft. "POW after POW, we shuffled up the gangplank, hurried along by Korean guards with sharp pointed bamboo sticks," recounted Cornford. "Half of the men were sent forward, the remainder aft. I went forward where there were three large cargo hatches. Hatches 1 and 3 were battened down full of cargo, hatch 2 was open and 10 feet deep with two decks built for soldiers. So, we were brutally forced down this hatch. Eventually the Japanese allowed half the POWs to stop up on deck. Luckily I was one of the POWs up on deck." The hold was designed to accommodate less than two hundred passengers, not several hundred: "after much jabbering and plenty of use of their rifle butts they [the Japanese guards] allowed 200 to stay on deck, that number increasing when darkness fell to 4 or 500."[8]

The other transport vessel, *Kachidoki Maru*, was loaded with approximately nine hundred British POWs. Finally, the ships slipped their moorings and got under way, setting a course for the Formosa Straits. They flew the Rising Sun flag but did not have a Red Cross symbol or any other indication of their human cargo: 2,218 Allied prisoners of war. "We set sail," wrote George

Ward later aboard *Pampanito*, "bound for a thrashing from the Yanks."[9]

Conditions on the Hellships

Having endured so much already, the POWs now found themselves housed in appalling conditions aboard the transports, hardly better than in the camps. Aboard *Rakuyo Maru*, the holds in which the majority of the prisoners were confined were subdivided horizontally by a false floor, creating two decks; this hardly solved the problem of creating more space, however, as neither deck had an overhead height of more than four feet. This arrangement left each POW a mere two square feet of space—not enough overhead space to stand, barely enough room to sit up, and certainly not enough room to lie down. The only way to sleep was by leaning against each other. Each man given one flimsy blanket; many ended up using pieces of their own clothing, if they had it, as additional bedding. Many of the POWs had nothing but a loincloth to wear—a skimpy garment that the men had taken to referring to as a "Jap happy," consisting of a piece of cloth passed from the front of the waist between the legs and to the back of the waist, held in place by a piece of string around the waist.[10] Port holes were sealed, leaving the air in the holds fetid and hot. The only source of ventilation was the hatch leading to the hold.

By the time Bill McKittrick climbed down into the hold, all of the spaces had been taken. Feeling distinctly unlucky, he settled down in the center of the hold, directly underneath the hatch cover.[11]

On *Kachidoki Maru*, one of the holds had had bunks installed inside it to accommodate the wounded Japanese soldiers, but the holds in which the POWs were confined, near the bow of the ship, were as bare and uncomfortable as those on *Rakuyo Maru*, leaving each man with barely enough room to sit or squat, and no room to lie down or stand up.

Aboard *Rakuyo Maru*, where some of the men had been allowed to remain on the ship's deck, sick men were brought up from the hold for fresh air and treatment by the two Australian doctors who were among the prisoners. The cook sergeant asked British soldier W. A. W. Mandley to help him in the galley during the voyage, which Mandley considered a great stroke of luck: "I was fortunate to stay on deck all the time, and sleep on the deck, not like the other chaps that were locked down in the holds of the ship with the cargo." The food was cooked in cooking boilers on the deck, in the open, and those who took part in preparing the food lived and slept on the deck, near the boilers. While on deck the conditions were less claustrophobic and the air much better to breathe, those living and sleeping on deck had to contend with the hot beating sun during the days, and the cold at night, as they tried to sleep on the bare deck with only their one thin blanket as covering. Some of the men found some canvas sails to sleep under to help keep themselves warm.[12]

Toilet facilities aboard many "hellships" consisted of buckets and cans placed in the corners of the holds. The POWs aboard *Rakuyo Maru* and *Kachidoki Maru* were perhaps more fortunate in that toilet facilities were on deck. This provided those stuck in the hold with the occasional opportunity to go on deck. The men who were locked in the hold were only allowed access to the deck when they had to use the latrines. The toilets, reported Bill McKittrick, "consisted of a row of boxes lashed to the rails over the water. At times

I wondered to myself what would happen if I untied the ropes and floated away." There was usually a continuous row of men lining up to go on deck and use these primitive latrines hanging off the side of the ship, not only for the chance to go on deck but because there were still many cases of dysentery among the POWs.[13]

The Japanese navy had written regulations for the behavior of prisoners on its transport ships, and any prisoner found disobeying the rules or orders on board was subject to punishment by immediate death. Forbidden behavior included talking or moving around the vessel without permission; displaying any antagonism or opposition to the guards; and touching any part of the ship's wiring, switches, or other equipment. There were even rules forbidding trying to take more food than was rationed to each individual, or using more than the one allotted blanket.[14]

On the morning of convoy HI-72's first day at sea, the POW officers informed their men of the rules that the Japanese expected them to follow while on board the ship, and—more importantly— about the eating arrangements. The men's last meal had been a full twenty-four hours ago. While on board the ships, the POWs would be allowed on deck in groups twice a day to receive their meals, each meal consisting of a small quantity of rice and dried fish. Jack Wall described the ration as "rice, with a small piece of dry, dirty fish, about half the size of your little finger. Since there was a shortage of drinking water aboard the ships, the POWs' rice rations were cooked in salt water, which made the prisoners even thirstier. Despite the shortage, the Japanese guards freely used fresh water to wash themselves, and did so in view of the prisoners. The POWs were only allowed a salt-water wash on deck each night, using the salt-water hose. Recalled Roy Cornford: "The geisha girls used to line up near us for a good look, holding their hands apart to show what size they saw."[15]

Crammed in a hold aboard *Kachidoki Maru*, John Huckins had felt a slight sense of relief as the ship finally pulled out of the harbor and got under way, and a slight breeze from the deck penetrated the hot and humid hold. As the voyage progressed, the POWs locked in the darkness of the hold lost track of the time. It was difficult to tell night from day. Ralph Clifton, also confined in one of *Kachidoki Maru*'s holds, felt like he was one of hundreds of sardines packed tightly in a can. The heat and stench in the holds grew from the sweat of hundreds of bodies until it was almost unbearable. To make matters worse, some of the men suffering from bad cases of dysentery weren't always able to make it to the deck latrines. Huckins tried his best to cope with the heat and smell. "At night we used to sneak up on deck and turn on the sea hoses to wash ourselves down. Once we were at sea the sentries used to sit down and fall asleep, they knew we couldn't mutiny as we were barely strong enough to walk."[16]

In the depths of the hold, the prisoners tried to stay calm, but the horrible conditions were unnerving and sometimes fear overtook them. Although these POWs had been selected for this journey because they had been judged to be the healthiest of all of those who had worked on construction of the Burma-Thai Railroad, many of the men were in fact ill, so ill that they were unable to eat even the tiny portions of rice and fish they were provided twice a day. Some died right there in the hold. "We had to tie them up in rice sacks that the Japs gave us and then our Padre would give them the last rites and drop them overboard. Judging by the Japs' treatment of us at this time it looked as though we would be very lucky if we ever reached Japan alive. We hoped that as time went on things would improve but they were to get even worse. Night time was the worst because we could not see anything. We had to urinate and do our business where we were and you could hear some of the poor fellows asking to die for they could not stand anymore."[17]

Day by day, the convoy steamed on. The weather was hot and clear, the seas calm. Norman Massey, on *Kachidoki Maru*, tried to keep his mind occupied. "My first recollection on going on board was of finding an abundance of pencils in the hold! These were like gold dust as we were not allowed writing materials, but we had no paper to go with them! . . . I had managed to obtain a book, Isaac Walton's 'The Compleat Angler' from somewhere, and a battered New Testament were my only reading material. I never did finish the Isaac Walton and have had no desire since to do so!" On the fifth day a torrential rainstorm filled the skies and poured down on the ships, a blessing for the parched POWs, who danced on the deck trying to soak in as much of the fresh water as they could.[18]

Meanwhile, as the convoy continued its journey toward Japan, the wolf pack of submarines known as "Ben's Busters" was searching for targets in the South China Sea. In the early morning hours of September 12, *Growler*, *Sealion* and *Pampanito* closed in on a Japanese convoy. It was HI-72.

The Sinkings

Aboard *Rakuyo Maru* that night, most of the POWs were asleep— or trying to sleep. About five hundred of them were spending the night on deck. Roy Cornford was one of those who couldn't sleep: he and three or four of his comrades were on the port side of the deck, near the railing, watching a Japanese destroyer flashing coded messages near the rear of the convoy. Suddenly he heard a loud explosion and saw a bright flash of fire. The Japanese guards who were on deck claimed it was an island on fire from gunnery practice, but suddenly there was another explosion and another bright flash of flame, followed by complete darkness. One of Cornford's mates muttered, "Hell, someone's pulled the plug out of that island." Soon ship sirens were sounding, depth charges were exploding, and Japanese sailors were running chaotically around the deck of *Rakuyo Maru*. Everyone aboard *Rakuyo Maru* was now wide awake. The crew rushed to battle stations, but as the forward gun crew began to fire, the flashes of light from the flares that were being fired revealed that most of the Japanese crew were already sitting in lifeboats, with their life jackets on, ready to abandon ship—and the POWs along with the ship.[19]

The POWs on deck relayed what was happening topside to the men down below in the hold. They began putting on kapok life jackets, although there were not enough for all of them. As they hurried about, gathering life jackets and relaying information to each other and to those still in the hold, the chaos around them increased. As Cornford watched, "one of the oil tankers only 500 yards from us exploded, lighting up the ocean. I could see Japanese 'cooking,' trying to get away from the tanker. That tanker lit up the entire convoy. Then there were two explosions forward of our ship and two transport ships sunk. By now the Jap escorts were zipping everywhere, dropping depth charges. Then another large ship got hit and it just sort of drifted into the burning tanker and burst into flame, just as the second tanker exploded again, lighting up the ocean with burning oil."[20]

Then it was *Rakuyo Maru*'s turn. The first hit on the transport struck just forward of the hold that housed the POWs. It hit instead a hold that was full of bales of rubber. The rubber absorbed most of the shock of the torpedo, thus probably saving the POWs from serious injury. As the ship slowed from the first torpedo hit, the bow of the ship began to sink downward, just as the second torpedo hit— so when the bow rose again the hole caused by the first torpedo was above the waterline.[21]

Suddenly, what seemed like a huge tidal wave of water washed over the deck, pouring around and over the stunned POWs on the deck, and nearly drowning some of them. The water flooded into number 3 hold, on top of the hundreds of POWs who were still crammed in the hold. They began to panic, thinking the ship was sinking. There was a mad scramble as the POWs struggled to get out of the hold and onto the deck. Most of them were soldiers, not sailors, and they were unprepared for this. *Rakuyo Maru* listed and sank ten feet down. She then settled, sitting about ten feet lower in the water and listing to port. Then she just floated. She would take twelve hours to sink.[22]

Ray Burridge had been living and sleeping on *Rakuyo Maru*'s deck for several days. Sometime after midnight on September 12 he was woken by a loud explosion and bright flash of light coming from somewhere ahead of *Rakuyo Maru*. He realized it was one of the escort ships being torpedoed. Next he watched in amazement as an oil tanker on the port side of *Rakuyo Maru* was hit and burst into flame. The night grew brighter as burning oil spread over the surrounding water. From his vantage point on the deck, Burridge was able to see the wake of a torpedo that appeared to be heading straight for *Rakuyo Maru*. He heard it strike the ship between the forward hold and the bow. He then heard the second torpedo strike amidships with a dull thud.

Burridge's first thought upon realizing that *Rakuyo Maru* was hit was for the welfare of those in the hold. The Japanese appeared to be "running around like madmen screaming and shouting, trying to get off what they thought was a doomed ship; no thought of prisoners locked down the hold with hatch boards fixed and unable to get out." He and some of the other POWs who had been on the deck helped to remove some of the hatch boards and help the men out onto the deck. Burridge then went looking for his friends Bill McKittrick and Max Curran, since he knew neither of them could swim. He noted the calm and orderly manner of the POWs now on deck, making preparations to jump in the water. But he was unable to find his two friends.[23]

Bill McKittrick was one of the POWs in the hold of *Rakuyo Maru* when the first torpedo hit. Crowded in the tiny space, in the pitch black of the night, hearing explosions all around but unable to see what was happening, all he could think was of the need to get out— and fast. McKittrick managed to climb through the hatch and onto the deck. On deck he found a scene of chaos. Dozens of men were already in the water. At that point the ship began to list, and he decided his safest option was to get into the water, rather than risk going down with the ship. He made his way down a rope, managed to grab a piece of timber in the water, and paddled away from the slowly sinking vessel. Soon he located a refrigerator door from one of the destroyed ships. He crawled onto it, and was soon joined by another man. Together they huddled, through the night, on the refrigerator door.[24]

When the POWs on *Rakuyo Maru* realized that the ship was not going to sink immediately, the panic in the hold diminished, and they began climbing up the ladder from the hold up to the deck in an orderly manner. As the Japanese rushed around the ship cutting down lifeboats with bayonets and throwing them into the water, the POW officers took charge of their men, telling them not to panic, to take their time.

W. G. Smith paid attention as one of the POW officers took charge and started directing the POWs on the deck. There was a sense of calmness now. "There was absolute quiet, and every man went to work," Smith recalled. "Morale of the troops was something to marvel at. Not one man panicked. In fact, most of us felt a sense of relief after the torpedo hit. We knew we had it coming, and when none of us was seriously hurt we felt a lot better."[25] In other cases, officers were not around to take charge and the scene was less orderly as the POWs, left to their own devices by the ship's crew, tried to get themselves organized and prepared to evacuate the ship.

Don McArdle heard one of the POW officers call out, "Every man for himself." There was a mad scramble then to get out of the hold, and a few broken bones in the process. Still, he couldn't help but notice that the POWs managed to remain calmer than the Japanese, who were "running and yelling like maniacs." The worst part, for McArdle, was jumping off the side of the ship into the water into the dark. "There were bodies everywhere, I remember when I jumped I didn't think I would ever come to the top, I thought my lungs would burst." Once in the water, the POWs feared that they would be swept by the waves into the oil that had leaked from the tankers and was burning on the surface: "It seemed that miles of the ocean was [*sic*] on fire."[26]

The Japanese crewmen, meanwhile, were preoccupied with trying to get themselves off the sinking vessel and to safety. They had already taken most of the lifeboats. Some just jumped from the deck into the sea. Soon the water was a chaotic soup of lifeboats from the sunken and damaged vessels, and men trying desperately to paddle away from the sinking ships and from the oil burning on the surface of the sea, to reach the lifeboats. "I saw one Jap boat drift into flaming oil and you could hear screams of men burning and drowning. On many of the lifeboats, the Japanese occupants used guns and bayonets to keep POWs from boarding," recalled Cornford.[27]

Seeing that their access to the ship's lifeboats would be limited, the POWs on *Rakuyo Maru* untied rafts that were on the deck and tossed them overboard, along with hatch covers and anything else they could find on board that they thought would float and that could function as makeshift rafts. In the meantime, some POWs were already jumping into the water. Cornford watched in horror as some of the POWs in the water were hit and killed by rafts being dropped from overhead.[28]

For those POWs who could not swim, the jump from the deck of the burning ship into the waters below really did seem like a huge leap of faith—like jumping from the frying pan into the fire. But the ships were sinking deeper and deeper and there was no other choice. Jack Wall, unable to swim a single stroke, jumped anyway, and to his great relief, after hitting the water he surfaced near a raft and managed to kick his way to it and pull himself aboard.[29]

Ray Burridge was still looking for his friends McKittrick and Curran when *Rakuyo Maru* gave a sudden and frightening shudder. He realized it was time to get off the ship. "The most terrifying part was to make the jump into the water from the deck which was quite a height, especially as the water was a mass of burning oil patches on the port side. There was no option and I jumped." He bumped into another Australian swimming toward a small dinghy that had two Japanese officers in it. Burridge swam toward it too. When the two men reached the dinghy and clambered aboard, the Japanese officers ordered them to start rowing away from the sinking ship. Instead, Burridge had a different idea. He said to the other Australian, "'When I count to three you take the Jap in front and I will take the one in back.' I guess they sank fairly quickly, being fully dressed, complete with their large swords—a case of 'fish food' for them, not us as they had taunted us in Kanchanaburi and Saigon." In the melee, however, the dinghy tipped over and capsized, leaving Burridge drifting with the current toward the tanker and patches of burning oil that swirled nearby. Swimming against the current was exhausting, seemingly impossible, so Burridge decided his best chances lay in trying to reach *Rakuyo Maru*. The looming hulk was still afloat, and Burridge thought that taking his chances aboard her seemed a better option than taking a chance at being burned alive in the ocean. Later, after he had been picked up by a Japanese rescue frigate, he knew he had made the right decision. He saw how horribly burned and scarred the survivors who had been picked up out of the flaming water were.[30]

A thoroughly exhausted Burridge finally managed to swim all the way back to *Rakuyo Maru*, only to find he barely had the strength left to climb her ladder. Struggling, he made it halfway up the rungs only to lose his grip and fall back in the water. On his second attempt up the ladder, he reached the top and climbed back onto *Rakuyo Maru*'s deck. Wandering aboard the vessel, he found a few of the other POWs trying to untangle a lifeboat that the Japanese crew had left behind in their panic. When the knots were finally loosened, the POWs sent the lifeboat crashing down into the water. They got in the boat and had already begun rowing away from *Rakuyo Maru* when they decided there was still enough time to go back aboard and grab some provisions. Two of them swam back to the ship, found some biscuits and some water bottles which they filled with water before returning to the lifeboat.[31]

Finally, most of the POWs had made their way from *Rakuyo Maru* into the water or onto rafts. Roy Cornford, however, was still on the ship's deck, along with six other POWs. There was one raft left. Four of the POWs were left to guard it, while Cornford and the other two went to find water, realizing they needed to prepare themselves as best they could for the ordeal that lay ahead. They found some hats, then scrounged their way into the ship's galley and scraped all the dry rice off of the bottom of the big basins they were cooked in. But they had no way to carry any food or water with them, so they hurriedly ate some of the rice, took one big, final drink of water, put on life jackets, tossed the raft overboard, and jumped into the swirling water after it.

The raft was a piece of wood six feet square, six inches deep, with ropes on the side for men to hang on to. The seven POWs grabbed the ropes and began to kick and paddle in an effort to get away from the slowly sinking *Rakuyo Maru*. "We had only got about 100 yards away when a Jap naval escort came back, flashing signal lights, when it also got torpedoed and exploded. That torpedo exploding made us sick, causing us to lose all of the water we had drunk." William Mandley and two or three other POWs on the deck of *Rakuyo Maru* had found an old wooden refrigerator and threw it overboard before jumping in after it. Mandley could already see *Rakuyo Maru's* bow dipping into the sea, while her stern rose higher and higher.

Most of the other ships had been sunk, and the sea was covered in oil. It didn't take long before the men in the water were all covered with oil—"black as the ace of spades." The men managed to get the wooden fridge open, and they climbed inside—but it soon became waterlogged and slipped under the waves. They desperately searched for something else to cling to, and found a raft. The raft had a piece of corrugated tin on it, an incredibly lucky find because in the days to come they would use the piece of tin to collect rainwater in its ridges to use for drinking.[32]

The POWs in the water tried to stay afloat any way they could, clinging to rafts, timbers, or other pieces of debris in the water. Ships around them were still in flames, and their first concern was to keep from drifting too close to the burning ships. As daylight began to break they spotted a small destroyer about three-quarters of a mile distant, heading toward the attack site, and signaling to another ship. Suddenly there was a huge explosion, a cloud of smoke, and the destroyer was gone. "We knew then that the submarine was still out there." The explosion was so close to the men drifting in the water that they could feel the impact: "The explosion of the torpedo hurt us like hell. My stomach seemed to click and I felt very sick. More of this was caused by the explosion of depth charges dropped by the only destroyer left. I think these had a bad effect on some of our chaps and caused their death the first night." James Campbell was lying in the water on top of a small hatch cover when suddenly he felt like someone was slamming him in the stomach with a sledgehammer. He realized it was depth charges exploding. Michael Deguarra, who had made it off of *Rakuyo Maru,* recalls how each exploding depth charge made them double up with pain and cause them to feel nauseous.[33]

Paddling on a plank in the water, Frank Farmer could see pieces of ship debris scattered in all directions. Some distance away, he saw a large mass of floating material drifted together in one area, with a large group of men clinging to it. "Dreading the loneliness that night would bring, I paddled my plank across to them. Before long I was sharing my plank with at least five or six others. With them I spent a night of sheer misery and continual torment."[34]

Meanwhile, as darkness turned into day, *Pampanito* continued to doggedly pursue the remainder of the convoy, determined to have her turn in sending some enemy ships to the bottom. By noon that day, September 12, she had located the convoy, and spent the rest of the day patiently tracking it westward. It was already night by the time *Pampanito* reached attack position. At 10:40 p.m. she moved in for the kill, launching five torpedoes from her forward tubes. Summers quickly swung the boat around and ordered four more fish launched, these from the stern.

Aboard *Kachidoki Maru*, most of the POWs were asleep when *Pampanito*'s torpedoes hit. Ralph Clifton, asleep in the hold, was jolted awake as he felt something hit the ship very hard. Suddenly the boards covering the hold were being forced apart. Just then the ship began to lurch to one side. He and the other POWs scrambled on deck. They heard a loud gunshot from the bridge of the ship, and news spread among the POWs that the captain of the ship had shot himself. The other crew members seemed to be in total disarray, shouting and running around the deck in a state of panic. Some of the POWs went over the side of the ship as soon as they emerged from the holds; this turned out to be an unfortunate strategy, as there was at that point very little debris in the water for them to cling to. Clifton's uncle had been a sailor, and he remembered him saying, "Never leave a sinking ship." Two other POWs, recognizing Clifton, hurried to his side. They informed him that they couldn't swim and wanted to stay with him aboard the ship. "They both seemed to have some inexplicable faith in me. I am at a loss to say where my courage came from, but I never thought I would drown. I just prayed that we would come out of it all right."[35]

Norman Massey had been lying asleep on a board when he suddenly had the strange sensation of rising into the upright position while still lying prone on the board. Instinctively, he leaped up the ladder from the hold leading to the deck. There he found a scene of mass panic, as Japanese crew members scrambled in confusion. He, too, heard the shot from the bridge. Trying to decide what to do, Massey hurried to the deck railing and looked down at the swirling waters below. The water seemed a long, long way down, but was there really any other choice? He jumped. The force of the water as he hit the surface destroyed his kapok life jacket, leaving him with the remnants of a pair of pants, the "gaudily coloured ladies pants" that had been issued to POWs by the Japanese in Singapore.[36]

In the water, Massey swam away from the ship, looking back as it disappeared under the waves. Fortunately, he found a piece of debris to cling to. In this way he floated for most of the coming day, until he noticed an empty lifeboat whose Japanese occupants had been picked up by a rescue vessel. He and several other POWs got in the lifeboat and tried to figure out a plan for what they should do next. The situation seemed hopeless. They had no water, no food, and no idea which way to try to steer.[37]

John Huckins was awakened from his slumber aboard *Kachidoki Maru* by the sound of explosions; then he felt the ship give a violent shudder. He heard screaming and shouting on deck in Japanese. Climbing up a few stairs of the hold ladder so that he could see out of the hatch, he was greeted by a chaotic scene: Japanese crewmen were running every which way, slashing lifeboat davits, shouting. Huckins waited about forty minutes, until the noise and chaos seemed to have subsided, and then he and some of the other POWs ventured out of the hold. They now found the ship deserted, except for a large number of POWs who were still aboard, unsure of what to do or where to go. The Japanese had taken all of the ship's lifeboats. The stern of the ship was by now underwater, and unlike *Rakuyo Maru*'s slow descent, *Kachidoki Maru* was sinking rapidly. The POWs gathered what little pieces of clothing they had, and many were able to find life jackets. Huckins headed for one of the toilets hanging over the side of the ship, figuring he could hang on to it before leaping over the side into the sea. The distance down appeared to be well over a hundred feet, and the bow of the ship was already well out of the water. Huckins steeled himself and jumped. It seemed like an awfully long way down. As he sank under the waves into the darkness, his feet became tangled in some wire ropes; after what seemed like an eternity, he finally managed to free himself and shot up to the surface "like a cork out of a bottle." Gathering what energy he had left, he began to swim as quickly as he could away from the ship. He had not gotten very far when *Kachidoki Maru* slid beneath the surface, not gracefully and quietly but with a series of bangs and explosions—possibly the ship's boilers bursting. The water was now full of debris, and Huckins grabbed a piece of timber—one of the hatch battens off the hold—and hung on for dear life. In the pitch blackness around him he could see very little, but he could hear screams and cries for help from every direction. He clung to the piece of timber even tighter and began to pray.[38]

Jack Goodman, in the hold of *Kachidoki Maru*, had not been sleeping. He and three other POWs were trying to play bridge, using a box for a table, when the torpedo hit. He soon heard one of the POW officers give the order, "Every man for himself." Goodman grabbed a kapok life jacket and went on deck. The ship was already going down, and Goodman slipped on the steeply sloping deck, getting caught under some deck machinery. He finally got clear, jumped off the deck and into the water, and came up near a lifeboat full of Japanese soldiers. A non-swimmer, he grabbed onto the side of the lifeboat. He remained in this position for hours, clutching the side of the boat, and feeling more and more ill as the waves bashed him around. Hours later, as the sun began to rise and a Japanese destroyer arrived to pluck Japanese sailors out of the water, Huckins finally was able to climb into the now-abandoned lifeboat. A few other POWs also clambered in. They lay there in exhaustion, covered in oil and dirt, nursing their wounds as the hot morning sun began to beat down on them.[39]

When *Kachidoki Maru* sank into the South China Sea, Ralph Clifton found himself pulled down with the submerging vessel, but then the force of the water released its hold on him and he rose to the surface. He saw one of his friends from the ship calling out to him from a raft. "The first sound I heard was my pal Tosh calling out to me that he had managed to climb on to a raft with someone else. He knew I was somewhere around as he could hear what he thought was me making the sound of a baby crying (which was a noise I often made to the amusement of my pals). I had to call back to him that it was not me making the crying noise but a real baby I had taken out of the water! I was swimming around trying to find someone to take the baby. I eventually managed to hand the baby to her mother but when I attempted to climb on to the raft I could hear shouts of 'Koora bugara' (English white pig) and a Nippon Officer made an effort to cut my hands off the raft, which was greatly overloaded. Luckily for me the baby's nurse made the Nippon Officer understand that I had saved her baby and they let me climb on. The woman thanked me by stroking my head and saying 'thank you English soldier.'"[40]

Hundreds of men were now struggling for survival in the South China Sea, most of them clinging to pieces of wreckage or debris as they tried desperately to stay afloat. Those who had been aboard *Rakuyo Maru* had now been in the water for nearly twenty-four hours. After two and a half years as POWs, they were no longer prisoners of the Japanese, but their next ordeal was only just beginning.

The Rescue

Day One: September 12

As darkness turned into dawn on September 12, the survivors of *Rakuyo Maru*, floating in the water, were amazed by what they saw. The sea was littered with pieces of wreckage. Large oil slicks covered the water's surface, and in some areas the oil was still burning. Men in small groups on rafts were scattered over a wide area. The only ship was to be seen was the listing silhouette of *Rakuyo Maru*, now miles off in the distance. She would not sink completely until that evening. John Huckins recalled: "When daylight finally broke after a dreadful night, the sight was indescribable. There was wreckage as far as the eye could see. That was the best dawn I have ever seen in my life." Despite the fact that they were clinging to bits of wreckage, in the middle of the South China Sea, the POWs felt lucky to be alive. They had survived the torpedoing; they had survived the sinkings; and above all, they were now free. They couldn't help but feel a sense of perverse pleasure in watching the hellship that had been their prison break into pieces and slide into the sea. Two and a half years of captivity were suddenly and unexpectedly ended. The men's optimism was partly fueled by an assumption that before too long Japanese rescue ships, searching for survivors of the attack on the convoy, would be steaming by to pick up them up. Still, the feeling of liberation—even if it was only to be temporary—was overwhelming. Some of the men felt such relief to be free of their Japanese captors that they began to feel giddy. A few started racing, rowing the planks and boards on which they sat. As the waves buffeted him, Ralph Clifton started to sing. He chose the song that seemed most appropriate to the immediate situation: "A Life on the Ocean Waves." His singing brought shouts from the Japanese sailors who were drifting on lifeboats nearby.[1]

But as the hours began to pass, the reality of their situation sank in. They were covered with oil, clinging to pieces of wreckage in the middle of the South China Sea, with no food or water, and still no sign of rescue was in sight. "When one is in the sea it was like being in a huge bowl with water rising from all sides and clear off to the horizon," recalled John Huckins. As the sun rose higher in the sky, its rays beat down on the men and began to bake the oil coating their bodies, increasing their discomfort. Some of the men had shorts and shirts to protect them from the sun; some had hats; some were entirely naked. Some had managed to bring along kapok life vests. Some of the rafts had only one or two men aboard, while others were crowded with bodies. The rafts, like the men, were covered with oil from the tankers, rendering them slippery and difficult to hold onto. The sea was rough, constantly threatening to dislodge the men from their rafts. If enough space was available, the men lay on their bellies on the rafts, or sat up, clutching the sides of the raft with their hands and bracing themselves with their feet to keep from toppling into the water as the waves rocked them. Some of the rafts, particularly those carrying several men, were floating beneath the surface, leaving their passengers up to their waists or even their necks in water. In the choppy water, the rafts and other floating debris bumped heavily into each other, leaving the men's legs bruised and sore. The salt water and the sun stung their faces.[2]

Occasionally some debris from the wreckage of the sunken ships floated by, which the men were able to make use of. Harold Martin of West Australia, known as "Curly" for his fair, tousled hair, had managed to join forces with a fellow soldier from his unit, Frank Farmer. Farmer had been swimming through the debris, collecting planks. He and Martin tied three planks together in a triangle using tapes from their life belts. This enabled them to sit about waist deep in the water, with their legs on the inside—saving them from being buffeted by other rafts or by debris bumping into them on that first night. During the next forty-eight hours they collected more planks and rafts, lashing them together, along with a wooden deckhouse. On this contraption they then tried to rig a sail. They used the only tool they had available, a pocketknife with a broken blade, to pry tacks out of the wood and used the tacks to secure an oar to the deckhouse as a mast. To this they attached a piece of canvas they had found. Farmer felt sure that with this makeshift sail in place, they would be able to make it to the China coast. Martin secretly felt that Farmer was being overly optimistic, but he was glad to have a task to occupy his mind. "Strangely enough, I never at any time thought that I would not survive, in fact I found keeping busy gave me no time to think at all, which was just as well." As they drifted they were joined by other men they encountered in the waves. There was at least a little bit of comfort in company, especially when darkness would begin to fall.[3]

Reg Bullock had been busily gathering rafts to tie together. He had found five, and, seeing a sixth floating nearby, swam off to fetch it. "When I came back there was a bloody Japanese officer sitting in the middle of them, and all the men were in the water watching him. I was pretty angry and said, 'why don't you get the bastard out,' and then they pointed behind me at a Jap destroyer only about 100 metres away watching us. Well, they sent a longboat over to pick him up, turned around and left us to our own devices. We thought they were going to machine gun us but they didn't."[4]

"We were just drifting about and passing the time away—sort of visiting each other, like you do at party," recalled James Campbell. At about midday he noticed a couple of Japanese ships in the area, picking up survivors. Campbell swam toward one of the rescue boats, but the Japanese would not let him board and he had to swim back to his raft. Roy Cornford's spirit soared when he saw two Japanese naval vessels appear on the horizon and slowly begin to nose their way through the oil and debris. He watched as lifeboats were lowered into the water, but soon his spirit sank again as he realized that only Japanese survivors were being picked up. One of the Japanese ships dropped a scramble net down the side of her hull. John Huckins and some other POWs who were close enough to grab hold of the net tried to climb up it to the ship's deck, but they were knocked back into the water with long poles.[5]

Throughout the rest of the day, the POWs watched as Japanese vessels patrolled the area, picking up Japanese sailors from lifeboats. Cornford saw fully clothed Japanese officers, still clinging to their swords, being helped out of the lifeboats. By dusk it was clear that the ships weren't going to be rescuing any of the POWs. The men began to realize that they were going to be left to their own devices.

Some of them concentrated on pulling life jackets off of the bodies of dead Japanese sailors in the water; these were given to the POWs who had not managed to find and take along a life jacket when leaving the sinking ships. Others swam to claim a place in the lifeboats that the rescued Japanese had left behind.

W. G. Smith of Queensland had been certain one of the Japanese vessels was coming to rescue them; when he saw that he was wrong, he grew defiant: "There were about 170 of us together, British and Australians, and as one of the destroyers took a final sweep for Nips, we all sang 'Britons never, never, never shall be slaves' and I don't think they liked it." George Ward was close enough to one of the Japanese ships to hear the sailors on board mocking the men they left behind in the water: "They said we would have to suffer for [the] damage our friends the Yanks had done." Ward was furious at the heartlessness of the Japanese, who were unwilling to help the POWs. "We thought, 'you lousy rotten bastards,' but at the same time we didn't mind because we preferred death to their treatment." There was at least one small act of kindness, however: Roy Cornford saw a Japanese officer give some of the POWs his water bottle just before he was picked up by one of the rescue ships.[6]

That evening, Cornford watched from his raft as his former prison, *Rakuyo Maru,* finally sank. Her stern lifted up high into the air as she slid into the South China Sea bow first, squirting water into the air. Cornford could see blocks of rubber flying high into the air and pieces of debris settling on the surface of the water. Watching the transport submerge, James Campbell gave up any remaining shreds of hope that the Japanese would return to the scene to rescue them.[7]

Rainstorms swept across the sea that night, but the castaways welcomed the fresh water, opening their parched mouths toward the sky, cupping their hands to their mouths, trying to quench their thirst with the precious drops. Sometime during the night, McKittrick spotted another Japanese naval vessel picking up survivors. His companion aboard the refrigerator door announced that he was going to swim to the rescue ship. McKittrick, a non-swimmer, could only wish him luck as he watched the man swim away. He never saw him again. McKittrick spent a lonely night huddled alone on the refrigerator door, keeping his hand forced through a ring bolt on the door to avoid sliding off into the rough waters during that long night. The stillness of the night was pierced with frequent cries from the rafts, as men called out, trying to locate their friends.[8]

Day Two: September 13

By the following morning, the rafts had drifted apart from each other. Many of the rafts now held fewer men, some having slipped off during the night, unable to hold on. As the sun crept higher and higher, some of the men began to get delirious in the heat and the constantly rocking waves. The rafts drifted through the oil slicks left by the sunken tankers, and the oil coated the men's faces, got in their eyes, and matted their hair. Ken Williams of Adelaide, who had spent the first night sitting on a plank, up to his armpits in water, spent the day collecting wreckage and rafts to put under the planks. With this increased buoyancy, he was at least a little bit more comfortable in the water. The next day a rubber-covered box would drift by; Williams and the other men who had joined him on his raft grabbed the box, stripped the rubber off its sides, and created a makeshift sail. Like Farmer and Martin, they hoped that, with the sail, they would be able to reach the China coast: "Little did we know that it was 400 miles away." Some of the men on other rafts had found some cases of dried fish, and used wood from the boxes to create makeshift paddles, about a foot and a half long and three or four inches wide. They rowed as enthusiastically as their tired and dehydrated bodies would allow during the day, and tried to rest up during the night; but it was impossible to get any sleep in their precarious positions on the rafts, and during the daytime the currents proved to be too strong. Finally, after two days of unproductive rowing, they gave up the plan. The dried fish proved to be of no use; these were too dry and salty to swallow. Still, in the middle of the sea with no land in sight, it was hard to leave anything behind, and the POWs towed the cases of dried fish along with them.[9]

Bill McKittrick was still clinging to the refrigerator door he had found, concentrating on paddling away from the patches of burning oil left by the tankers. He saw other men, in small groups, floating on pieces of wreckage. One of the men recognized McKittrick. Knowing "Mac" had served in the British Merchant Marine as a youth, he yelled out, "Hey! You've been on ships. What should we do?" McKittrick thought their best strategy was to stick together as best they could. He instructed the men to gather all available pieces of wreckage from the water. Those who were decent swimmers paddled out and returned with an assortment of items: a large bundle of bamboo, some hatch boards, a boom from a boat, as well as pieces of driftwood. They lashed these together with the refrigerator door to create a platform—a crude raft, on which sixteen men then floated together. It at least kept the upper part of their bodies out of the water. Glad to have each other's company, they talked about the possibility of rescue. And they concentrated on the task of hanging on—and of trying to stay awake. Sleep could be fatal. Those who fell asleep tended to lose their grip on the raft and floated away. "Being eaten by sea lice and in shark infested seas, our hold on life was becoming very weak," McKittrick recalled. "There seemed little else to do but pray and this was difficult as lack of water had caused tongues to swell and throats to constrict. We just thought about prayers and about our past life—there did not seem to be any future to think about. There was nothing to see but the sea for miles."[10] As men continued to drop off the raft, McKittrick found it harder and harder to watch. He felt helpless and angry at the situation they had found themselves in. "It was sad to look at these poor wretches, and think that they had once been soldiers—proud and upstanding."[11]

As another night closed in, the cries for help diminished as the rafts drifted further and further apart in the darkness. Some distance away, the POWs from *Kachidoki Maru*, sunk the night before, also struggled to survive. John Huckins found himself hanging onto a piece of furniture of some sort—a cupboard or wardrobe. Another POW clutched it from the other side. The interior of the cupboard was full of water. Suddenly Huckins noticed a body floating inside. "We pulled him up and hung his arms over the edge, as he had no life jacket on. Whether he was alive or dead we didn't know. The chap that was with me without hesitation took off his own life jacket and put it on the other man, and said to me, 'I am going to try and swim for that light,' which he thought might be a lifeboat or a raft. I said stay here but he insisted on going whereupon I wished him luck. Whether he made it or not I don't know for the distance to that light could have been anything from 100 yards to a half-mile away. I never knew the man, couldn't see his face properly in the dark, but one thing for certain he is the bravest man I ever met in my life." Huckins never saw the man again. Drifting in and out of consciousness, he passed another long night in the sea.[12]

Day Three: September 14

Another day dawned. Some of the men on the rafts began to hallucinate. They told their raft mates they could see a creek with fresh water in it, could hear running taps of water. Some described a luxurious hotel that they had seen under the waves. Some of them let go of the rafts and began to paddle out toward the mirages. The others tried desperately to convince them that the images they saw really weren't there, that they should stay with the rafts. They tried to pull them back when they swam toward the visions. But the images were so real, the fresh running water in the distance so tempting, that many of the delirious men struggled to reach them. One man tried to swim after a raft mate who had drifted off toward a mirage; when he grabbed him to pull him back to the raft, the man hit him and continued swimming.[13]

James Campbell was one of the stronger swimmers, having been a member of the Sydney Lifesaving Club before enlisting in the Australian Army, and he took on the task of swimming after men who tried to abandon the raft and dragging them back. In one day he made twenty-five such "rescue" swims, but the exertion was taking its toll. He wondered how many more he could save, as more and more men around him began to show signs of delirium, while others just started simply giving up. As more and more men disappeared under the waves, the group's hopes sank deeper and deeper as well.[14]

At one point during the course of this long day on the rafts, Roy Cornford's group came across a large freezer box, drifting in the waves. The box was approximately ten feet square, with a flat iron roof, atop which sat a lone figure. Cornford recognized him as an Australian, a fellow known by the nickname "Rabbit." Rabbit appeared to be guarding the contents of the freezer—crates of dried fish that were too salty to be edible—and refused to leave the freezer to join the other men on the raft. He did give them one of the crates of dried fish, however, and tore off a piece of the metal roof for the men on the raft, who folded it and used it to collect rain water for drinking.[15]

As the minutes turned into hours, more men, either from physical weakness or madness or sheer hopelessness, let go of the rafts and drifted off. Three days of thirst was becoming unbearable. Some began to drink the seawater as their resistance began to fade away. William Mandley watched as one of his raft mates went over the side, telling him he was going to go get a cup of tea; another informed him he was off to do his washing, and disappeared under the waves. Before long, Mandley was all alone on his raft.[16]

Roy Cornford saw many bodies floating by, bobbing in the waves in their life jackets. "Some were dead while others were alive with far away looks in their eyes. They just floated away." Of the eighteen men on his raft, only seven would survive. His good friend Pat Linnane, who had seemed to be the strongest of them all, quietly disappeared from the raft one night. Cornford wasn't even aware his friend was gone until the following morning.[17]

When night finally came, the mirages did not stop. Some of the men thought the reflection of the moon on the water might be a track leading through some trees to fresh water. Bumped by the waves, the men were constantly slipping off the greasy rafts into the water. The efforts, repeated at least fifty times throughout each day, of hauling their bodies back onto the rafts took every ounce of energy and will they could muster. For those without life jackets, the biggest challenge was staying awake. Some men drifted off to sleep and unconsciously slipped into the water and under the sea; each morning, there were fewer and fewer men on the rafts. Those who could muster the energy dipped themselves into the cold water occasionally to keep from falling asleep.[18]

The oil that made the rafts too slippery to hold onto also coated the men's faces, getting into their mouths and making their eyes burn; some of them could barely open their eyes. There was no way to clean off the oil. They tried scraping it out of their eyes with their fingernails. Some men tore open their life jackets and picked out pieces of kapok with which they tried to swab the oil out of their eyes, but without much success. At night, the coating of oil on the men's bodies did at least offer some protection from the cold; and in the heat of day it deflected some of the burning rays of the tropical sun.[19]

That night the sky cracked with lightning, and when it started to rain the men turned their faces upward and cupped their hands to their mouths, trying to slake their thirst.[20]

Day Four: September 15

Yet another sunrise, and another day of trying to cling to life in these most unsurvivable of conditions. Don McArdle knew better than to drink seawater, despite his almost unbearable thirst. He did, however, allow himself to periodically rinse his mouth out with the seawater, which made him feel at least a little bit better. By the end of this fourth day, however, his resistance was slipping. The seawater began to taste fresh and cool, and he had to will himself not to gulp some down.[21]

In the meantime, the rafts drifted with the tide, moving miles and miles away from the sinking site, and further away from each other. James Campbell's raft drifted by two others that afternoon, but instead of trying to reach the men on those rafts, as they would have done a day or two earlier, "we just said 'good-day' to them and drifted on. The only way to stop drifting was by paddling with our hands and we were too weak to do that." That night, Campbell, like McArdle, had to fight against the temptation to drink seawater. The weather had begun to get stormy, and he held onto the edge of his raft desperately. "There was only one other chap left, and he said, 'There's a hut over there. I know the night watchman. He'll give us a drink.' He swam off, and I went after him. I managed to get him back six times that night, but finally he pulled off his life-jacket and sank."[22]

Their ranks thinned considerably by now, the survivors bobbed up and down on their rafts on the swell of the South China Sea. The rafts had now drifted so far away from each other that to Roy Cornford some of them appeared merely as black dots far in the distance. By now there were only seven men left on Cornford's raft of the original eighteen. The oily rafts were becoming increasingly hard to sit on, and the remaining survivors leaned on top of each other, occasionally dozing. When Cornford saw a dead Japanese body float past with a water bottle around its neck, he jumped in the water and swam to get the bottle, only to find it uncorked and full of salt water. Disappointed, he barely had the energy to swim back to the raft.[23]

Occasionally Cornford saw sharks in the water, but didn't see any of them attack any of the POWs. McKittrick also was aware of the sharks that circled nearby, but from his perspective they were the least of his troubles. Besides, he related later, "When there are more than 1,000 people in the water they can take their pick." There was safety in numbers; the sharks tended to go for men who were isolated, sitting alone on a piece of wood.[24]

On board their raft, Frank Farmer and Curly Martin assessed their situation. They agreed that they might have the strength to survive another two or three days, but not much longer. Suddenly one of the men on their raft claimed to have spotted a ship in the distance. The others, aware that this man had been hallucinating earlier, paid little heed, until Martin himself saw what looked like two ship's masts in the distance. Farmer leaned on Martin and slowly pulled his weak frame into a standing position to take a look. He recognized the "masts" as the twin periscopes of a submarine. The men watched in disbelief as the submarine emerged from the water and moved toward them. "Moments later, the huge vessel powered past, leaving our flotilla of rafts jostling in its swash. Rescue had miraculously come, and gone. . . . As the sound of the submarine's engines receded, each man suffered his own peculiar agony. For me it was a terrible resignation, a feeling that there would never be a second chance."[25]

Suddenly the submarine was seen turning back. Hope returned and was just as quickly dashed again as the POWs saw that the men on the deck of the submarine were pointing guns at them. "Every one of us reacted in his own way to this unexpected development," recalled Farmer. "Some shouted and pleaded, others sensing the danger, slid off the raft into the sea, while others like myself stood transfixed, mesmerized by the sight of the guns." Farmer raised a hand with his fingers formed in a "V for Victory" sign, hoping it would be interpreted as a friendly gesture. Martin took off his hat and waved it frantically at the boat, revealing his fair, curly hair.[26]

Suddenly Farmer saw a heaving line being tossed toward him by one of the men on deck. It fell short. Farmer was not going to lose this opportunity. He plunged into the water and managed to swim close enough to the line to grasp it. He felt himself being towed through the water and dragged onto the saddle tank of the submarine. From the deck a strong hand reached down and pulled him up. "My earnest 'thank you' brought to his face a look of complete surprise, and his shout of, 'They're English, sir' confirmed that we had been found by friends."[27]

As soon as Farmer, Martin, and Ken Williams had been pulled off this raft and were safely on board, the submarine began searching for other survivors. The men learned that in the past four days they had drifted approximately sixty miles from the site of the convoy attack.[28]

As the sun began to slip away at the close of that fourth long day at sea, Don McArdle also saw an unexpected sight: a periscope coming out of the water, just yards away. As quickly as it had appeared it vanished again. He assumed it was a Japanese submarine and that it, like the other Japanese vessels that had steamed through the area, was going to leave them where they were, to die. But the submarine reappeared. It slowly rose out of the water and headed closer to the rafts. In the last rays of the late-afternoon sun, the sub looked gigantic. It must be a German U-boat, the POWs thought—until they heard a voice call down to them from the submarine's deck in English, with a distinctly American accent.[29]

A large figure on the bow of the submarine stood with a gun trained at the men on the rafts. One of the POWs on McArdle's raft tried to shout out at him. They could hear words being exchanged on the deck of the sub. The next thing they knew, the large man on the bow had put down his gun and was diving into the water, grabbing the men one by one "and throwing us on top of the sub as if we were pieces of cork." When McArdle and the other men from the raft were safely on the sub, they were surprised to find other survivors already on board. They had thought they were the last ones remaining alive.[30]

Figure 4. One of the rafts sighted by *Pampanito's* lookouts in the South China Sea. Because the men on the rafts were completely covered in oil, it was initially difficult for the submariners to identify them. U.S. Navy photo.

K. C. Renton, drifting on his raft, had been certain it was the end. Two of his raft mates had succumbed to thirst and lapped up some seawater. Soon afterwards they threw themselves over the side and disappeared. Renton had just about given up hope when the submarine appeared. Watching it approach, he felt a mixture of joy and trepidation: "That afternoon between four and five the marvellous and wonderful thing happened—a submarine was making straight for us, but we did not know to whom it belonged. . . . My eyes were paining with oil and I could not see clearly, but when it was right opposite I saw a couple of men with machine guns pointing them at us. I did not care because it would have been a quicker way out and believe me they looked tough. But instead of lead we got a rope and was taken aboard."[31]

On another raft, Claude Longey was sure he was one of the last remaining survivors. By day four, his original group of forty-eight had dwindled down to nine. His last remaining ounce of hope seemed to be dwindling as well, when suddenly the submarine appeared a few hundred yards away. As quickly as it had appeared, the sub turned and went away. "Then I thought it was the end of my life; she was only like a bird on the horizon, when she turned and came back to us. She had been picking up the ones and twos as we could be seen more easily." Finally, the sub veered toward Longey's raft. He heard a voice from the sub yell a reassuring, "We'll get you, boys!" Then he saw a tall sailor near the bow of the boat jump into the water, followed by another crewman from the stern. Swimming out to the raft, they grabbed it and towed it to the side of the submarine. Longey and the others were all lifted aboard.[32]

Floating on another raft, Michael Deguarra thought he must be delirious. At around 6 p.m. on the fourth day, he thought he saw a ship. But he also saw buildings and trees, so he told himself it was only a mirage. But the mirage sailed closer. Soon it was only a hundred yards away. He could still see the buildings and trees, but the ship looked like a real ship. "I had never seen a submarine and so I still couldn't work it out." When it was fifteen yards away, he began waving and shouting at it. He saw men on the deck. Deguarra was almost completely convinced he was delirious when he heard one of the men speak: "Okay, bud. We'll pick you up in minute." But soon he felt himself being lifted up and carried aboard a submarine. "I said to the sailor who carried me down, 'Are you Japs?' He said, 'To hell with the Japs. We sunk all the . . .' Then I knew I was among friends. I broke down and cried like a kid."[33]

Harry Chivers couldn't believe his luck. "We kept saying while there is life there is hope and we done quite a lot of praying for something to come along." But the little hope, and life, that remained in the exhausted bodies on the rafts had begun to run out. "It is a terrible experience to be floating around on water all the time and knowing if you drink it you will go crazy. Unless you have been through it you can't realize how it is. Then we sighted the wonderful submarine *Pampanito* but we did not know who it was until we were helped on board by the men. My words were 'Thank God for the Americans.'"[34]

Reg Bullock was one of twelve men remaining on a raft that had originally held thirty. The others had either died or just swum away. When Bullock saw the submarine, his reaction was immediate: "I jumped in and swam like mad towards it." Getting closer, he saw bearded faces on the sailors lining the deck, and his joy turned to panic. "Oh no—they're bloody Germans!" he thought.

Then he heard one of them yell, in a slow American drawl: "Man overboard!"[35]

There were eight men left on Bill McKittrick's raft when he heard a strange sound in the falling darkness. It sounded like engines, and the men looked up, expecting to see a plane. Nothing. The sound faded away, but soon it resumed, accompanied by a large, dark shape that rose as if out of nowhere. McKittrick recognized the sound as that of diesel engines, although he still wasn't sure what this vessel coming at them was. "As it came closer we could see it was a submarine and to us on the raft, only eight now, she looked big and beautiful. She went past us and as she did a voice called out 'Stay with the raft.' One didn't and now we were only seven." This overly eager POW ended up in the propeller of the submarine.[36]

The gray-painted vessel looked huge to McKittrick from the raft. He thought she must be three times bigger than the *Queen Mary*. As she sailed past, one of the men asked McKittrick, "What if it's a Jap?" McKittrick replied that he had never seen a Japanese sub that big. He was sure by now that the submarine—this big, beautiful miracle of a boat that had come out of nowhere—was American. Then, to his dismay, the sub turned around and began sailing away from them. His stomach sank. After a few minutes he realized that the sub had not left but was simply moving from raft to raft, picking up other survivors. They waited, and eventually the sub turned around and came back toward McKittrick's raft, stopping about twenty feet away. By now it was completely dark, but McKittrick could see the shapes of crewmen standing on the saddle tank of the sub. Two of them dove into the water, swam to the raft with lines, and pulled the men to the boat and onto the saddle tank. From there two other crewmen grabbed them and tossed them onto the deck. After two and a half years of near starvation, the POWs felt like sacks of feathers to the well-fed submariners.[37]

Roy Cornford was still wearing what remained of his life jacket. While on the raft, he had torn kapok out of the vest in order to try to wipe the oil out of his eyes and off of his badly burned arms. All at once he saw many eager hands reaching down from the submarine to help him aboard. As he held up his hands to them, he begged them not to grab him by the arms, which were blistered and painful. His skin was worn raw from sunburns and the constant rubbing of the life vest against his chest. Bob Bennett pulled him aboard as tenderly as he could.[38]

One small raft that was sighted had just one man on it, lying motionless on his back. Thinking the man might still be alive, one of the submariners dove into the water and began to swim to the raft with a line. All of a sudden the figure on the raft sat up, looking startled, and started to go over the side. The submariner who had swum out to him persuaded him to remain on the raft until he could be helped onto the sub. The man appeared to be semi-conscious and nearly blind. On board the submarine, he fell into unconsciousness and remained that way.[39]

As the rescuers continued to haul aboard men from the rafts, they were too preoccupied with the monumental task at hand to be aware that they were being filmed. Paul Pappas was on watch down below when he heard that some people were being brought on board. Like the other submariners, he assumed they were going to be Japanese prisoners—until the "guests" started coming below, and Pappas heard one of them say, in English, "They told us to go all the way aft." Suddenly he heard Captain Summers's voice on the loudspeaker:

"Pappas, bring your camera to the bridge." While personal cameras and photography, like personal journals, were forbidden on board U.S. Navy ships, almost every vessel during the war was allowed to have cameras on board for "official purposes which will further the war effort." Some larger ships were also allowed to carry lab equipment and chemicals to develop the film. *Pampanito* carried both a 16-millimeter motion-picture camera and a 35-millimeter Eastman Kodak still camera. Pappas was an electrician's mate, but he was also

Figures 5 (*opposite*) and 6 (*above*). *Pampanito* electrician's mate Paul Pappas, a professional photographer in civilian life before the war, used *Pampanito*'s camera equipment to document the rescue in both still and motion pictures. The films were developed two weeks later. U.S. Navy photos.

Figure 7. Volunteers from *Pampanito*'s crew swam out to the rafts, holding lines with which to tow them to the side of the sub, where other crewmen helped lift the exhausted and feeble POWs from the rafts and aboard the submarine. U.S. Navy photo.

skilled in photography, having worked since the age of ten back home for his father, a professional photographer. (After the war, Paul Pappas would return to commercial photography.) Captain Summers, aware of Pappas's expertise, chose him to document the rescue.[40]

Roy Cornford was in the third-to-last group pulled aboard the sub, and McKittrick was in the next-to-last group. One final man, alone on a raft, was pulled in after that. William Mandley, a Brit, was the last man to be picked up by *Pampanito*, at 7:57 p.m. Fifteen minutes later, *Pampanito* terminated the search.[41] She had seventy-three rescued POWs now on board.

After he was gingerly hauled on deck, Roy Cornford found to his surprise that despite his poor condition, he could manage to stand up and walk. The survivors gathered on the deck were instructed to remove their ragged, oil-soaked clothes. Then the naked men, assisted by the submariners, lined up on deck and began moving toward the hatch to be helped into the sub. Suddenly they heard one of the American voices shout, "Planes, planes!" At the sound of these words, any slow and orderly movement of the POWs down the hatches stopped. Submariners grabbed the POWs, dropping them down the hatch, until a voice yelled, "It's okay—only birds."[42]

From his raft, Bill McKittrick had felt two sailors grab him and literally toss him onto the deck. McKittrick was wearing only an undershirt; while on the raft, he had removed his underpants and put them on his head to try to protect himself from the merciless sun. A submariner cut the undershirt off his body and he was lowered down the hatch, wearing nothing now but a thick layer of oil.

One by one the rest of the survivors were assisted down through the hatches and into the sub. Throughout the night, *Pampanito*'s sailors worked at swabbing the oil off of their new passengers and listening to the astounding stories the men told of their ordeal. They talked of their past four days on the water, of the Japanese rescue ships which had left them there to die, of the hot beating sun and their astonishing, unbearable thirst. One man related how, when one of his raft mates had died, he and the others drank his blood.

Figure 8. Men from the rafts were hauled onto *Pampanito*'s deck, where crew members wiped the oil from their bodies and helped them through the hatch into the submarine. U.S. Navy photo.

Another man had cut his own throat and slashed his wrists before falling into the water, saying he just wanted to "get it over with." Ironically, this happened just one hour before *Pampanito* appeared on the scene.[43]

All was not lost yet for the other POWs still in the water, those who had not been so lucky as to have been picked up by *Pampanito*. At 5:08 p.m. on September 15, USS *Sealion* had received a radio message from *Pampanito*, requesting assistance in rescuing POWs

Figure 9. *Pampanito* crew member Bob Bennett (*left*) cradles the unconscious body of John Campbell. U.S. Navy photo.

from the water. *Sealion* changed course immediately and increased her speed to eighteen knots as she headed to the rescue area. Forty minutes later her lookouts could spot pieces of debris from the wreckage, and they knew they were getting close. Fifteen minutes later, the sub passed through a heavy diesel oil slick, and a few minutes later, according to the skipper's notes in his patrol report, they passed "the first of many dead bodies floating on the surface." They were approximately forty miles northwest of the site of the torpedo attack on the convoy three days before. Soon they could see *Pampanito*, still circling through the wreckage, which was spread over an area of at least ten miles square. At 6:31 p.m. *Sealion*'s lookouts finally spotted a life raft with "living, shouting, beckoning" men aboard, and began the rescue, all the while acutely aware that time was short. There was only one hour of sunlight left. *Sealion* began maneuvering into position to reach the raft while her crew quickly organized themselves into rescue teams: a party of three swimmers, a "hauling out" party, and a "delivery and stripping" party. Ten minutes later the first survivor was hauled on board and sent below deck for medical treatment. By now several other rafts with survivors had been spotted, and the rescue became a race against the oncoming darkness. The swimmers swam out to the rafts with lines to tow the rafts to the sub, where the oil-coated, half conscious men were grabbed by the life jackets or under the arms and hauled onto *Sealion*'s deck, which was soon slippery with the oil left by the survivors.[44]

The "delivery and stripping" party removed the survivors' scraps of clothing, then led or carried them below deck. For the next two hours, *Sealion* continued moving slowly through the boxes, timber, and debris, picking up men from rafts until fifty-four were on board. Then darkness fell and no more rafts could be seen. It was nearly 9 p.m. As *Sealion* reluctantly turned away from the rescue area and steamed with her new cargo toward Balintang Channel and Saipan, her skipper was aware that somewhere, in the darkness, hundreds of men were still praying for rescue. "It was heartbreaking to leave so many dying men behind," he wrote in his patrol report. Before the sub reached Balintang Channel on September 17, three of the survivors had died; a fourth passed away on board on the nineteenth. Leading Seaman Norman Hunter, who had helped pull men out of the water, now assisted in burial parties as the four dead men were buried at sea en route to Saipan.[45]

Hundreds of the ex-POWs were indeed still in the water, scattered over an area of miles, still clinging to rafts. W. G. Smith of Queensland was finding it unbearable: "During the day we fried in the sun. . . . Sores were breaking out all over our bodies, and my lips felt like two sausages." When they saw *Sealion* picking up survivors, they struggled to get her attention. "Our hopes ran pretty high then, and we waved and coo-eed like hell. It came within about 200 yards of us, and then changed course to pick up other men who were closer. Then it turned around and went off into the dark. That was without doubt our greatest disappointment."[46]

Days Five and Six: September 16 and 17

Another long night on the rafts, and the fifth day at sea dawned. That day it rained, and Smith, along with his raft mates, lay on their backs, "with our mouths open like codfish," trying to drink in the rainwater. But the rain was sign of an ominous turn in the weather. The next day—Smith's sixth on the raft—brought rough waves and hints of an oncoming typhoon. The men knew they could not last on their flimsy rafts and in their weakened condition in the swirling waters of a typhoon. But at 5 p.m. that day, the unexpected happened. Another submarine appeared. The POWs knew it was their last chance at survival. "Boy did we wave! We took it in turns to wave as our energy was about gone, and at last they headed for us. We were pulled aboard, but found we couldn't stand up." The submarine, USS *Queenfish*, managed to pick up eighteen men off the rafts and bring them aboard. Smith couldn't believe what was happening. "Although we were smothered in black oil, they wrapped us in snow white blankets. Then they washed our faces a bit, gave us a small drink of water, the first for 144 hours, and let us have a little warm soup. We washed more of the oil off, had a hot bath and were put to bed. . . . Tired as we were, no-one could sleep. It was too much to think that we were not only saved from the sea, but were no longer prisoners of the Japs."[47]

Jack Pearson, afloat on a raft, had watched as *Pampanito* stopped picking up survivors from the water, then turned and steamed away. What he did not know was that *Pampanito* had called for help. Now, here he was, two days later and still alive—and being rescued by another American sub. One song began to play repeatedly in his mind: "God Bless America." Pearson was wearing a Dutch green jungle hat when *Queenfish's* crewmen lifted him out of the sea. The hat not only protected his head from the sun but had very likely kept him alive, as he was able to use it to catch some water when rain squalls passed over the rafts. Now he didn't want to surrender it. "Believe me it took the sailors some time to wrest that hat from my head. I still wanted to catch water."[48]

Alone on another raft, James Campbell was in the process of giving up. "I felt myself starting to go. The raft was just drifting, and I couldn't do anything. There was no-one else in sight. I could see a slit trench at the side of the raft, and I made up my mind that if it came close enough I would jump into it and have a sleep." Suddenly he noticed some ships on the horizon. He began paddling furiously toward them, but when he looked again they had disappeared. He tried to pull himself together, but was finding it hard—too hard. The typhoon winds were picking up around him. When, at about 7 p.m., he saw a submarine in the distance, he knew it was a mirage again—that is, until the submarine came close and picked him up out of the water.[49]

The submarine that picked him up was USS *Barb*. *Barb* was on her ninth war patrol, operating as part of Task Group 17.6 with *Queenfish* and *Tunny*. Skippered by Commander Eugene B. Fluckey, *Barb* had amassed an impressive record and a reputation as an aggressive warship. In the early morning hours of September 16, *Barb* and *Queenfish* had been tracking a convoy north of Luzon when they received an urgent radio message to proceed for rescue operations to the area in the South China Sea where *Pampanito* and *Sealion* had sunk some Japanese transports out of a northbound convoy, carrying Allied POWs. Now the two subs were overloaded with POWs and needed help badly. Fluckey assessed the situation in his patrol report: "We now have over 450 miles to go to reach this point and must naturally give up the search on present convoy. The latter is not regretted, but the fact that the *Barb* and *Queenfish* were within 70 miles of the convoy on the night of 12-13, and are now 450 miles away is regretted." *Barb* received the radio request for assistance at 4 a.m.; at 4:01 she was already steaming to the area at a rapid clip of nineteen knots. En route, her crew prepared to take on extra passengers, converting each empty torpedo skid into bunks for three men each.[50]

Four hundred and fifty miles was a long detour. Along the way *Barb* had to dive several times to avoid enemy aircraft. The skipper's biggest concern, however, was the weather. "The seas had calmed down with a long slick. It was just that uneasy feeling in the air. The barometer was steadying, then dropping, indicating an approaching typhoon. We had to get there before the typhoon did." At the same time, however, it made no sense to hurry. Arriving at the rescue area in darkness would result in a fruitless search, so Fluckey ordered a reduction in speed. They were now two hours ahead of schedule for a dawn arrival. With some extra time on their hands, when *Queenfish* picked up another convoy, *Barb* was more than willing to join in the attack. *Barb* sank a tanker and an escort aircraft carrier. Fluckey's warrior instincts told him to go back to verify that the carrier had been sunk, but his mind also raced at the thought of the POWs in the water, awaiting rescue. Again, Fluckey quickly assessed the situation: "With one torpedo remaining forward and two aft would like to chase the remains of this convoy to get rid of them. However we would probably be held down during daylight when we must rescue survivors. The seas have been rising and if we don't reach the survivors today, their fifth day in the water, there will be none left alive. With a plum being dangled before my eyes, it is obvious after due consideration of all aspects, that our primary mission now is the search for survivors. We have already lost 5 hours by sidetracking to attack this convoy."[51]

The commander of Task Group 17.6, Captain Ed Swinburne, issued orders for *Barb* and *Queenfish* to abandon tracking the convoy and proceed to the rescue area. *Barb* had only three torpedoes remaining, and *Queenfish* had expended all of hers. Besides, noted Swinburne, the main task had been achieved: "The three biggest plums in this convoy had been plucked and sunk." Fluckey had no qualms in complying. He would later remark in his patrol report: "As an afterthought inserted here, having seen the piteous plight of the 14 survivors we rescued, I can say that I would forego the pleasure of an attack on a Jap Task Force to rescue any one of them. There is little room for sentiment in submarine warfare, but the measure of saving one allied life against sinking a Jap ship is one which leaves no question, once experienced."[52]

By 10 a.m. on September 17, *Barb* was passing through the wreckage of the sunken convoy. At 11:41 a.m. lookouts sighted several naked, bloated bodies floating in the waves; these were identified as Japanese. Finally at 12:55 p.m. two small wooden rafts, with a total of five survivors aboard, were spotted. From the bridge of *Barb*, Fluckey tried to get a good view of the men: "At the time they looked very dark to us and we thought, 'My God, we've run into Japs instead of our Allied prisoner of war survivors.'" *Barb* drew closer to the raft, and Fluckey saw the men on the rafts turn their heads toward the sub, then turn away. "We were sure then that they weren't Allies because the Allies would have been glad to see us and would have been screaming their heads off." But these unfortunate men had been in the water two days longer than those who had waved at *Pampanito's* crew. They had been at sea on rafts, with no food, for almost five days; they were dazed, almost lifeless, and by now utterly devoid of hope. Even as *Barb* moved closer until she was only fifty feet from the men, they still refused to believe that the big gray shape in front of them was anything but another mirage. "One of them kept tapping his buddies' back we could see, and telling him that certainly he could see something, if they couldn't. They would turn around with this dazed stare and then turn away again, certain that it was all a mirage. Finally, they held him up, he was barely able to struggle to his knees, and he just screamed, 'Hey, Yank.' Well, we knew what that was. That was the Allies. There was no mistaking that Australian call."[53]

Barb's rescue team picked them up, and the sub continued searching for other rafts. By now there were few rafts to be found, and most that were spotted were empty. The sub passed by more floating bodies, many of them the bodies of Allied soldiers. *Queenfish* was also still searching madly, cognizant of the coming typhoon. The rescuers were running out of time.

Fluckey watched the men being taken on board his submarine and was struck by their reaction to rescue. "The expression on their faces is something that is hard to describe. They were so thankful for being picked up. Most of them couldn't talk, but would just cry; even in their condition they had a few tears left. In their glazed, oil-soaked eyes you could see the expression of gratitude as we picked each one up." *Barb* continued searching for rafts and picking up men until 3:30 that afternoon.[54]

Like the crew of *Queenfish*, *Barb*'s men had organized themselves into rescue parties. Fluckey referred to it as a "production line." There was a "deck party" to pick up the men from the water, consisting of four men. After stripping the clothes off the survivors, they passed them on to the "transportation gang," whose job was to get the survivors safely below. Once below decks the survivors were transferred to the care of the "cleaners," who did their best to wipe the oil and grease from their bodies, handed them over to the "doctors and nurses" for first aid, and then to the "feeders"—"and finally to the sleepers who carried them off and tucked them in their bunks." In this manner, fourteen survivors found themselves safe and dry, lying in torpedo racks aboard an American submarine.[55]

The next day, September 18, *Barb* was patrolling on the surface, continuing to look for survivors. She was now, however, in the tail end of a typhoon. The wind had picked up to thirty-five knots, and the sea was rocked by waves as high as thirty or forty feet. *Barb*'s crewmen who were on lookout tied themselves to the superstructure with a length of line to keep from being washed overboard. It was clear that any POWs still out there clinging to small wooden rafts would not be able to survive a typhoon of this magnitude. The lookouts spotted many more rafts, but every one was empty. "Even the dead people had been washed off the rafts that they had been on," noted Fluckey. Finally, at 7 p.m. *Barb* abandoned the search and set course for Saipan.[56]

The next morning, in the early hours, one of the rescued men aboard *Queenfish*, who had remained unconscious since being picked up, died. At noon that day he was buried at sea. Late that evening a second POW died, also having never regained consciousness. He was given a burial at sea the next day. Their deaths were noted in *Queenfish*'s action report: "Neither evidenced a conscious lucid moment since having been recovered but it was with the utmost regret that we watched them draw their last breath, in no apparent pain, and later committed their bodies to the deep." *Queenfish* then continued with the remaining sixteen survivors to Saipan.[57]

The POWs aboard the Subs

Torpedoman Hubert Brown was off duty. He was in his bunk aboard *Pampanito* when the word was passed to "Stand by to take on prisoners of war." Brown quickly got out of his rack, pulled his clothes on, and hurried to the forward torpedo room, not knowing exactly what to expect. He was standing at the bottom of the deck ladder as a near-naked, oil-soaked man clambered down. Brown assumed he was Japanese—until the man turned around and said to him, "Hi, Yank!" Brown then went topside to join in the operation of pulling more POWs out of the water and onto the sub.[1]

As the POWs were assembled on *Pamp*'s deck, the submariners used rags to try to wipe the men clean. But the coat of crude oil covering their bodies was so thick—about a quarter of an inch thick, observed Richard Sherlock—that the submariners began dipping the rags in the sub's own diesel fuel and using that to wipe off the oil. In some cases the diesel fuel proved too strong, removing some skin along with the black tanker oil. They would have to wait until they got down below for a more thorough cleaning.[2]

Pampanito's pharmacist's mate, Maurice Demers, was on deck, frantically trying to perform triage as the POWs were brought on board. He administered morphine to those suffering from extreme shock. Next, the forward and after torpedo room hatches were opened, along with the after battery hatch, which led into the crew's mess, and the POWs were lowered through the open hatches into the submarine. Still covered in oil, they were slippery and difficult to hold onto. Woodrow Weaver was in charge of the forward torpedo room and could not leave his station to go topside, but soon his torpedo room became a flurry of activity. Weaver helped care for the sunburned, oil-soaked men who were being brought down the ladder into the compartment, cleaning

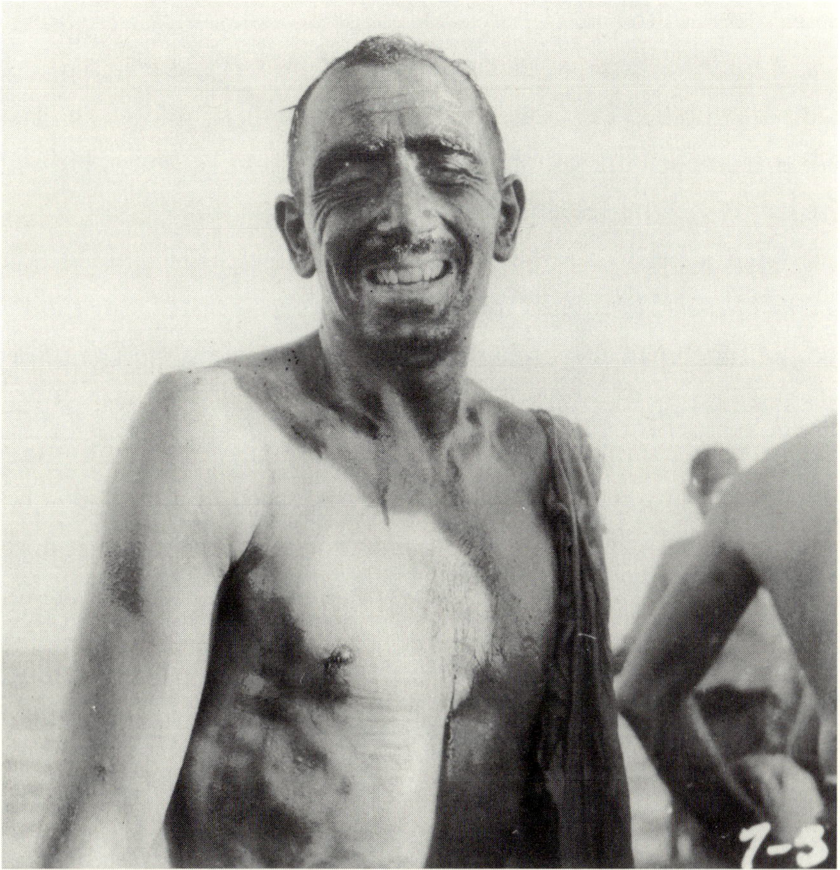

Figure 10. This man smiles as he realizes he is no longer a prisoner of war but safely aboard an American submarine. U.S. Navy photo.

up as many as they could right there on the spot, using rags soaked in torpedo alcohol.[3]

Radio Technician Spence Stimmler was also off duty, and was in the after torpedo room, where his bunk was. He helped carry the POWs who were being handed down the ladder, and then assisted in cleaning oil off of their skin. He remembers not just the oil but the many large sores covering the men's bodies. Quartermaster Johnny Greene was also taken aback by the sores, burns, and oil that covered the POWs' bodies. He watched as the survivors were lowered into the crew's mess: "I wasn't in the handling department. But I came in the galley here and one of the fellas, they were bringing him down through the hatch, turned around and seen a pad of butter, I guess on the table. And he said, later on he told me, he said his eyes opened up, you know, like he wanted to get some. He said he hadn't seen butter since the beginning of the war."[4]

When a head count was finally done, it was determined that *Pampanito* had brought a total of 73 survivors on board. The sub set course for Saipan at four engine speed. Down below, the first priority was finding room for the POWs. On this, her third war patrol, *Pampanito*'s complement was an even larger than usual 89 officers and men. Now, with the POWs on board, there were 162 men on that tiny vessel. Space had to be made somehow. To complicate matters, all the POWs had been exposed to contagious diseases. Captain Summers was concerned about keeping the survivors segregated, as much as possible, from the submarine crew until their health had been assessed and they had been checked for contagious diseases.

Pampanito's crew had to get creative. The six POWs whom Demers assessed as being the most critical cases were placed in bunks in one corner of the after battery compartment—the main sleeping quarters for the crew. The rest—sixty-seven men!—were crammed into the small after torpedo room. There were several bunks in this compartment, wedged over and between the torpedoes; normally fifteen crewmen slept here. Some of the POWs were laid in the bunks; it was particularly challenging getting them into the upper-level bunks. Blankets were spread on the deck of the compartment to accommodate some of the others. By this point, late in the war patrol, *Pampanito* had expended all eight of the torpedoes from her after torpedo room, so the submariners made use of the empty torpedo skids as well. Blankets were laid on the skids and each could hold three men; they were so thin and emaciated that each man took up very little room. The submariners had wiped as much oil off the POWs' bodies as they could by this point, but by no means were the men clean yet. Survivor Roy Cornford noted, "with us black with oil and water-crinkled skin, what a mess we made of those sailors' bunks and bedding."[5]

The head located adjacent to the after torpedo room—one of only four on the sub—was made available for the POWs' exclusive use. Rather than teaching the POWs how to operate the head, one of the torpedomen was assigned to operate the discharge valves to flood and discharge the head after each use. This proved to be a considerable task, since most of the POWs were suffering from diarrhea. "One would get in and use it, and as soon as he'd get out another one. And so this poor guy was there operating this head for four solid hours." Woodrow Weaver compared it to having sixty-five men lined up in your hallway at home to use your bathroom, all at the same time.[6]

Three other crewmen were assigned to a similarly unpleasant task: they stood round-the-clock shifts caring for a bedridden POW who

Figures 11, 12, and 13 (*above and opposite*). On board, most of the POWs were housed in the submarine's after torpedo room. U.S. Navy photos.

had a particularly bad case of dysentery and needed a clean bedpan available constantly. "Doc" Demers noted: "This task would have been distasteful to a professional nurse but these men did their job with a smile on their faces reassuring the patient and the other survivors that they had done their part in the war for freedom and it was their turn to help."[7]

When asked, more than fifty years later, how the submarine crew coped with this situation, Hubert Brown remarked: "I thought about

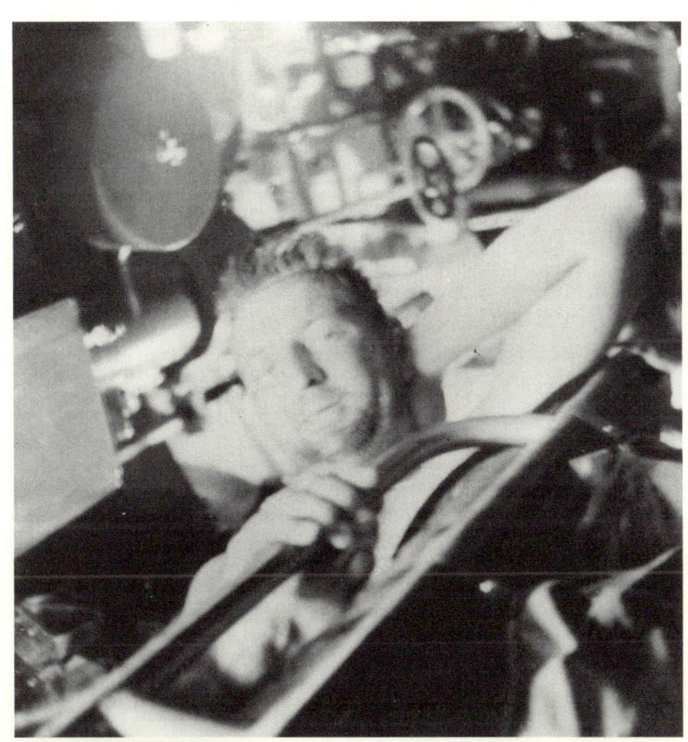

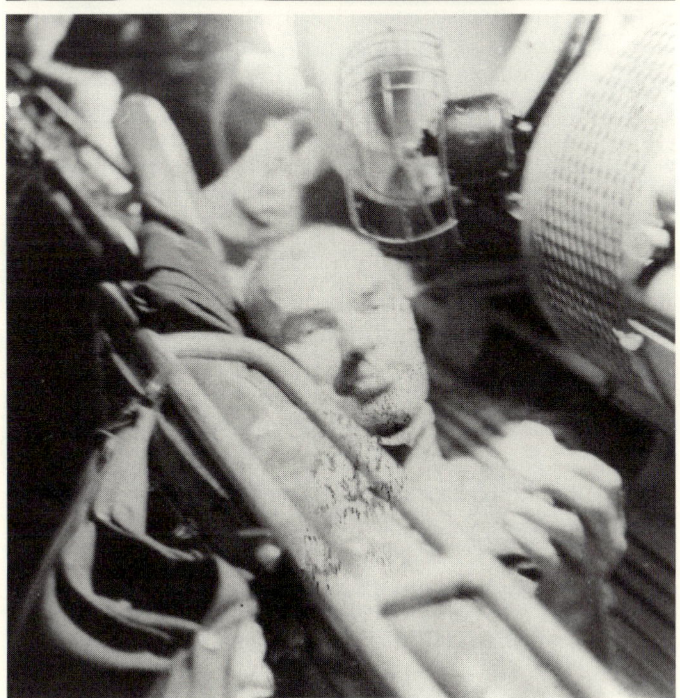

that later, you know? We was busy taking care of them, cleaning them up, feeding them. . . . I don't remember how I slept. . . . I don't remember how we served chow, I just think we grabbed something wherever we could." When it came time for his turn as lookout, Brown climbed to his perch on the periscope shears with a sense of relief, glad to have a chance to go topside, to get some fresh air and to get away for a little while from the confusion and commotion down below.[8]

Once bunk space, of one sort or another, had been created for the seventy-three POWs and they were settled in, the next priority was dealing with the dehydration suffered by all the men during their ordeal at sea. Initially they were given water through wet rags, until it was felt they could handle something more substantial: hot tea, broth, or soup. Spence Stimmler recalls seeing "Doc" Demers running back and forth between the six men in the crew's quarters and the rest in the after torpedo room, checking to see who needed what.[9]

"Doc" Demers Takes Charge

Maurice Demers, who until now had only had to deal with minor emergencies on board, suddenly had seventy-three seriously ill and malnourished patients under his care, all in need of immediate medical attention. Captain Summers admitted that Demers "was over his head in work." Once the POWs were settled below decks, Demers's main task was to conduct a more thorough examination of each man to determine the extent of the injuries and sicknesses. He discovered that every one of the POWs was partially blind, either from disease or from crude oil irritation. One of his first priorities was to give each man an eye irrigation, to clear their eyes of the painful and blinding oil. He then proceeded to give emergency treatment to the worst cases. Next, he went on to deal with the other ailments he found among the men. All were suffering from acute exhaustion, exposure, shock, starvation, and skin sores. Approximately 70 percent of them, reported Summers in his action report, had drunk sea water, urine, or blood during their four days on the rafts. Nearly all of them still had a coating of crude oil on their bodies.[10]

Demers threw himself into his role without hesitation, and without stopping for rest. Within twelve hours of the rescue, every one of the POWs had been examined and had had his wounds cleaned and dressed. Demers had also collected information from the men about their ailments and the diseases they had suffered or been exposed to while POWs.

Demers administered medications to the men every four hours as needed. About a quarter of the POWs were given sedatives. Three of the men were found to have severe cases of malaria—one of them was in a state of delirium for four hours after being rescued. Woodrow Weaver noticed that one of the men brought down into the torpedo room was burning up with fever: "you could just put your hand over him, you could feel the heat." He was laid down in one of the torpedo skids where the man started to shake with severe chills. Unsure what to do, the submariners tried piling blankets on him to ward off the chills, but he kept switching from chills to fever and back again.[11]

One man, Demers discovered, had an injured back and a broken rib. He found himself at a loss as to how to bind the injury, as the man had an acute tropical dermatitis infection covering 50 percent of his body. Demers decided to focus on treating the dermatitis in order to make the man as comfortable as possible in his bunk.[12]

Demers, like several of the other *Pampanito* crew, kept a diary. On September 15, 1944, he made a brief entry stating that seventy-three ex-POW survivors had been picked up by the sub approximately one hundred miles off the coast of Hainan. Not surprisingly, he made no more entries until September 20, the day *Pampanito* delivered the survivors to the hospital at Saipan. *Pampanito*'s crew, as well as the POWs themselves, were amazed at Demers's stamina during the five days the POWs were on board. The British intelligence liaison officer who questioned the survivors upon their arrival at Saipan noted in his report that Demers worked tirelessly: "Survivors say that he did not seem to sleep during the whole time they were on board."[13]

Years later, when retired rear admiral and former submariner Tommy Dykers approached Demers for information about the rescue, to use as the basis of an episode of his television series *The Silent Service*, Demers provided his memories of those five days in much greater detail. In a 1958 letter to Dykers, he opened up about how the rescue had affected him: "as I examined and treated each one," he wrote, "I could feel a deep sense of gratitude, yet their faces were expressionless and only a few could move their lips to whisper a faint 'thanks.' Their eyes were like dead men's eyes, dim, lifeless, as though they had lost everything but their souls."[14]

"The *Pampanito* Story"—the episode of *The Silent Service* that was based on the attack on the convoy and subsequent rescue—depicted Demers as drinking lots of coffee and taking amphetamines to keep himself awake while the POWs were on board. In fact, as Demers remarked when the episode aired, he was one of the few sailors in the Navy who *didn't* drink coffee. (He never commented about the veracity of the claim about the amphetamines.) But his son, Larry Demers, believes it was his father's strong will at work, keeping him awake as he tended to his seventy-three patients: "I think he just felt that it was his duty and he had to do that and he just did."[15]

While the bulk of the task of caring for the patients fell to Demers, the willingness of the rest of the crew to assist in whatever way they could was ultimately the answer to the question of how a submarine could manage to accommodate and care for so many ill passengers over a five-day period. As Summers noted in his patrol report, soon after the men were brought aboard, the "problem of caring for men began to solve itself. Lieutenant T. N. Swain, USN, took over supervision and care of survivors." Ted Swain, together with Ensign Charles Bartholomew, immediately took the initiative and began to assign duties to the rest of the crew. Several crewmen were assigned to nursing detail. Under "Doc" Demers's supervision, they treated the POWs with eye irrigations, cleaned their sores and skin ulcers, and helped feed the men.[16]

Cleaning the oil from the men's bodies would be a long process. Over the next three days, survivors were escorted to the forward or after engine room, where the sailors who were on "cleaning watch" worked around the clock trying to remove every last drop of oil from the men's bodies. Demers assumed that cleaning up the survivors was his job, and was gratified at the way the crew pitched in willingly, without being asked—coming off four hours of watch and then without complaint spending the next four hours in the engine room, cleaning oil off the POWs' skin. One bucket of water was allotted for the cleaning of two men—fresh water is in short supply on a submarine at sea! First the hair was washed—a challenging task, because of the thick oil that stuck in and matted the men's hair. Demers and his assistants took pride, however, in the fact that they were able to sufficiently wash the oil out of the men's hair, so that shaving the POWs' heads or cutting their hair was not necessary. Cotton swabs were used to clean the oil out of ears, noses, and other hard-to-reach areas. By the second day, all of the POWs had had shampoos and shaves. The six most critical cases were given sponge baths in their bunks in the corner of the crew's quarters.[17]

The skipper instructed the rest of the officers and crew, those who were not assigned to assist with the survivors under the supervision of Swain and Bartholomew, to avoid contact with the POWs, in order to avoid contamination. They needed to focus on their duties, as *Pampanito* was now going to make a high-speed surface run in order to deliver the patients to Saipan and full-scale medical care as quickly as possible. A surface run would require extra vigilance, as it would expose the submarine to a greater risk of being spotted by enemy aircraft en route. To help ensure that the crew would remain in good health and be able to fulfill duties, other precautions were taken. The POWs were provided with separate eating utensils, which were washed and stored separately from those of the crew.[18]

But even those officers and crewmen who were not directly caring for the POWs wanted to do whatever they could to make the patients as comfortable as possible. No sacrifice was too great. Officers and crewmen cheerfully gave up their blankets for the men, and donated clothing for them to wear. Soon every POW had underwear, a shirt, trousers, and socks, and most even had acquired shoes or sandals. "Hot bunking"—the practice of two or three men sleeping in a single bunk in shifts—was increased in order to provide room for the POWs. Again, not a single complaint was heard.

The cooks worked tirelessly preparing food for the patients. After being examined, each survivor was given one cup of either water, tea with milk and sugar, cocoa, or soup every hour for twenty-four hours. The men were hungry after four days on the rafts, but after the minimal diet they had endured for the past two and a half years, their stomachs were unaccustomed to the food now available to them on the sub. Food rations to the men were increased gradually, and vitamin pills were also provided. Peder Granum teamed up with Bob Bennett, and together the two torpedomen-turned-nurses helped to spoon-feed the patients, still in their bunks, a little bit at a time.[19]

Demers was surprised when one of the healthier survivors, who had come aboard off the first raft, asked him for a Coca-Cola almost immediately after coming aboard. "Of course we had none," he recalled, "but to me it seemed a strange request after enduring so many deprivations." Later that night when making rounds of the patients he found the man vomiting, and after some questioning the man admitted that, craving more than the broths he was being fed, he had "swiped" some solid food from the crew's mess. Thirty-six hours later, however, the man's hunger had not subsided and Demers spotted him eating a huge hamburger, this time with no ill effects. "There is no doubt this Australian was rugged since he was the only one who tolerated solid food during the four days on board."[20]

Pampanito, meanwhile, continued on course, heading east toward Saipan. She traveled on the surface for maximum speed until the afternoon of September 16, when a four-engine bomber was spotted by a lookout, forcing the sub to dive until the bomber cleared the area. She then resurfaced and resumed her course to Saipan.

On board, many of the POWs were now feeling better. They had graduated from sips of water to sips of pineapple juice, and by the second day some of them were enjoying a meal of scrambled eggs on toast. Demers had to experiment with food rations, trying to determine which of the foods available on the sub would be best to bring back the men's strength and health. He soon discovered, for example, that the fruit juices were irritating to the men's stomachs, and he stopped allowing them for the POWs. Gradually the POWs' diet was increased to include beef bouillon, bread and butter, chicken broth and crackers, tomato consommé, eggnog, canned fruit,

Figure 14. Bob Bennett and rescued POW Bill Cray (*right*) aboard *Pampanito* in September 1944. The men would keep in touch after Cray returned home to England. By permission of Robert Bennett.

and finally soft-boiled eggs and hash. Multivitamin pills were given every fifteen hours, as well as a small amount of soft chocolate.[21]

Most of the POWs were soon ambulatory, and despite the captain's best efforts to keep them separated from the segment of the crew that was not assigned to nursing detail, many began to wander through the submarine, into the crew's quarters and mess.[22]

Burial at Sea

One of the seventy-three men rescued, however, never fully recovered consciousness after being pulled from the water. For twenty-four hours he drifted between an unconscious and a semiconscious state. At 6:30 p.m. on September 16, John Campbell of the Gordon Highlanders' Regiment, British Army, died on board—probably due to a combination of acute exhaustion, exposure, shock, dehydration, and possible internal injuries. Intravenous injections of dextrose and saline solution had been attempted, recorded Summers in his patrol report, "but without success due to the failure to locate a vein or even a drop of blood." In addition to these injuries, the crew had noticed that Campbell had "a big chunk taken out of the instep of one foot." This hole—two inches wide and one inch deep—on the bottom of Campbell's left foot was believed to have been caused by the nibbling of fish while he was in the water.[23]

Two hours after Campbell passed away, *Pampanito*'s crew held a small ceremony on deck and committed Campbell's body to the deep as the sub passed through Balintang Channel. Fellow POW Douglas Cresswale reflected on the death of his friend: "I am sorry Jock Campbell was so far gone that he couldn't be saved but at least we can tell his folks that his last hours were spent on an American submarine and that he was free." Bob Bennett, who as part of the rescue team had brought Campbell aboard and laid him down on the deck, was one of the crew members who now participated in his burial. Paul Pappas conducted the ceremony. There was some debate among the crew as to the most appropriate way to weigh down Campbell's body before committing it to the deep; in such situations, a five-inch shell was usually used. But the crew chose instead a spare part from one of the engines—a heavy connecting rod—which was in fact many times more valuable. According to Machinist's Mate Mike Carmody, the crew, as a tribute to Campbell, wanted to commit him to the deep with something of more value than a shell. Campbell's body was wrapped in a mattress cover and taken topside through the after battery hatch. On the deck, which was still slick with oil from the previous day, Pappas led the submariners in a prayer before Campbell body's was dropped into the waters of Balintang Channel. "Meanwhile, we kept our fingers crossed, hoping not to have an engine breakdown," recalled Carmody.[24]

Demers, meanwhile, completed an official certificate of death for submission to the Bureau of Medicine and Surgery at the Navy Department in Washington, D.C., for Campbell, filling in what little information he knew about the man. Under "cause of death" he listed "exhaustion from over exposure" as the principal cause, and starvation and deprivation of water as contributing factors.[25]

The Crew Gets to Know the Survivors

On September 17, the survivors' third day aboard the submarine, *Pampanito* continued to make her way through Balintang Channel.

Most of the remaining seventy-two survivors were much improved by now, and some were moving around the boat, taking a look around and becoming better acquainted with the crew. Summers noted that the survivors seemed to be in good spirits, enjoying the food and the company, listening to the phonograph and radio with the crew. Reg Bullock spent the time exploring the ship from stem to stern, regretting only that he could not climb up into the conning tower, which was strictly off limits for the survivors. Bill McKittrick was particularly awed by the torpedoes in the forward torpedo room—"the destructive weapons which had caused our trouble." Still, he found himself starting to feel a strong attachment to this vessel, and crew, which had saved his life: "for five days I became part of the '*Pampanito*' and she became part of me." Roy Cornford remembers listening to music played on the phonograph in the crew's mess. "They had only two records on that sub I think, as all day they played Vera Lynn singing 'Be like a kettle and sing' and 'Pistol packin' Mama.'" Curly Martin, whose fair hair had helped the crew identify the POWs in the water as other than Japanese, remembered a very large crewman who used to sit in the bulkhead doorway and talk to the survivors, promising he would take them to all of the "low dives" in Honolulu. "That did not eventuate, probably just as well."[26]

Pampanito's crew also took advantage of this opportunity to talk to the POWs about their experiences. Gordon Hopper found that at first the POWs seemed somewhat quiet and apprehensive, but once they started to recover and relax, they became more willing to talk about what they had been through as POWs. Some of their accounts were typed up by *Pampanito*'s yeoman, Charlie McGuire, and appended to Summers's official report for this patrol. Individual crewmen, in the meantime, were busy collecting names and home addresses of the men in their journals and notebooks, and many new and lasting friendships began. In addition to their contact information, many of the men jotted down messages of gratitude to the submariners. "I wish to thank the officers and men of this sub for saving myself and fellow men from the deep. God bless them all." "Officers and men of the USS *Pampanito*, I thank you with all my heart for everything. May you have good hunting and a safe return." "Best of luck and good shooting to the officers and men of USS *Pampanito*." Some of the messages asked the submariners to exact vengeance on their behalf: "I cannot find words to thank you and your mates for saving us from sure death. But I wish you all the luck in the world and may you put the Nips where they belong." "Wish you the very best of luck and a merry Xmas and prosperous New Year. Also hope you find plenty more Japs and put them to the bottom."[27]

Many wrote of how grateful they were to be finally free. They spoke of the sadness that filled them when they thought of their comrades who had been lost at sea, and of their eagerness to recover fully so they could resume the fight against the Japanese. "Big Bill" Cunneen wrote in Quartermaster John Greene's journal of his feelings about being torpedoed by the American subs in the early hours of September 12: "An early reveille, I must say, but despite the loss of life of our comrades, we still say as we said when we were first hit: 'Bloody good shots, these fellows!,' and we raise our hats to you and your devotion to duty." British survivor Charles Perry was philosophical about the sinking of *Rakuyo Maru*: "This is my third smash up at sea and here's hoping it's the last."[28]

Over and over again, the POWs thanked the submariners for

the kind and caring treatment they had been given while aboard the sub. They issued invitations to the submariners to visit them in Australia and England. "A sure welcome for every member of the sub *Pampanito*," wrote David Flinn when he jotted down his address in Roger Bourgeois's journal. "My home is theirs. We owe them everything." "Come to Aussie and the first week's fun is on me," promised "Big Bill" Cunneen. Some of the messages the survivors wrote were just simply and heart-wrenchingly to the point. "Many thanks for our freedom and life," wrote F. E. Wiles. "You made me very happy when I saw your sub come in sight to pick us up," wrote Thomas Taylor. Harry Chivers, in the account he wrote in Torpedoman Leonard Baron's journal, remarked: "Thank God for the Americans. We had got away from the Japanese at last after two and a half years of misery and hell. Our luck had changed at last."[29]

The destroyer USS *Case* (DD-370) was on interisland escort duty in the Marianas Islands area on September 16 when she received a secret dispatch with instructions for a rendezvous mission with two submarines, USS *Pampanito* and USS *Sealion*, to give assistance as deemed necessary by the subs' skippers in caring for a group of rescued Allied survivors. *Case* immediately set course for the area. Just after noon on the eighteenth, *Case* sighted and approached *Pampanito*. The original intention was to transfer the survivors from the submarine to the destroyer, and have *Case* deliver them to Saipan as quickly as possible. It was quickly decided, however, that despite the limited space and lack of medical facilities aboard *Pampanito*, it would be best not to transfer the survivors, in their weakened condition, to *Case*. Weather conditions were not ideal for such an operation, the sea was too rough; and in any case, the survivors were being cared for suitably aboard the sub. Instead, *Case's* medical officer, Lieutenant Commander Paul Waldo, and Chief Pharmacist's Mate Lynn Wilcox went aboard *Pampanito* to examine the survivors and bring additional medical supplies for Demers, as well as blankets and clothing.[30]

Arrival at Saipan

By now, almost all of the survivors aboard *Pampanito* had recovered enough to be able to walk through the sub. According to Summers, "This was encouraged so that our men plus a few of the healthiest survivors could do some cleaning up in the After Torpedo Room." At five minutes to nine on the morning of September 20, *Pampanito* sailed into Saipan's Tanapag Harbor, where she tied up next to the tender USS *Fulton* (AS-11). As doctors came aboard to assist in the transfer of the survivors from the sub to the tender and then to the island hospital, fresh fruit and ice cream were delivered for the survivors to enjoy. A few of the men were stretcher cases, but most were able to climb up to the deck and walk off the submarine unassisted. They were neat, clean, and dressed like American submarine sailors. And it was just starting to dawn on them that finally, their long ordeal was really over. "When they came alongside the big tender at Saipan and they lowered those big beautiful oranges down to us and the cans of ice cream, we knew we were home," recalled Roy Cornford. "That was it."[31]

Fulton had relief crews standing by; as soon as the POWs were transferred off the sub, they came aboard to decontaminate and thoroughly clean the sub. All contaminated clothing and soiled bedding was removed and replaced. Each *Pampanito* crewman received a new set of dungarees and "skivvies." *Pampanito* then took on fresh provisions and fuel, and by 4 p.m. she was under way again, en route to Pearl Harbor, where this momentous and memorable patrol would come to an end. It is likely that each member of *Pampanito's* crew felt an extraordinary sense of accomplishment at the end of this patrol. This feeling was best described by Demers: "When the survivors were picked up they were disease ridden, spirit broken men, like slaves in despair. Four days later they left the ship happy and smiling, men who found life was worth living. I feel that the vast change in these men was not all attributed to the fact that they were once again men, nor to the medical treatment they received, but to the friendliness and devotion shown by the ninety some odd men who were on board at the time."[32]

Sealion Arrives with More Survivors

Two hours after *Pampanito* arrived at Saipan, *Case* steamed into the harbor, accompanied by *Sealion*. *Sealion* had picked up fifty-four survivors from the South China Sea after being radioed by *Pampanito* for assistance. *Sealion's* pharmacist's mate, P. J. Williams, with a team of eight "volunteer nurses," had tended to the patients. Relieved of all other duties, these men had spent the next five days caring for the survivors in shifts: eight hours on, eight hours off.

Some of the men, upon being taken aboard *Sealion*, were unable to even hold down water, and blood plasma was administered to them. Williams performed triage and administered morphine to a few of the survivors. Once all were settled in as comfortably as possible, the operation of cleaning the oil from their bodies began in earnest. The "nurses" used mineral oil; when the supply of mineral oil ran out, they tried using detergent emulsion, then light hydraulic oil. All the men who could stand up were given a warm shower. Williams treated their skin sores. He also identified signs of malnourishment, malaria, sunburn, exposure, shock, and exhaustion. "After this we decided to cut everyone's hair. I didn't see any lice; I figured that they had probably been killed by the oil with which their hair was matted." Laurie Kearney of the Australian Imperial Force, one of the survivors taken aboard *Sealion*, remembered little about the actual rescue or the first day aboard the sub: "The first I remember was being sat on a toilet with the crewman endeavoring to remove the oil from my body and cut all my hair off as it was matted with oil."[33]

By the morning of September 16, all of the POWs had consumed a small amount of food and were sleeping a restless sleep, tossing and turning in their racks. The lights were turned down to help them rest. After some rest, the survivors were more responsive and even cheerful. They were given milk, vitamins, and quinine. Four were unconscious and never came to. They passed away on the submarine. Williams had been unable to find any external injuries on these men, and thought they may have been suffering from internal injuries from the force of the depth-charging they had endured while in the water. The crew conducted burial services for them, and the four were buried at sea.[34]

On September 17, Williams felt the remaining POWs were recovered enough to start getting three meals a day. These were limited to soft foods, such as soup, soft boiled eggs, toast, and ice cream. They seemed to tolerate the food quite well.[35]

Even those members of *Sealion*'s crew who had limited contact with the survivors did what they could, donating clothes, mattress covers, toothbrushes, and cigarettes for their use. There was ample food on board for everyone, but *Sealion*'s crew and officers ended up eating sandwiches for the next five days, simply because the galley was kept so busy preparing food for the POWs.[36]

The skipper's action report for this patrol noted of the survivors: "They were a scrawny, scabrous lot of human beings, but, on *Sealion*'s arrival in Saipan on 20 September 1944, the care given them by the nursing gang brought most of them around—only six of the fifty remaining survivors required stretchers."[37]

At 4 p.m. on September 18, *Sealion* rendezvoused with *Case* approximately seven hundred miles west of Saipan. A medical officer and a pharmacist's mate reported aboard for temporary duty, to examine and treat the survivors. Soon both vessels were heading for Saipan. On September 20 the ships arrived at Tanapag Harbor, where *Sealion* was moored to *Fulton*, and the fifty remaining survivors were transferred to the U.S. Army hospital on the island. *Sealion* was cleaned and disinfected, and the next day she was under way for Pearl Harbor.[38]

Queenfish and *Barb* Arrive

The other two submarines called in to assist in rescuing POWs, *Queenfish* and *Barb*, arrived on the scene later than *Pampanito* and *Sealion*. The men they pulled from the water had been in the South China Sea, without nourishment, for five days. The one advantage was that the subs had forty-eight hours' advance notice and were able to prepare the submarine for the taking on of survivors. *Queenfish* picked up eighteen men: three of them were semiconscious and slow to respond; one was unconscious. Pharmacist's Mate Harold

Dixon found them to be suffering from malnutrition, fatigue, and exposure, as well as pellagra, conjunctivitis, and tropical ulcers. Their skin was covered with rashes and was itching from exposure to the fuel oil and salt water. Many showed skin pigmentation from the oil. *Queenfish*'s crew chose to use the forward torpedo room as a sick bay, since there were sixteen bunks in that compartment, and immediately adjacent was the officers' head and shower, which was designated for the patients. Two of the men, those without bunks, were laid in blankets on the deck.

Like the other submarines' pharmacist's mates, Dixon did his best with this gigantic and unexpected task that was thrust upon him, experimenting along the way. He tried giving the men stimulants in the form of hot coffee, then brandy, which was not well tolerated by the patients. He experimented with other fluids throughout the first day. It was a challenging and sometimes frustrating situation for Dixon: "Treatment of these men was complicated by the fact that for three days after we picked them up typhoon weather prevailed. The men were seasick and were kept awake by the storm." Through-out the first night, he found it difficult to administer intravenous fluids to his patients: it was difficult to keep a steady flow, as the ship was constantly rolling, sometimes at an angle of as much as thirty-five or forty degrees. The rough weather, noted Commander Charles E. Loughlin grimly in his patrol report, "effectively sealed the fate of any possible remaining survivors and materially added to the discomfort of those on board." He also noted, however, that not a single word of complaint was heard from the survivors.[39]

Of the eighteen men rescued by *Queenfish*, two did not make it to Saipan. When brought aboard, both were unconscious and suffering from a high fever. Their temperatures never dropped, and they never regained consciousness. One died during the first night, about ten hours after the rescue; the other about thirty hours after being rescued. Dixon believed the deaths were at least partly caused by internal injuries, caused by the underwater explosions from the depth charges dropped after their ship was sunk.[40]

By the second day the patients were eating soft food, and by the fourth day Dixon was able to report that "they were receiving their regular chow." Warm soap and water were used to remove the fuel oil from the men's skin, as was the submarine's supply of diesel oil. After three days, most of the survivors were able to stand and walk, and were moving around the sub, enjoying the company and the care being extended to them, and getting their first news in years of the progress of the war. W. G. Smith of Queensland asked the skipper one morning if they had any bread aboard. "'Sure,' he said, 'we baked extra bread for you last night.' I was pretty doubtful about this, and couldn't imagine bread being baked on a submarine, but at breakfast time in came the bread and butter. Yes, tinned Australian butter! If you give up eating bread for two and a half years, like we did, you can imagine how we felt. It tasted good." Soon the survivors were gaining weight. The crew contributed clothes, shoes, toothpaste, soap, towels, cigarettes—anything they could think of—for the survivors' use. Smith was amazed by the generosity. "It kind of made lumps in our throats. We weren't used to things like this. I smoked 10 cigarettes without a stop. From there, the trip was just a succession of surprises, with men vying with each other to do kindnesses for us. The crew watched us all night, just in case we asked for anything. America can be very proud of her submarine men."[41]

On September 25, *Queenfish* rendezvoused with *Case* and proceeded to Saipan in the company of *Case* and *Barb*. The remaining sixteen survivors rescued by *Queenfish* were delivered to the to U.S. Army hospital on Saipan safely, cleaner, rested, and each weighing ten to fifteen pounds more than when they had been picked up out of the sea. *Queenfish*, meanwhile, reloaded fuel and torpedoes and departed Saipan the next day.[42]

When *Barb* had arrived at the rescue site, the fourteen men she was able to pluck out of the sea had been in the water for six days and seven nights. Pharmacist's Mate William Donnelly had had two and a half days to make preparations for taking survivors on board. He chose to use the crew's quarters, in the after battery compartment, for the patients, and one of the crew's heads adjacent to the after battery. The mattresses were covered with canvas to protect them from the oil. Next, Donnelly laid out what medical supplies he had at hand: saline, plasma, sterile gear, morphine syrettes, and adrenalin. Buckets, soap, mineral oil, and alcohol were gathered for cleaning the men. When the POWs were brought aboard, a procedure was already in place: Donnelly stood "in the receiving position," at the bottom of the ladder in the crew's mess, where two mattresses were laid on the deck on which to lay the survivors. All of the POWs were initially extremely weak and required assistance to descend the ladder. Only one of the fourteen could even sit up. Eight of the men were semiconscious, and the rest were reasonably alert. Donnelly examined them and found multiple skin abrasions covering their bodies from their uncomfortable positions on the rafts. He saw open sores caused by exposure to salt water, oil, and sun, and large skin ulcers on many of the men. The men were also suffering from dehydration, pellagra, beriberi, and malnutrition.[43]

After checking for fractures and other injuries, Donnelly gave the men sweetened water, three tablespoons at a time, and washed their eyes with boric acid solution, followed by a few drops of mineral oil. Again, experimentation was the key: "We found that giving them a little brandy in coffee seemed to make them rest more easily and to tolerate better the cleaning up." Attempts to remove the oil covering the POWs' skin, because of the many abrasions on their bodies, was quite painful for them. Donnelly feared that using fuel oil as a cleanser would only cause more pain, so buckets of warm water and soap were prepared to finish the cleaning process. He then treated and dressed the skin abrasions, and cut the men's hair because it was so heavily matted with oil.[44]

Because the POWs were so dehydrated, Donnelly administered liquids carefully. At first, in addition to the sweetened water and coffee, he gave them chipped ice cubes and small sips of water. The second day he tried fruit juice, but found that the men did not tolerate it very well. Later that day, the men were consuming soft foods—soft boiled eggs, toast, eggnog, ice cream. By the third day the men were eating normally, although still suffering stomach upsets, unaccustomed as they were to a normal diet. The men were also affected by seasickness as the ship rolled in the force of the typhoon. By the fourth day, most of the men were looking and feeling better, and able to move around the boat. Soon Donnelly gave up on trying to keep them isolated from the rest of the crew. The crew took a great interest in their passengers, inquiring of their ordeal and collecting signatures and stories. Each POW was constantly surrounded by a circle of sailors, listening to his stories of the surrender of Singapore, the building of the Burma-Thai Railroad, and the journey aboard the hellships. Aware that the survivors had nothing, the sailors donated food and clothing. Before the voyage to Saipan had ended, they also pooled together their money and presented it to the survivors: a total of three hundred dollars.[45]

Gene Fluckey, *Barb*'s skipper, was impressed by the unbounded gratitude displayed by the survivors and regretted that they hadn't been able to take aboard more. "Even those who couldn't talk expressed themselves tearfully through their glazed oil soaked eyes. . . . On the amusing side, the following remarks were recorded as the survivors were being carried to their bunks. 'I take back all I ever said about you Yanks.' 'Three bloody years without a drink of Brandy, please give me another.' 'Turn me loose I'll run to that bunk.' 'Be sure to wake me up for chow.' 'Matey, we're in safe hands at last.' 'As soon as I can I'm going to write my wife to kick the Yankee out—I'm coming home!'" Fluckey was also impressed by the vehemence with which the survivors' appetite returned. Before long he noticed that they were eating heartily, each one sporting a "pot belly" by the end of the five-day journey.[46]

On the morning of September 25, *Barb* rendezvoused with *Case*, in company with *Queenfish*, and together they proceeded to Tanapag Harbor, where *Barb* moored portside to *Queenfish* alongside *Fulton*. The POWs were now in decent shape; all but one were able to walk off the submarine unassisted. Fluckey wrote in his patrol narrative: "We had only one ambulance case and when he saw the rest of them walking out he'd be damned if he'd be left to be the only man to go out on a stretcher, so he got right out of the stretcher and walked off. It took a lot of courage to do that because he was in no condition to walk. He could hardly do it and the people had to support him at times."[47]

Captain Ed Swinburne, commander of the task group that included *Barb* and *Queenfish*, was aboard *Barb* and observed the rescue and the care of the POWs by the submariners. He was impressed by the men's remarkable recovery and return to health under the patient and tender care of the crews of the two subs. "How versatile a submarine enlisted man can be!" he remarked in his action report. But it is perhaps the reflections of *Barb*'s CO, Gene Fluckey, that best sum up the real impact of the rescue: "These boys are very grateful, it gives you an insight into humanity to see what people have gone through and come out of it. I mean some of them would wake up nights screaming. When we had nurses these other men, these tough submarine men that were now meek as a lamb acting as nurses for these prisoners who would wake up in the night screaming and not know where they were, and somebody would explain to them that 'You're on the submarine *Barb* now. Don't worry fellow, you're doing all right. We're taking care of you,' and all he would say was, 'Well, thank God I'm in safe hands at last,' or something like that. Very touching scenes aboard there."[48]

After the survivors were disembarked at Tanapag Harbor, *Barb* took on one torpedo forward and twenty gallons of fuel, and by 7:45 the next morning she was steaming out of Saipan.

8

Saipan

Five days after the rescue, on the morning of September 20, *Pampanito* reached Saipan with her load of ex-POWs and tied up next to the submarine tender USS *Fulton*. The seventy-two men were all assembled in the after torpedo room, where Captain Summers addressed them. The CO, as one of the POWs recalled, told them that he "regretted the circumstance which had put us in this position and hoped that we would continue to try and achieve the object of the allies which was to defeat our common enemy—THE JAP."[1] The survivors then went up on deck, for the first time since the night of the rescue, and lined up to await transfer to the tender. Five of the men were stretcher cases, but the rest were mobile and appeared greatly recovered from their ordeal.

While the men awaited transfer, ice cream and fresh oranges were distributed to them. Fresh fruit and dairy products were usually brought aboard when a sub came in from patrol; after sixty days at sea, the sailors looked forward to such items. But for the ex-POWs, it was truly an unexpected luxury, giving them, as *Pampanito*'s skipper noted in his report, "their finest treat in over two and one-half years." Bill McKittrick remembered the tubs of ice cream and the baskets of oranges, as well as the crew of *Fulton* waving and cheering the survivors: "it was wonderful because we were free and we felt like the crew of the *Bounty* did when they arrived in Tahiti."[2]

When the small boats for the transfer arrived, those confined to stretchers were moved first. Then the remaining sixty-seven men were loaded onto two boats and shoved off, as the men waved, cheered, and gave thumbs-up signs to their rescuers. On the cigarette deck, Paul Pappas, the unofficial ship's photographer, stood by again with camera in hand to document the transfer. Survivor Reg Bullock took a final look back at the submarine, and at the hull number on the nose of the vessel: "383." It was a number he would never forget.[3]

The survivors were now fully dressed, in clothes mostly donated by the submariners, looking like American submariners themselves. Maurice Demers recalled: "When we arrived in Saipan many of the survivors looked better than the crew. As a matter of fact one of our Cooks who worked tirelessly preparing the proper nourishments and serving it to the survivors in the after battery and after torpedo room, and who is naturally thin, was almost forced in one of the boats going to the hospital. This Officer who took charge of evacuation thought our ship's cook was trying to pull a fast one." As the cook insisted, "I'm not one of them!" his fellow crew members laughed and shouted, "No, he's one of them, take him away!"[4]

Demers was particularly proud of the fact that not only were the disembarking ex-POWs now fully dressed and clean, but their heads had not been shaved. The POWs aboard the other rescuing submarines had had the oil-matted hair from their heads cut as part of the clean-up process. Demers recognized that his decision not to

Figures 15 (*above*) and 16 (*opposite*). After five days aboard *Pampanito*, the rescued POWs, wearing items of clothing donated by the submariners, lined up on *Pampanito*'s deck to await transfer to the sub tender USS *Fulton* at Saipan. U.S. Navy photos.

shave the men's heads resulted in their being able to feel proud that they now looked like military men, not POWs.[5]

When *Sealion* arrived at Saipan a couple of hours after *Pampanito*, she moored outboard of *Pampanito* to discharge her cargo of fifty survivors. They were transferred aboard *Fulton*, where they, along with the survivors delivered by *Pampanito*, were examined by the ship's medical officers, who substantiated all of the observations and conclusions made by the subs' pharmacist's mates: "It is our opinion

that they are to be commended for their resourcefulness and skill in meeting the sudden emergency thrust upon them."[6] After it had been determined that the ex-POWs were free of any quarantinable diseases, they were taken to the U.S. Army 148th General Hospital on Saipan.

Meanwhile, *Pampanito's* compartments were cleaned and disinfected, and four hours after the POWs had disembarked, the sub departed Saipan. At long last, Doc Demers could rest. He recalled: "The Captain called me to the wardroom, gave me two ounces of brandy, told me I could take a shower and go to bed. By this time my ankles and legs were swollen twice their size and I had some difficulty walking." The crew, noticing this, helped Demers to his

Figure 17. Survivors waiting on *Pampanito*'s deck. Frank Farmer stands in the forefront. U.S. Navy photo.

rack, where he fell asleep immediately and slept for thirty-six hours straight. "I doubt that even a depth charge would have awakened me."[7]

Just days after *Pampanito* returned to Pearl Harbor at the patrol's end, Captain Summers recommended Demers for promotion to warrant pharmacist rank in recognition of his exceptional and outstanding service while the POWs were on board. It was a huge responsibility for one man, and Demers had handled it with true dedication, stamina, and professionalism. Many of the survivors rescued by *Pampanito* owed their recovery and indeed their lives to

Figure 18. Maurice "Doc" Demers, *Pampanito*'s pharmacist's mate, helps a POW off the submarine at Saipan. U.S. Navy photo.

Demers's care and professional skill. Based on the CO's observations of Demers in action, "he is considered in every respect as fine officer material," concluded Summers in his recommendation memo to the chief of the Navy Bureau of Personnel.[8]

COMSUBPAC Charles A. Lockwood Jr. agreed. In his endorsement of Summers's recommendation, he remarked: "The outstanding professional ability of Demers undoubtedly saved the lives of many British and Australian survivors. The Force Commander fully concurs in the recommendation for advancement of Demers to the

Figure 19 (*above*). One of the rescued men is helped up the ladder, through the hatch, and onto the deck of the submarine. U.S. Navy photo.

Figures 20 and 21 (*opposite*). Those survivors, unable to walk yet, were transferred off of the submarine on stretchers. U.S. Navy photos.

rank of Warrant Pharmacist." In June 1945, Demers would also be recognized with the awarding of a Navy and Marine Corps Medal by Fleet Admiral Chester W. Nimitz. The citation was forwarded to him at the U.S. Naval Hospital in Brooklyn, New York, where he was stationed as of May 12, 1945.[9]

Summers also recommended other personnel for awards for the third patrol, including Silver Star Medals to Lieutenant Junior Grade

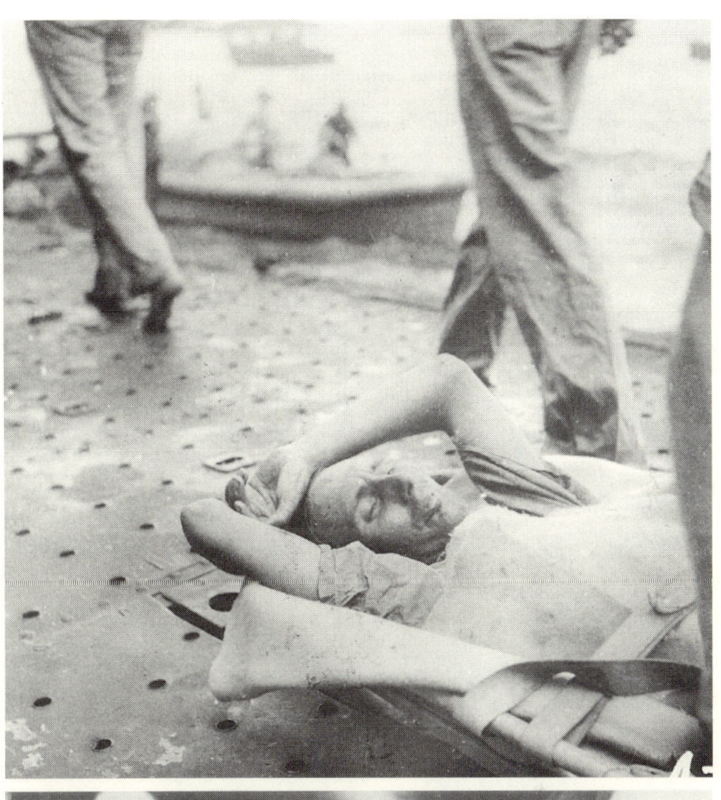

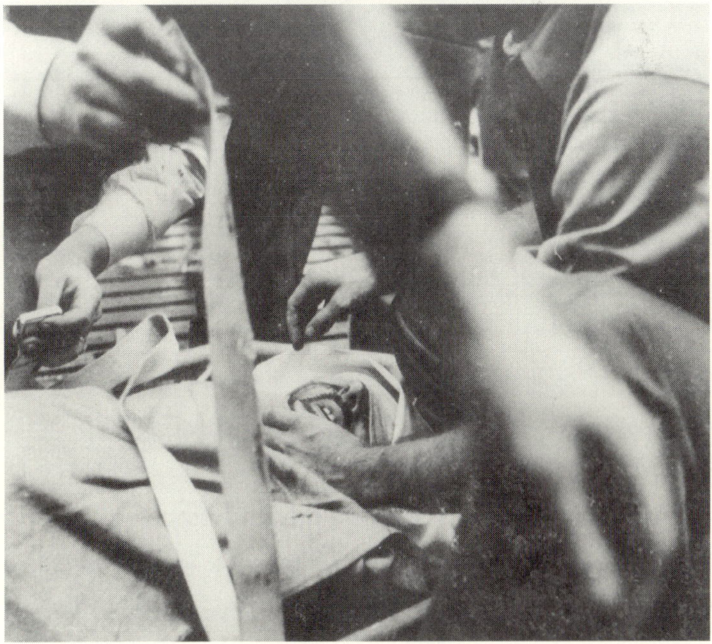

Figure 22. While awaiting transfer at Saipan, the rescued men enjoyed a treat of fresh oranges and ice cream. U.S. Navy photo.

Francis M. Fives "for gallantry and intrepidity in action, as Torpedo Data Computer Operator and Assistant to the Approach Officer"; to Lieutenant Commander Landon L. Davis Jr. for his performance as OOD and assistant approach officer during the night surface attack against the convoy; and to Radio Technician George Moffett for "his alertness, excellent judgement, and efficiency in operating the radar equipment" during the night surface radar attack against the convoy. Summers recommended the awarding of Bronze Star

Figure 23. The submariners help the survivors onto the boat that will transfer them to the sub tender USS *Fulton* at Saipan. U.S. Navy photo.

Medals to Lieutenant Commander Clifford Grommet, as first plotting officer and assistant to the approach officer in the same attack; to Lieutenant Howard Fulton, as junior OOD during the attack and for his role in making emergency repairs to the forward trim tank of the sub prior to the attack; to Gunner's Mate Tony Hauptman, as battle lookout during the attack as well as for his role in the trim tank repair operation; and to Chief Motor Machinist's Mate Clarence Smith, as chief of the watch and hydraulic manifold operator during the attack. Several other officers and men were also

Figure 24. A last heartfelt wave to their rescuers as the former POWs are transferred by boat from *Pampanito* to *Fulton*. U.S. Navy photo.

recommended for recognition, among them Lieutenant Ted Swain as "officer in general charge of survivors." Summers felt that Swain deserved the Navy and Marine Corps Medal for his role in caring for the POWs: "He exhibited outstanding ingenuity in devising accommodations for the 73 survivors in the small compartment available and excellent supervision of the treatment and care of the men." Members of the rescue party were recommended for awards, as well as those crewmen who had served as "nurse maids" to the patients.[10]

Barb and *Queenfish* arrived at Saipan midmorning on September 25 with their cargoes of patients. Together, the four subs had rescued 159 men. Seven of the men died later. The next day, *Barb* and *Queenfish* departed for Majuro.

The POWs in the Saipan Army Hospital

The 152 former POWs were taken ashore in small boats to waiting ambulances, which delivered them to the 148th General Hospital on Saipan. Here the men were showered and dressed in clean pajamas, and finally able to rest on spring mattresses, away from the roar of diesel engines. Occasionally they could hear the sounds of combat: small pockets of Japanese resistance were still fighting the Americans on the island.[11]

The 148th was the only general hospital on the island, housing its patients in tent wards on a hilltop. Smaller medical units on the island serviced Japanese civilian internees and the non-Japanese native population. Although hospital staff was informed about the incoming POWs, nothing was said about their nationality or their condition prior to their arrival. Hospital staff members were shocked by the men's condition. "We were dismayed and angered by the terrible physical condition of the [men]," recalled Army medic Andrew Hart. The men appeared to be nothing but skin and bones. "Like other patients, they got the very best care that we could provide. Unlike the others, they received many visits from well-wishing hospital personnel as well as many gifts of money and other items."

Hart had joined the Army in February 1943 and was trained as a lab technician in the Army Medical Corps. When the POWs were at Saipan, his duties included taking blood samples from them and conducting some of the tests that were run on them, such as checking red and white cell counts. He took the opportunity to talk to the men, especially after discovering that he shared a surname with one of them, Reginald Hart. He noted that the newly arrived patients were reluctant to talk about their experiences but eager for updates on the progress of the war. "To me they did not appear overly depressed or withdrawn; rather, they were composed, uncomplaining, and—not surprisingly—lacked any exuberance."[12]

Doctors at the 148th took careful medical histories of the survivors. They were able to determine that the average age of the survivors was twenty-nine and that their average weight loss as POWs had been sixteen pounds. Ninety-five percent of the survivors stated that they had contracted malaria, and 65 percent said they had suffered from recurrent dysentery. Ninety-five percent reported signs of vitamin and nutritional deficiencies during their imprisonment. The ex-POWs told the doctors and hospital staff about the cholera epidemic and the typhoid fever that had swept through the POW camps, killing many of them of their comrades. One-fifth of the survivors rescued by *Pampanito* and *Sealion* had acute bronchitis, it was discovered. But, with treatment and rest, all of the men responded favorably.[13]

When news of the rescue was received at Pacific Fleet headquarters, the British Intelligence liaison officer, Captain D.N.C. Tufnell, was dispatched to Saipan to interview the sub crews and the rescued POWs and gather what information he could. Tufnell left Pearl Harbor on September 17; however, due to delays with the aircraft, he did not arrive on Saipan until the twenty-first, the day after the arrival of *Pampanito* and *Sealion*, and was unable to meet with their crews. Tufnell visited the former POWs in the hospital, but he found that many were in no condition yet to be questioned. "The experiences of 150 men would fill a book, and countless more facts and details will be obtainable when they arrive home and can be interviewed individually, and when they have time to recall facts which come to their minds," he wrote in his report. A list of all of the survivors at Saipan was compiled, and photographs were taken of each one. These were forwarded to military authorities. The POWs were able to provide some information about Japanese military positions, as well as the shocking details of the horrors and atrocities inflicted on them by the Japanese in the POW camps.[14] "They were a remarkable crowd of fellows," Tufnell noted, "cheerful in the most, but quiet and subdued, modest and in no way claiming anything for themselves; universally in praise of the wonderful work done by their own doctors and other officers during the past 2½ years, and especially of their reception by their American rescuers." He was impressed by their conduct, courage, and rapid recovery—not just in health, but in spirit.[15]

While on Saipan, the ex-POWs were issued complete sets of uniforms and boots, and full kits. They relished the care and attention given to them by the Army doctors, and especially by the nurses. They were showered with gifts of cigarettes, candy, and ice cream. There was an open-air theater set up for use of the military on Saipan, where the survivors attended a showing one night. Jack Flynn, one of the men rescued and brought to Saipan by *Barb*, expressed some concern to one of the American soldiers at the screening that the bright lights of the theater might attract the attention of enemy Japanese forces still on the island. The American responded: "Don't matter where we are, Bud. We gotta have our movies!"[16]

The ex-POWs remained in the hospital on Saipan for one week.

Pampanito Returns to Pearl Harbor

Many years later, when asked what the best thing in a submariner's life was, Torpedoman Hubert Brown of *Pampanito* replied without hesitation: "Getting back into port." No doubt the end of *Pamp*'s third war patrol was greeted with a huge sense of relief by the crew. After dropping her passengers off at Saipan, the sub returned to Pearl Harbor for refit, arriving at Subase on September 28. The crew turned the boat over to a refit crew while they retreated to the Royal Hawaiian Hotel on Waikiki Beach for two well-earned weeks of R&R. Each crew member received the Submarine Combat Insignia for having completed a successful war patrol. L. H. Chappell, commander of Submarine Division 281, in his October 3 endorsement of *Pampanito*'s third war patrol report, congratulated her skipper, officers, and crew and noted that *Pampanito* had returned from patrol clean and shipshape, and her crew in excellent health and spirits.[17]

Sealion's crew was not so lucky, healthwise: four of her "nursing" crew were so exhausted they immediately checked in to sick bay upon arrival in port. Several men developed mild cases of fever, and many had severe colds and sore throats. Noted the sub's captain in his patrol report: "The outbreak probably resulted from over crowding, loss of sleep, and irregular meals and routine while the survivors were aboard."[18]

After the rest period for *Pamp*'s crew, preparations began for the sub's fourth war patrol. Pete Summers had been granted an extended leave, and he headed to the mainland for a rest. He was replaced as CO by Captain Frank W. Fenno Jr.. The news came as a surprise to the crew members returning from their R&R at the Royal Hawaiian, but it was met with a positive response. The men had heard of the "legendary Captain Mike Fenno." Gordon Hopper recalled: "This was cause for celebration. Not only did Mike Fenno have a distinguished war record as captain of the USS *Trout* (SS-202), but he was widely reputed to be an 'enlisted man's captain.' The latter proved to be true." Still, recalled Hopper, their new captain was tough on them, taking them "through rigorous preparation that made prior training runs look like picnics."[19]

Pampanito's Fourth Patrol

It was Fenno who took *Pampanito* out on her next patrol, departing Pearl Harbor on October 28. She headed for the Hainan area again, in the South China Sea, as part of another wolf pack. On this run the sub would be plagued by rough weather: "Mountainous seas and overcast skies made it an arduous patrol." In spite of the conditions, *Pampanito* would manage to sink one Japanese ship and damage another on this patrol. She then received orders to proceed to Fremantle, Australia, arriving on December 30. A pleasant surprise awaited them upon their arrival: they were greeted at the port by several of the former POWs rescued by *Pampanito* three months earlier. The reunion was a joyful one. Recalled Gordon Hopper, "Did anybody ever see a New Year in like we did that one?"[20]

A number of U.S. submarines were operating out of Fremantle, and the Navy had contracted a couple of local hotels as R&R centers for the sub crews. *Pampanito*'s crew stayed at the Ocean Beach Hotel and again enjoyed a pleasant two weeks of rest, during which time they were able to visit with more of the former POWs from the Fremantle and Perth areas. The Aussies held numerous parties in honor of the submariners who had saved their lives. "Doc" Demers was delighted to see many of his former patients, and to meet their family members, who of course could not hold back their gratitude: "We were invited to meet their mothers, fathers, wives, etc., and we were greeted, hugged, and kissed with such affection that a more emotional greeting would be hard to encounter. The little we were able to do for these men was more than compensated."[21]

For the former POWs, having spent their first Christmas at home with their families for the first time in several years, it was now doubly wonderful to have their submariner rescuers visit. The Australians went out of their way to make the submariners' stay in their country as enjoyable and memorable as possible. Some of the men went rabbit hunting. Jack Cocking took Tony Hauptman and two other *Pampanito* crewmen on a kangaroo-hunting expedition. December is the height of summer in Australia: the day was exceptionally hot, and the men walked miles in the bush, searching for kangaroos. They found none, but saw hundreds of rabbits. Motor Machinist's Mate Walter Madison, a farm boy from Nebraska, was thrilled when one of the former POWs, who owned a number of high-quality race horses, let the submariners ride them.[22]

For many of *Pampanito*'s crew it was their first time in Australia, and the presence and hospitality of the survivors made it all the more memorable. It was a "dream R&R," recalled Gordon Hopper.[23] When it ended and the crew reassembled on the boat, some were less than thrilled to learn that Pete Summers was back in command, having been flown in to Australia for the start of the fifth patrol. They would miss the personable, down-to-earth Captain Fenno, as well as XO Jeff Davis, who had been replaced by Lynn Orser.

Pampanito's Fifth and Sixth Patrols

Pampanito departed Fremantle on January 23, 1945, and headed north toward her patrol area: the Gulf of Siam. Early in the patrol, lookouts sighted a small, heavily escorted convoy. *Pampanito* succeeded in sinking one of the transports, then watched as USS *Guavina* (SS-362) torpedoed one of the others. The following afternoon, *Pampanito* encountered a single ship with two escorts—a contact that resulted in the sinking of a Japanese tanker. As the patrol wound down, *Pampanito* headed for Subic Bay, where she arrived on February 12 for refit. She was to be the first submarine refitted at this base. On February 25 she departed Subic Bay, headed again for the Gulf of Siam. On this, her sixth run, she found no targets, before finally wrapping up the disappointing patrol and returning to Pearl Harbor on April 24. She then proceeded to the U.S. Naval Drydock at Hunter's Point, California, for an overhaul. On May 24, Commander Donald A. Scherer relieved Summers as CO of *Pampanito*. The overhaul was completed by August 1, and *Pampanito* headed back to Pearl.

Home

All I want to do now is go home on leave, and
forget the whole business.

Rakuyo Maru survivor James Campbell

The former POWs recovered swiftly under the care of the doctors and nurses at the 148th General Hospital on Saipan. By September 28 the medical staff felt that most of the men were now healthy enough to send on the long journey home: to Australia for some, Britain for the rest. What lay ahead for them upon their return was still undetermined; what was certain was that, after two and a half years in the hands of the Japanese, the one thing that ex-POWs needed and wanted more than anything else was to see their families again.

A handful of the men were deemed not yet fit enough for travel, and they remained on Saipan until late October. Among them was twenty-two-year-old Roy Cornford, who would stay on the island for a total of six weeks before being allowed to begin the journey home. Although the medical authorities had determined that Cornford was not well enough to travel, after a week he was feeling much better, enough so to be up and about: "And probably after a week I came good. So I had five weeks of good times on Saipan Island with all these American nurses." When he began to recover, he was taken on a tour of the U.S. Army camps around the island, where he gave a couple of lectures on his experiences. At the end of October, he and the other remaining POWs were transported to Guam, then boarded a large hospital plane, accompanied by a nurse, for the rest of the journey home. "As we flew over the Caroline Islands, the crew said they would go down low and let the Japs fire some flak at us. They said they wouldn't hit us, but we said we are too close to home now."[1]

On the morning of September 28, now fully outfitted with clothing and kit, supplied with cigarettes, and in greatly improved health, the other survivors were loaded into ambulances and driven to the wharf. The Brits would be traveling home via the United States. They boarded the liberty ship *Cape Douglas* for the voyage to Pearl Harbor. In Hawai'i they boarded another ship, which took them to San Francisco. From there they traveled by train across the country—through Chicago and to New York City. The Cunard ocean liner *Queen Mary* carried them from New York to England.

The Australians, meanwhile, were headed for the South Pacific. The vessel designated to transport them from Saipan was a liberty ship, *Alcoa Polaris*, which was carrying U.S. Marines to Guadalcanal. The weather was good for the journey, and the ship's crew was attentive to the men; while on board they enjoyed good food and became well rested. The ship's crew normally ate two meals a day— meals that seemed unbelievably huge and rich to the survivors. Still, the ship's crew were concerned that this wasn't enough food for the ex-POWs, and insisted on preparing sandwiches for them between meals. The men slept on comfortable canvas bunks. The ship's sick bay attended to any outstanding medical needs. There were even movie screenings on board to help pass away the time and to distract the men from the anxious thoughts of homecomings. While on board, the ex-POWs were also kept busy with the assigned task of compiling lists of all the names they could remember of men who had been with them aboard the Japanese transports.[2] *Alcoa Polaris* traveled to Eniwetok in the Marshall Islands, and from there headed to Guadalcanal in the Solomons chain. Here there was an unexpected delay, and the ex-POWs spent two impatient weeks on Guadalcanal, aware only that there were some complications in the negotiations between U.S. and Australian authorities regarding their transportation and repatriation. In fact, up to this point the survivors had not seen any Australian officials or officers, only Americans. They were housed at the island's military hospital during this time. They underwent more interrogations about their POW experiences, but also had the opportunity to tour the island, to see its aerodrome and aircraft, battle zones and cemeteries. Bill McKittrick was astonished at the rows and rows of graves. In spite of the horrors he had already witnessed, the costs of war still hit him hard: "It was most distressing to see all the crosses, and on the landing beaches all the evidence of the killing that had taken place."[3]

But still, no sign of or word from any Australian officials. The ex-POWs had no idea what the future held for them. Edith Monks Stark, an American Red Cross worker on Guadalcanal, saw a group of the former POWs pass by in a truck, and she was struck not only by how thin and emaciated they looked but also by how sad they seemed. Unable to comprehend why these men, who were finally going home, looked so sad, she pressed for information and was told that the sadness was "because nobody expects them." Finally the survivors were gathered together by a senior U.S. military of-ficial, who apologized for the delays in getting the men back home. "I think you chaps deserve a better deal," he said, and offered them a proposal. The U.S. Navy had a minelayer that was scheduled to depart Guadalcanal and return to the United States for refit. The Navy was willing to divert the ship from its scheduled route and let it instead carry the ex-POWs to Brisbane—if the ex-POWs were willing to "rough it" and sleep in empty mine racks. "It will be rough but we will get you there," the officer told them. The men were impatient to get home, and willing to endure virtually any conditions—after all, they had already slept in torpedo racks on a submarine. Traveling on a minelayer hardly seemed like an incon-venience, especially if meant leaving immediately. A vote was taken, and the ex-POWs unanimously agreed to travel by minelayer.[4]

And so the survivors boarded USS *Monadnock* (CM-9) on Oc-tober 13. The journey to Brisbane would take five days, and the minelayer did prove to be a less-than-ideal passenger vessel. The seas were choppy, and many of the men became seasick and unable to eat. Bill McKittrick was bothered by the loud, clanging noises made by two large doors in the after section of the vessel through which the mines were dispatched. However, the kindness and attentiveness of *Monadnock*'s crew toward the ex-POWs more than made up for such inconveniences.[5]

Finally, *Monadnock* sailed up the Brisbane River and up to New Farm Wharf, arriving on October 18. As the former POWs walked down the gangway and onto Australian soil for the first time in more than two years, a military band played the national anthem. The men were glad to be home. "It made us all feel as though we wanted to stand up and sing," said one of the men. "It was good to

Figure 25. Rescued POWs arriving at Brisbane, Queensland, aboard the minelayer USS *Monadnock*. Australian War Memorial Negative Number 088958.

feel that we were Australian soldiers again, instead of being kicked around by the Nips."[6] They did notice that no civilians were on hand to meet them; only military officials. These were the first Australian military officials they had encountered since their rescue.

Security had been tight throughout the entire journey, with armed guards on the ship and at the wharf to prevent anyone from speaking to the survivors. Efforts were made not to reveal to anyone along the way who these gaunt and tired-looking men were. They were herded into windowless vans and taken to a secret location. They later learned it was a Catholic convent named Stuartholme, on a hilltop overlooking Brisbane. Army huts had been erected on the grounds of the convent to house the men. The pleasant surroundings were countered somewhat by the high walls around the facility, along with guards who ensured that the men had no opportunity to leave. Even the few among them who were Brisbaners were not allowed to see their families during this time, or even to let their families know that they were there. They were told that because there had been a lack of information about men in Japanese hands, any information leaks could create a panic.[7]

The men were given comfortable rooms and were thrilled to find themselves under the care of Australian nurses. They then began undergoing a long series of medical exams. A mobile pathology lab was set up to conduct tests for all possible diseases they might have been exposed to in the POW camps. Dentists checked the men's teeth, finding most of them in surprisingly decent condition, despite the meager diets and lack of nutrition in the camps. The ex-POWs attributed this to the POW dentists in the camps, who, like the doctors among the POWs, cared for the men as best as they could.

For recreation there was tennis, badminton, table tennis, and a library filled with books, newspaper, and magazines, as well as official accounts and maps of the war. A mobile movie theater was set up for the men's enjoyment and showed a new film every night, including features such as *Kokoda Trail* and *The Battle of the Bismarck Sea*. After a few days at this camp, the men received some mail. For most of them, this was their first mail call since they had been captured and as such was an exceptional treat. Letters were passed from hand to hand for everyone to share and enjoy.

At Stuartholme the men underwent more interrogations, this time by Australian military officials. They were asked about their treatment by their Japanese captors and were urged to recall the names of as many fellow POWs as they could. They were also able to supply a substantial amount of information about the locations of Japanese POW camps as well as Japanese military supply depots. And while their families were as of yet unaware of their presence, they did receive visits from government and military officials, including General Sir Thomas Blamey, Commander in Chief of Allied Land Forces in the Southwest Pacific and Commander in Chief of Australian Military Forces, who praised their courage and endurance in the ordeals they had undergone. Personalized telegrams welcoming them home were received from the king, the governor-general, and the minister for the navy. Sir Leslie Wilson, the governor of Queensland, and Lady Wilson sent flowers to brighten the hospital wards; so did the Red Cross, which also supplied shoes and slippers, cigarettes, and candy for the men. A four-gallon keg of Australian beer was provided daily, courtesy of General Stantke, the commander of the Queensland region. Nuns of the convent held a garden party to help entertain the men. Before long they were allowed on organized trips to the local beaches.[8]

But as pleasant as the surroundings were, the men still didn't feel like they were truly "home," for they still had not been able to meet with, or even talk to, their families. In fact, armed guards continued to patrol the premises, ensuring that there was no contact between the ex-POWs and the outside world. No photography of the men was allowed.[9]

While at the convalescent camp, six of the POWs approached an officer and informed him that they had saved a lot of money since being away and would like to put it into war bonds. "The officer told the men that he thought they had already made their contribution by fighting in Malaya, spending 2½ years on a starvation

Figure 26. The first three POWs picked up by *Pampanito*—(*left to right*) Ken Williams, Frank Farmer, and H. D. "Curly" Martin—during convalescence in Brisbane, October 1944. USS *Pampanito* (SS-383) Collection, San Francisco Maritime National Park Association.

diet in prisoner of war camps, working like slaves for the Japs and surviving days in the waters of the South China Sea. They said they still wanted to buy bonds. 'And we're going to have another crack at the Nips after we've had some leave,' one added." More than forty of the survivors did purchase war bonds, worth just over a thousand pounds.[10]

During their second week at Stuartholme, the survivors were herded once again into trucks and taken to an army depot, where they were issued with army uniforms. They were delighted to find that the uniforms included the color patches of their original units. However, they were not so happy when officials tried to insist that the men turn over the clothes they were wearing—the American uniform items they were given while aboard the U.S. submarines and while they were at Saipan. The men refused. Bill McKittrick had a visit from a crew member of *Monadnock* and complained to him about the situation. The next day, the survivors received a surprise visitor—*Pampanito*'s skipper, Pete Summers. Summers provided paperwork stating that the U.S. uniforms the survivors possessed were a gift from the U.S. government, and thus the personal property of the ex-POWs, and could not be confiscated.[11]

News of the POWs' Return

The ex-POWs spent three weeks at Stuartholme. In the meantime, the Australian, British, and U.S. governments sat on the story of the returned POWs, trying to decide whether and how to reveal their appalling ordeal to the public. Up until now there had been very few first-person accounts of the conditions in Japanese POW camps available, and over the years the governments had struggled with the question of whether to withhold atrocity stories from the general public. But now a relatively large group of former POWs had returned, and they could not be kept in isolation indefinitely. These men were entitled to some leave. Even if they could be kept isolated, their stories would surely leak out one way or another. The tales these men had to tell would certainly shock and horrify the public—particularly those who had relatives who were still missing and believed to be prisoners of the Japanese. Government officials realized that years of pent-up frustration over the lack of news about missing relatives might be unleashed upon these returnees, and so it was decided not to release their names. The U.S. government, meanwhile, had been pressuring Britain and Australia not to release the men's stories, as they feared the release of information might jeopardize a U.S.-Japan POW exchange they had been trying to negotiate.

Statements announcing the rescue and the return of the POWs were finally released on October 31 in Britain and Australia, but these were purposely kept brief and very general. The Australian Navy arranged for press interviews with some of the men but specified that the interviews were to be held under controlled conditions and that certain topics were to be avoided, including how the men were rescued and the conditions of their internment.[12]

On November 18, 1944, Australia's acting prime minister, Francis Forde, made an announcement to the House of Representatives in Canberra. Similar announcements were made in London and Washington, D.C. A Japanese transport carrying about seven hundred Australians and six hundred Brits had been torpedoed in the western Pacific on September 12, Forde said. U.S. submarines had rescued 152 of them, but the chances of survival for the rest were slim. Members of the House sat in shocked silence as Forde read the statement in a quiet, dignified voice. He proceeded to reveal some of the information gathered from the returned survivors: the brutal conditions in the Japanese POW camps and aboard the hellships; the horrific details of the torpedoing of the transports; and the men's ordeal as they drifted in the water for days. He also added the grim news that it was believed that two thousand out of ten thousand Australian POWs in Japanese hands had died.[13]

Members on both sides of the House immediately raised questions about the wisdom of sharing this information with the public, pointing out the distress and anguish it would likely cause to relatives of men who were still believed to be prisoners of the Japanese.

Forde assured them that the decision had not been taken lightly by the government and that it had involved consultation with the governments of both Britain and the United States. The potential impact of this news was understood, he said, but it was also recognized that, with some of the survivors now back in Australia, the news would leak out before long, and it was best to disclose now what information was available. This was the hardest statement he had ever had to make in the House, he confessed. He promised, however, that the government would try to determine the fates of the rest of the men now known to have been, based on the interrogation of the returned POWs, aboard *Rakuyo Maru* and *Kachidoki Maru*—Could they have made it to land somehow? Were they still alive?—and asked relatives of POWs to refrain from bothering the returned POWs personally for this information, and to let them enjoy a well-deserved rest and reunion with their families. Forde concluded by saying: "The Government regrets that these disclosures have to be made, but it is convinced it is necessary that the Japanese Government should know that we are in possession of the facts and will hold them responsible."[14]

Surprise and joy at the news of the survival and return of these men was soon followed by shock and confusion. A statement issued by the Australian government reflected what many could not help but feel upon hearing the stories of atrocities in the POW camps: "The story of their experiences underlined what Australia had learned to believe—that the Japanese were savage barbarians with a burning hatred of the white races." Prime Minister John Curtin credited the returned POWs with being bearers of critical information: "They have thrown a spotlight into the heart of the Japanese Empire which shows to all the world the nature of the enemy we face." He expressed the hope that once the POWs were sent home on leave, they would not be bothered by people seeking information about their own relatives who had been taken prisoner at the fall of Singapore. The survivors, he pointed out, were seeing their families for the first time in three years, and, more than anything else, wanted to forget their war experiences now rather than be asked to talk about them. Curtin stressed that the men had already been questioned and that the information obtained from them about other POWs would be shared with the next of kin as soon as possible.[15]

The press immediately picked up on the news, and the story appeared on the front page of newspapers across the nation. In the days following the official announcement, articles appeared on a regular basis, each revealing more and more unbelievable details about the men's ordeal. Reports chided the conduct of the Japanese and praised the gallantry of the American submarines that rescued 152 of the POWs and, in doing so, not only saved lives but enabled confirmation of the atrocities that were being committed by the Japanese in the name of war. The *London Times* demanded retribution: "The conscience of mankind will be satisfied with nothing less than the punishment of those proved responsible in the Japanese Army." Official protests were made to Japan concerning the treatment of Allied POWs through the protecting power, Switzerland. On December 6, Japanese authorities responded by announcing that Japanese ships had rescued 136 British and Australian POWs after the September 12 torpedoing, and denied Allied charges of the maltreatment of the POWs aboard the transports. This caused additional consternation among families of POWs, and on December 16 Forde felt compelled to make a public statement explaining that this information was doubtful. The Japanese government had refused Allied requests to provide names of the rescued POWs, he explained. Furthermore, the Japanese claim conflicted with the statements provided by the returned POWs, who had confirmed that Japanese rescue ships had made no attempts to rescue Allied POWs from the water, and in fact had refused to pick them up. Forde warned relatives not to build hopes on the basis of Japanese statements.[16]

Up until now, the families of Allied POWs in Japanese hands had been unaware of the details of the conditions under which the POWs were being held. It has been suggested that this was in fact a good thing; that if they knew the truth, it may have driven them mad with frustration, helplessness, and grief. Instead, they were glad at the knowledge that their relatives were alive, and assumed the best, sending letters and parcels through the Red Cross (very few of which every actually reached the POWs). Major-General Gordon Bennett, commander of the Australian 8th Division, who had escaped from Singapore, was quoted in Australian papers in early March 1942 saying that there was no reason to believe Australian POWs would be mistreated, and encouraging relatives not to worry. The Australian Prisoners of War Relatives Association, formed in 1942, was accused of presenting an overly optimistic picture to its members. Sydney Smith, the group's leader and editor of its journal, *P.O.W.*, responded that it was not appropriate to heap more anguish on families.[17]

The government's announcements in November 1944 constituted the first time the Australian public heard in detail of the horrors of Japanese POW camps. It was only after the official announcements had been made and the news of the men's return appeared in the newspapers that they were allowed to talk about what had happened. As word of the return of a group of survivors spread, the men were indeed flooded with information requests from anxious families of soldiers missing in action in the Pacific, hoping to learn about the fate of their own loved ones. Rescued POW Frank Coombes wrote in a letter to a *Pampanito* crew member that month: "I have been very busy. We all arrived home on the 30th of October and I have done nothing else but answer questions for people who have boys still over with the Japs. Each day I receive about twenty letters and I have got so tired of answering them that I have got my father to help me now." Frank Farmer also received dozens of letters from relatives of missing servicemen, asking if he had encountered their relatives and if he knew if they were still alive; he spent many hours slaving over responses, agonizing over what to write, what to say, how it should be phrased. Bill McKittrick, who had been asked by the local POW Relatives Association to talk to the families of missing servicemen, also found it consumed a great deal of his time and was by no means an easy task. "You have [had] to be very careful what you said. You couldn't cause distress to people. And it's not a nice thing for people to know that their relations had died, let alone how they had died. 'Cause there's no way of describing it, it's a terrible way to die."[18]

Jack Wall, home on leave in Hopetown, Victoria, was interviewed for the local paper. While he could not offer much solid information to relatives who were still wondering about the fate of their missing loved ones, he had words of encouragement: wherever the missing men were, he knew their Aussie digger spirit would see them through, no matter how brutal and inhumane their treatment at the hands of their Japanese captors: "I can safely say that that spirit will remain with the boys so long as they are able to stand up. And until they are released, no matter what treatment they receive, no Jap will break the spirit of an Aussie soldier."[19]

At a meeting of the Prisoners of War Relatives Association held at the Sydney Town Hall in January 1945, which included seventeen recovered POWs (five of them from *Rakuyo Maru*), three thousand people attended. During the proceedings, the stage was rushed by approximately one hundred of the attendees, desperate for information. One soldier collapsed in the ruckus. Finally, the ex-POWs were escorted to a back room, only to be mobbed again when they tried to leave building.[20]

After the official announcements of their return had been made, the ex-POWs were given the standard two months' leave. On December 8, Acting Prime Minister Forde announced that the men would be allowed a "special leave" of ninety days. This, he explained, would allow more complete medical rehabilitation before the men had to decide whether to stay in the service or accept a discharge from the armed forces. News of this "special treatment" for the former POWs caused almost as much controversy in Australia as the news about the horrors of the camps. Other returnees, including ex-POWs released from German and Italian POW camps, had only been allowed sixty days' leave; nor did they receive the option of a discharge. The extended leave also meant that the continuation of the interrogation process would be delayed, thus further delaying the transmission of information to relatives of other POWs.[21]

After the survivors returned from their leave, they were assembled in Melbourne. Here, each day they were taken to Army Headquarters, where they underwent more interrogations, lasting from ten in the morning until four in the afternoon, for six weeks. "It was most thorough, and any guess work made more questions. Checking—cross-checking—where now—where last seen—state of health etc. etc."[22]

From the time they were in the hospital at Saipan, the former Australian POWs had endured weeks of debriefings and interrogations, much of it trying to remember and identify other POWs and MIAs believed to be in Japanese hands. Intelligence information obtained from the survivors included details of the locations of camps along the Burma-Thai Railroad, and this information was used in selective bombing of the railway, thereby probably saving the lives of many POWs still working in those camps. The American interrogator at Saipan seemed most interested in military aspects: information about the various Japanese military installations the POWs had been employed on, and their locations: airfields, ammunition and supply dumps, docks and wharves, anti-aircraft defenses. "While we were still in Saipan the Americans made the first bombing raids on some of the targets we gave them as we pinpointed them. And they don't mess around, the Americans, you know." The most intense interrogations were during the six weeks at Melbourne, where the ex-POWs were questioned continuously for six hours each day, six days a week. They were asked to name every fellow POW they had seen or known, where they were, what they were doing, whether they thought they would come home. All the while the survivors were warned not to talk to anyone about any of this information.[23]

An interrogation report based on interviews with the ex-POWs was issued on November 10, 1944. It used information about factors such as the locals' attitudes in Burma, Thailand, French Indochina, and Malaya toward the Japanese and toward the POWs in order to gauge possible levels of support for the Allies from the civilian populations in these areas in ousting the Japanese presence. The POWs proved unable to provide much information about levels of Japanese security. It appeared that troops guarding the POWs in transit had received instructions not to talk to each other in order to avoid revealing any security information in the presence of the prisoners. Information provided by the former POWs regarding conditions in the camps and the treatment of POWs would be used to urge the Japanese government to allow inspections of the camps.[24]

The six weeks the POWs spent in Melbourne were not all work. The staff of the Red Cross tried to ensure that the men had some amusements and recreation as well, and took them on outings and to the theater. On weekends, they went on picnics. While at Melbourne, after their six weeks of interrogations and debriefings were finished, the survivors, in full uniform, were marched to the War Memorial for a service, then to Government House, where they attended a reception in their honor, hosted by the governor-general, the Duke of Gloucester.[25]

Readjusting to Life at Home

From Melbourne, the men were sent back to their home states. The New South Wales men were loaded on a troop train and sent to Sydney's Central Station. But this time too there was no cheering crowd to meet them. Other troops on the train headed out with leave passes in hand, but not the ex-POWs. They were herded once more into windowless vans, escorted by military police, and driven to Ingleburn Military Camp, approximately thirty miles southwest of Sydney.[26]

Leave was over, and interrogations were over. At Ingleburn they were put to work. The ex-POWs were eager to return to service, but what they had expected was to get back into the fight. "We had of course talked among ourselves, and those of us who had been passed as fit wanted only one thing and that was to give back to the Japs some of what they had given us." What they got was not at all what they expected, or wanted. Bill McKittrick and Pat Smith were assigned to whitewash stones along the roadway. After a couple of days they asked to see the officer in charge, and complained about this seemingly useless and boring task. "Among other things he informed us that we were an inconvenience to him, times had changed since our day, the war had changed—the army had changed, and this was a young man's war and it was impossible to fit us in. You are no longer of any use, and I can only use you as I see fit now that you have been sent here. He laughed when we said that we had only wished to get back into things and meet the Japs again but this time be on the winning side." At least he took them off whitewashing detail. However, the next assignment wasn't much better. The next day, they were issued brooms, spades, and wheelbarrows, and instructed to sweep up all the loose gravel along the roads and respread it. Thinking they were being tested, they dutifully did the assignment for a while, until, unable to stand it, complained again. The next morning they were issued ten-gallon tanks filled with chemicals, which they were to carry on their backs as they patrolled all the creeks and ditches in the area and spray them for mosquitoes. This time, when they complained, the officer in charge offered a different solution. "You know, you fellows could be preparing for a civilian life," he told them. "I think you would be better out of the army." He produced a stack of discharge forms for them to sign.[27]

Now a new round of medicals and other tests began. Aptitude tests were conducted to determine the most appropriate civilian calling for each man. McKittrick scored 98 percent in the tests and was recommended by the testing officer for a full-time trade course. The captain in charge of making the assignments, however, refused, stating that enrollment in the trades course was limited to those who had studied languages, taken correspondence courses, or otherwise tried to improve themselves while they were POWs. McKittrick, he pointed out, did not appear to have attempted any of these things. The absurdity of the situation was too much for McKittrick. "I explained to him that this was due to the different circumstances, and the apparent animosity that existed between the Allies and the Japanese, [so] that the mail service was very erratic, and I would be most happy to receive from him the names of those POWs of the Japanese who were doing great things." The captain reminded him he was still in the military and not to be impertinent.[28]

McKittrick's difficulties and frustrations in finding employment continued. After seven months he felt like he was going around in circles: "Other than relatives I never met anyone who knew about or cared about the POWs in Japan. In fact it seemed the authorities were ashamed, and were trying to cover it up." He was beginning to feel that the POWs were regarded not as heroes, not as soldiers, but simply as a nuisance. Eventually, most of the ex-POWs, when given the choice of staying in the military or being discharged, opted to be discharged.[29]

The ex-POWs had not seen their families in years. James Boulter of Victoria, upon his return home on leave, met his three-year-old daughter for the first time. She had been born on September 12, 1941—two months after he left for Malaya. During her first two birthdays, he had been a POW. On her third birthday, the transport he was aboard was torpedoed. He had survived that day largely due to the efforts of his friend and raft mate Reg Bullock: Bullock had tied Boulter to the side of their raft to keep him from sinking into the sea. Years later, Bullock recalled Boulter saying to him while they were in the water, "You know, Reg, my daughter's three years old today and I've never seen her."[30]

The homecomings were joyful, but rarely easy. Most Australians, in the fall of 1944, in addition to being unaware of the conditions in the camps and the treatment of the prisoners within the camps, also did not know how to deal with the returned POWs. The ex-POWs themselves tended to feel ashamed, angry; they expressed fears of becoming a burden to their families and to society. Australian military headquarters issued a secret memo concerning the reception, treatment, and disposal of the ex-POWs. The memo reported on the physical and mental conditions of returned POWs. While the physical problems were numerous, the report stated, military authorities considered them nothing that couldn't be solved. As for the mental condition of the former POWs, the report found that these men displayed the following symptoms: a "lack of balance in reaction to ordinary episodes of life"; "extravagance, undue gambling, *etc*"; "irritability"; "resistance both to command and suggestion"; "lack of concentration and initiative"; "apathy and depression"; "defensiveness"; a "sense of guilt, disillusionment, bitterness"; and, "passive hostility." Military medical authorities warned family and friends of repatriated POWs to expect signs of emotional unrest, instability, and introspection.[31]

Physical problems lingered for some of the men. But dealing with the memories of the suffering they had experienced and the deaths they had witnessed was another challenge altogether. Raymond Mawby, one of the survivors, explained what he and surely many of his fellow ex-POWs were going through: "Perhaps at times you want to remember and then other times you feel you want to forget."[32]

To help the relatives of the survivors cope with these symptoms, in May 1945 the military issued a letter to family members of repatriated POWs. The letter began: "You have been hearing a lot of talk about strangeness and so on, and may be a bit worried through your happiness." The following words of advice were offered: "Don't worry, he is still the same chap. Treat him as he is, a normal person. . . . Don't worry if he is a bit moody and irritable for a few weeks. . . . Life in a PW camp is different. . . . If he does snap at you, if he is stubborn . . . it is not because he wants to hurt you, but because he can't all at once break formed habits. Never mind him, time and love will remake the man." Some of the advice seemed almost contradictory: "Help re-establish habits of daily routine on him as early as possible. . . . But don't try to *force* a routine on him." And if this weren't enough for overwhelmed family members to handle, the letter suggested that it all be done furtively: "Let him see that all you do is for love of him. Don't give the impression that you are following a set of rules, or even these suggestions."[33] Clearly, the reintegration of the returned POWs was not going to be easy. They had been rescued and they had survived, but their difficult journey was still far from over. Still, these men were tough. They had endured and survived the unimaginable. Now they turned their attention to readjusting to civilian life.

The effects of their ordeal would affect them in all sorts of ways. Don McArdle experienced recurring nightmares. Frank Jesse experienced nightmares for years after the rescue—always the same dream of being in the water and calling out for help to a submarine. He made sure his children learned to swim from an early age, telling them about at time when he had had to swim away from a sinking ship. "The story scared the hell out of us," confessed his daughter Pam. Roy Cornford also encouraged his children to learn to swim at a young age, stressing that learning to swim was as important as their schoolwork.[34]

Bill "Mac" McKittrick, who had no family in Australia, met a girl named Sybil at a welcome-home party for one of ex-POWs. They married soon afterward. Mac was a jovial and happy-go-lucky sort; Sybil thought him "cheeky" when she first met him. He would sometimes tell some of the more lighthearted stories from his POW days, but Sybil found he generally talked very little about the camps, even when she asked him questions to try to coax some information out of him. Generally, it seemed, Mac tried not to dwell on his POW years, not to make a big deal out of it. One time, however, and just once, Sybil saw an unexpected and severe reaction from her husband: he "fell apart," as she put it, when a woman at a dinner party inquired about a relative. Mac clearly recognized the relative's name; but instead of answering, he jumped up from the table and hurriedly left the room. Sybil thought that Mac might have seen this man beheaded while in the camps. But for the most part, McKittrick seemed to be able to put the past behind him, and turn his attention to raising a family. "He was the best husband in the world and the greatest father," said Sybil.[35]

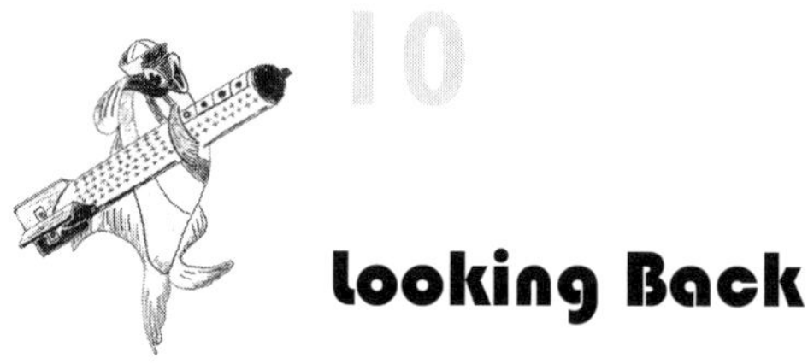

Looking Back

Pampanito spent a good portion of the summer of 1945 in San Francisco, undergoing an overhaul at the naval shipyard at Hunter's Point. The crew drew lots to determine who would get the first thirty-day leaves and who would have to wait for the second round. Gordon Hopper was pleased to be among those who would be going on leave first. He flew home and, while on a stopover in Kansas City, heard the news that Germany had surrendered. He hoped this meant that before long the war in the Pacific, his war, would end as well. He enjoyed visiting with friends and family, particularly his girlfriend, Dorothy; still, he found himself eager to return to *Pampanito.* "I felt a vague uneasiness, away from the boat, crew, and submarine life."[1]

The overhaul was completed by August 1, and soon *Pampanito,* with Commander Donald Scherer as her new CO, headed back to Pearl. In Hawai'i, as the boat and crew prepared for their seventh patrol, Hopper couldn't help but notice the huge fleet assembling at the naval base in preparation for the invasion of Japan. "And word was that we were to be part of it. Not a prospect to our liking." The Navy had lost so many ships during the Okinawa campaign that it had been decided to use submarines as radar pickets for the planned invasion of Japan, scheduled for October 1945. At Pearl Harbor, preparations for converting *Pampanito* to radar picket and training the crew for picket boat duty were soon under way.[2]

On the evening of August 15, a few of *Pampanito*'s crew were at the outdoor theater on Subase, waiting for the evening's feature film to start. "Suddenly, from the moored fleet, whistles screamed, flares burst in the night sky and we heard cheering that grew in volume. An announcement over the movie's P.A. system informed us of the Japanese surrender. It was a night of celebration and immense relief," remembered Hopper. And it seemed to him that ten major Fourth of July celebrations were taking place simultaneously that night, so great was the commotion and excitement. The sailors staying in the Subase barracks ran out of the building, shouting wildly, running circles around the swimming pool. Woodrow Weaver saw the Subase CO drive up hurriedly in his jeep, step out of the vehicle, and insist that the men quiet down and get themselves under control. In response, the celebrating sailors picked him up and threw him in the pool. Realizing this was a celebration that could not be stopped, the humiliated CO crawled out of the pool and got back in his jeep, leaving the submariners to their festivities.[3]

And so, as the summer of 1945 ended, instead of heading out for a seventh war patrol, *Pampanito* was headed back across the Pacific to San Francisco. The war was over, and the whole atmosphere aboard the ship was something different. As *Pampanito* steamed along the surface toward San Francisco, her crew spent as much time as they could topside, relaxing, even sunbathing on the deck. "It was just a new way of traveling on a submarine," recalled the skipper.[4]

Pampanito had amassed an impressive wartime record: six enemy ships sunk (totaling 43,600 tons) and four damaged (totaling 26,100 tons). Four of her six patrols had been designated "successful" by COMSUBPAC for the award of the Submarine Combat Insignia to her crew. She had received six battle stars for her World War II service. One Navy Cross and two Bronze Stars had been awarded to her COs. But as she cruised back across the Pacific to San Francisco, all the way on the surface with her battle flag flying high, her crew was undoubtedly proudest of the red cross with the number "73" on that flag, and of that day of the war when they had been able to save lives instead of take them.

Pampanito after the War

At Hunter's Point, *Pampanito* was deactivated and entered into the reserve fleet. In the 1960s she served as a training ship at Mare Island, California, until she was stricken from the Navy List in 1971. She could have ended up the same way as some of her sister submarines—as scrap—but *Pampanito* was one of the lucky ones. In 1976 she was turned over to the National Maritime Museum Association (now the San Francisco Maritime National Park Association), a nonprofit educational group, for restoration. In 1982 the submarine was on "active duty" again: not as a warship, but as a museum ship. Moored at a popular San Francisco tourist area, Fisherman's Wharf, she was opened to the public as a museum and a memorial to the submarine fleet of World War II.

The other three subs that had rushed to *Pampanito*'s aid that September in 1944 met very different fates. *Barb*, having completed twelve patrols and sunk seventeen enemy vessels during the war, was converted to Guppy class and served until 1954, when she was transferred to the Italian Navy. There she served under the new name of *Enrico Tazzoli* until 1975, when she was finally scrapped. *Sealion* and *Queenfish* were used for target practice and sunk. A small piece of *Queenfish*—a pressure gauge from her forward torpedo room—was kept by one her World War II crewmen, who eventually took it to Perth and presented it to one of the rescued POWs.[5]

The preservation of *Pampanito* came as a surprise to some of her crew. Gordon Hopper was living in California, just south of San Francisco, when he took some visitors on an excursion to Fisherman's Wharf. One of his guests remarked, "Hey, there's a submarine over there." Hopper went over to take a closer look and was overcome when he saw the hull number on the boat: 383. It was his old boat.[6]

Since *Pampanito* found a new life at Fisherman's Wharf, her World War II crew has gathered aboard her numerous times for crew reunions—to reminisce, to enjoy the camaraderie that still exists among the crew, and to spend time on board the sub. For them, "This is home away from home."[7]

In 1991, Bill McKittrick took his wife, Sybil, on a trip to the United States, which included a stop in San Francisco. They visited the usual tourist attractions, including Fisherman's Wharf. Sybil noticed the submarine first. "I happened to turn left and I said, 'There she is.' My husband said, 'Who?' 'The *Pampanito*.' And we both cried." At the admission booth, as they purchased tickets to tour the sub, "Mac" McKittrick couldn't resist mentioning to the cashier that "the last time I came on this submarine I got on for nothing." He and Sybil boarded and went down below, pausing in the after torpedo room. "I looked at the torpedo and I said, silently to myself, I slept on top of that torpedo but how the hell did they get seventy-two people in here? How did they do it?"[8]

Pampanito, resting calmly in the waters of San Francisco Bay, remains a tangible piece of history, a living reminder of that fateful day in September 1944. She serves as a strong symbol for the former POWs who were rescued by her and by the other submarines, but also for their families, who feel a tie with the submarine as well—a debt owed that they feel can never truly be repaid. "Without her I wouldn't have a husband," says Sybil McKittrick. "I wouldn't have had two daughters. I wouldn't have had six grandchildren."[9] In later years the McKittricks would bring their children and grandchildren to San Francisco to see the submarine that played such a key role in all of their lives. Although many of the children and grandchildren of the men she rescued were not even born in September 1944, many of them recognize the significance of *Pampanito* in their lives. The grandson of ex-POW Harry Pickett grew up listening to his grandfather's war stories: "He always has a smile on his face when he talks of the *Pampanito* and her crew. The *Pampanito* and her crew was the stuff of legend to us kids."[10]

The first POW pulled out of the water by *Pampanito* on September 15, 1944, Frank Farmer, visited *Pampanito* after the war. Years later, after Frank's death, his son Tim visited the vessel and attended a crew reunion with the men who rescued his father. Indeed, the bond was so strong that when a terrorist attack was launched against the United States on September 11, 2001, shocking both Americans and others around the world, Tim's first thoughts were of *Pampanito*. From his home in Wales, he sent a message of concern and sympathy to *Pampanito* staff. His father's connection with the sub that saved his life had compelled him to make contact, to send "thoughts and sympathy." His father, he noted, had often referred to September 15, 1944—the day of the rescue—as his "second birthday."[11]

Pampanito has also been visited by relatives of men rescued by one of the other submarines, as they try to get a better sense and appreciation of what their fathers or grandfathers went through. *Pampanito* serves as a worthy substitute. When the daughter of a survivor rescued by *Sealion* toured *Pampanito*, a sea lion swam by the sub as she watched from the deck—as if the animal was acknowledging the connection.

Pampanito has even been visited by a relative of a Japanese senior officer who had been aboard *Kachidoki Maru* on the night that ship was torpedoed. The nephew of Suke-Hiko Hosoya made a point of stopping in San Francisco for three days after a visit to New York in 2001. He visited *Pampanito* on each of those three days. Hosoya was a commander of the First Maritime Guard. When the ship began sinking, he ordered the evacuation of passengers, but he himself refused to leave the bridge, going down with the ship. Almost fifty years later, his nephew found himself in the torpedo room of the submarine that had sent *Kachidoki Maru* to the bottom. "Of course, I was deeply moved, and at the same time I had mixed feelings, especially when I stood in front of her torpedo tubes, thinking of September 12, 1944," he told museum staff. Yet he felt deeply gratified to make this connection with a part of his family history, and his relatives back home in Japan were equally grateful for the information he brought back to them about *Pampanito* and his visit aboard her.[12]

Reunions

After the war, many of the POWs kept in touch with their rescuers, having exchanged addresses while aboard *Pampanito*. Bob Bennett received a letter from Bill Cray in December 1944, just a few weeks after Cray's return to England. Over the years, Bennett kept up a correspondence with some of the other POWs he had pulled out of the South China Sea, including Roy Cornford and Frank Farmer.[13]

Some of the encounters occurred entirely by chance. Woodrow Weaver continued serving in the Navy after the war. By 1968 he had put in twenty-eight years, and was serving in San Diego with the Pacific coast section of the Naval Board of Inspection and Survey when he was assigned to conduct acceptance trials for an Australian destroyer, HMAS *Brisbane* (D-41), which had been constructed in a U.S. shipyard. The trials involved a demonstration of a sonar buoy. When time came for the demonstration, an announcement was made over the ship's intercom system that Lieutenant Cocking would be overseeing the event. The name rang a bell, and stuck in Weaver's mind throughout the day. When he got home, he pulled out a list of names of the POWs rescued by *Pampanito* in 1944, and sure enough, one of them was Jack Cocking, of Perth, Western Australia.

Back aboard *Brisbane* to continue the trials the following day, Weaver searched out Lieutenant Ron Cocking, who proved to be indeed the son of the rescued man. In fact, before the lieutenant left for the United States, his father had given him a small black book in which he had listed some of the names and addresses of *Pampanito*'s World War II crew. The son had attempted to look them up while on the east coast, but found that the addresses were no longer current, and finally gave up. Finally, through sheer luck, he had made

Figure 27. Former *Pampanito* crew member Lieutenant Woodrow Weaver (*right*) in 1968 during a chance encounter with Australian Navy lieutenant Ron Cocking, son of Jack Cocking, one of the POWs rescued by *Pampanito* on 12 September 1944. This photo, in which Weaver is showing Lieutenant Cocking pictures taken during the rescue, appeared in the *San Diego Union-Tribune* on May 20, 1968. San Diego Historical Society.

a contact. Cocking's son visited with Weaver and his wife at their home over the weekend, where Weaver shared with him photos of his father's rescue, and was able to tell him details about the rescue that his own father had never spoken about.[14]

Some of the reunions occurred in Australia. In 1979, Tony Hauptman and his wife, Betty, visited Australia, where they made an effort to look up as many of the former POWs as they could find, through the assistance of the local POW association. They were able to locate several of them and had rewarding visits with them and their families. As in Fremantle that Christmas season of 1944, the visiting Americans were treated like royalty. The Hauptmans continued their visits to Australia, spending time with the POWs as well as their children, who were just as thrilled to spend time with the man who helped rescue their fathers. Hauptman never ceased to be amazed by their kindness and hospitality: "It seems as though we picked up the best people over there. Every one that we visited was just the best—nicest guys, and we really enjoyed them."[15]

In 1988, *Pampanito* crew member Norm Arcement also made the journey to Australia, where he and his wife tried to look up as many of the survivors as possible. He sent letters to Russell Booth, ship's manager at the *Pampanito* museum, with updates on the rescued men. Ken Williams was eighty-two years old and preparing to celebrate his sixtieth wedding anniversary. Harry Pickett would be celebrating his fiftieth. Ken Williams also wrote to Booth about the informal reunion. He and Frank Farmer, Claude Longey, and Ray Gainger all gathered together to spend a day with Arcement. "We had a wonderful day; after 43½ years there was plenty to talk about."[16]

Upon his return to Australia, Frank Farmer had resumed his work as a teacher before the war had even ended. Although he had kept in touch with several of his fellow POWs, he had lost contact with the crew of *Pampanito*. His young son Tim was only vaguely aware of the significance of the American sub named *Pampanito*. He knew his father had souvenirs, mementos given to him by the crew. In fact, Tim himself had a white USN sailor cap, given to his father aboard the sub. Like many other former POWs, Frank tended not to talk much about his wartime experiences, and it was only because he was interested in sailing and things nautical that in 1983 a friend mentioned to him in passing that on a recent visit to the United States he had come across a World War II fleet submarine on exhibit in San Francisco. Her name was *Pampanito*. Suddenly a rush of memories was triggered in Frank. He waited until September, and on the fifteenth a telegram from Australia arrived at the submarine. It read: "Greetings. Best wishes on the 39th anniversary rescue POW South China Sea," and was signed, "First found—Frank Farmer." The telegram began a tradition that Frank would continue until his death. Also, every September 15 Farmer would make a phone call to Pete Summers, the skipper who had ordered the rescue, called in the other submarines, and risked his boat and crew to save as many men as possible.[17]

In 1985, perhaps inspired with the contact made by Farmer, Russell Booth began a concerted effort to locate and make contact with all of the POWs rescued by *Pampanito*, to document this outstanding episode in the history of the submarine under his care. With the assistance of the Australian Consulate General in San Francisco, notices were placed in various publications, including the newsletters of the Far East POW Association's branches in Britain and Australia. Booth began collecting their stories, the firsthand accounts of their experiences as POWs, and their memories of their rescue. He also invited the former POWs to a reunion with *Pampanito*'s wartime crew aboard *Pampanito* in San Francisco. Frank Farmer attended, renewing his bond with the submarine that had saved his life.

The November 1993 reunion of the crew, celebrating the fiftieth anniversary of *Pampanito*'s commissioning, was a huge occasion, marred only by the passing earlier that year of Pete Summers. The

Figure 28. Two of the POWs rescued by *Pampanito*, Reg Bullock and Frank Farmer, reminisce in *Pampanito*'s torpedo room during a visit to San Francisco, c. 1990. USS *Pampanito* (SS-383) Collection, San Francisco Maritime National Park Association.

reunion was attended by thirty-three members of *Pampanito*'s World War II crew and two of the survivors from Australia: Bill McKittrick and Roy Cornford. The men enjoyed four days of events, including a ceremony in which the sub was rechristened, and the gathering of oral histories. The sub seemed to come alive again, particularly on the morning of November 5 when breakfast was prepared on board. Soon the crew's mess was filled with the smell of coffee, bacon, and freshly baked biscuits, along with a host of familiar voices that had not spoken together in this space since 1944. McKittrick and Cornford easily recognized some of the crew: there was the photographer, Paul Pappas; and the swimmer who had pulled Cornford aboard the sub, Bob Bennett. When McKittrick was introduced to Gordon Hopper, he said: "You're the one who swam out and brought our raft in." Hopper had no recollection of who was on the raft he had brought in. "How in the world could you remember that?" he asked. McKittrick didn't hesitate in his reply: "How could I forget it?" Their gratitude to the crew was unwavering. Said Cornford, "They gave us their beds, they gave us their clothes, they gave us everything. And most of all . . . they gave us freedom."[18]

One notable absence was that of Maurice "Doc" Demers, who had passed away in 1990. Rheumatoid arthritis had kept him from attending crew reunions, although he stayed in touch with the boat and her crew. After his passing, his two sons, Larry and Kevin, kept up the ties, attending some of the reunions in their father's place. After the death of Bill McKittrick, his widow, Sybil, took up for him, corresponding on his behalf with the man who had pulled him out of the water, Gordon Hopper. In 2005 she brought some of her children and grandchildren to a crew reunion at the sub: "so they can see why they're alive," she explained. *Pampanito* was as meaningful to her as it had been to her husband; and as for *Pampanito*'s crew—well, said Sybil, "*Pampanito* was crewed by angels without wings."[19]

Over the years, the rescued POWs displayed their gratitude in many ways. Some kept a photo of *Pampanito* hanging on the wall in their home or workplace, a reminder of the one bright shining light in their wartime experiences. Frank Farmer sent a Western Union

Figure 30. *Pampanito*'s World War II crew gathers aboard her at San Francisco in 1993 as they commemorate the fiftieth anniversary of the boat's commissioning. Standing to the left and right (respectively) of the battle flag are rescued POWs Roy Cornford and Bill McKittrick. USS *Pampanito* (SS-383) Collection, San Francisco Maritime National Park Association.

Mailgram to *Pampanito* in San Francisco each September 15, thanking her crew annually for the rescue. His wife, Mary, began a correspondence with "Doc" Demers and his wife, and every September she would thank Maurice for giving her her husband for another fifty years.[20]

Frank Farmer took his gratitude even further. Feeling that *Pampanito* and her crew deserved formal recognition of their good deeds, not just individually from him and the other survivors, not just from the American government, but from the nation of Australia, he wrote to Australian Prime Minister Bob Hawke in 1989, requesting that he consider rectifying what Farmer considered an "inconceivable lack of chivalry" on the part of the government. "Prime Minister," he wrote, "our failure to 'Honour when Honour was due' the submariners involved in this stirring episode had been of considerable concern to me for the past forty years, and now with my time running out I am seeking your help with the earnestness and hope that I sought the help of Lieutenant Commander Summers so long ago. I trust that you will respond with the same immediacy and magnanimity." Finally his efforts paid off. He received word from the Australian Defence Department in Canberra that the government was preparing a commemorative plaque to present to *Pampanito* in recognition of the rescue as well as the valuable intelligence information obtained as a result of the rescue. The plaque, from the Australian Defence Force, was presented to *Pampanito* and the National Maritime Museum Association in a ceremony on July 23, 1990, in San Francisco. The event was attended by the Australian consul-general, David C. Rutter, as well as ten of *Pampanito*'s World War II crew, including Pete Summers.[21]

Scott Thiele was fascinated by the experiences of his grandfather Ken Williams and the *Pampanito* crewmen he got to meet when they visited Williams in Australia. He, too, began to feel a strong connection with *Pampanito*. "Perhaps it was my serving in the Australian Navy for 14 years and my travels to Singapore and Thailand over the years where I have re-traced his steps that has strengthened my resolve to never let the memory of that submarine go. In fact while I served in the Navy one of my journeys at sea took me to the very area where he was rescued." In 2002, Thiele visited *Pampanito* and presented a plaque in memory of his grandfather and in honor of the efforts and bravery of the men of *Pampanito*—as engraved on the plaque, "on behalf of a grateful family."[22] Both plaques are now part of the *Pampanito* artifact collection, along with photographs, journals, and other items donated by the crew to document the rescue.

The rescue also strengthened bonds between three Allied nations: Britain, Australia, and the United States. Bill McKittrick was unabashed in his praise of the Americans: "Every time I see the American Declaration of Independence, about life, liberty, and pursuit of happiness, I think of the submarine because that's what it gave us. It gave us life, it gave us freedom, it gave us a chance to pursue our happiness again. So America means a lot to us. . . . We can only say, God bless *Pampanito* and God bless America, and the Americans." Australian Robert Collins, one of the *Rakuyo Maru* survivors who was rescued by *Sealion*, was more direct: "Anyone who says 'Go home, Yank' within my hearing is looking for a thick lip."[23]

Epilogue

Like the rest of the U.S. submarine fleet in World War II, *Pampanito*'s main purpose was to seek out and destroy enemy shipping. And this she did: although launched relatively late in the war, in only six patrols she succeeded in sinking six Japanese ships and putting another four temporarily out of commission. Yet it is the story of her third patrol, of the rescue of the seventy-three Allied POWs, that has become her "claim to fame" and that is regarded as her most outstanding achievement.

This is not surprising. It is a gripping and dramatic narrative that shows the human and personal side of war. And it is certainly easier to tell a group of young schoolchildren touring the submarine about such a rescue than about the actual ramifications of the six sinkings executed by the submarine they are aboard. And, it makes good official history: Vice Admiral Charles Lockwood would refer to *Pampanito*'s third patrol as a mission "unique in submarine history."[1] For a soldier or a sailor, to be able to lay claim to having saved lives in the midst of war seems to strike a ready chord, and indeed many of *Pampanito*'s crew members recall the rescue as their most memorable experience of the war. Yet what is often glossed over in the various retellings and accounts of this story, be they official accounts or personal reminiscences, is the fact that the men fighting so desperately for their survival in the South China Sea during those days in mid-September 1944 were there because *Pampanito* had helped put them there, during her attack on the Japanese convoy on September 12. A few days later, *Pampanito*, along with the three other submarines called in to assist in the rescue operation, picked up 159 POWs. Yet that ill-fated convoy was carrying more than two thousand POWs.

How much "heroism" is there in the rescue of a few of the victims of one's own attack? Or in selectively choosing whom to rescue? Japanese survivors in the water would not have been picked up by the submarines. Furthermore, *Pampanito*'s CO made an effort to look for Americans in the water first, to give them priority in being rescued by an American sub.[2] Then there is also the question of the legality of sinking merchant vessels at all—an issue, in fact, over which the United States had entered World War I. (Incidentally, the fact that the United States had condemned German U-boats' use of wolf pack techniques during World War I did not stop COMSUB-PAC Charles Lockwood from introducing wolf packing into the U.S. Submarine Service in World War II.)[3]

If one accepts the premise that in wartime, enemy victims will be left in the water to die, what about helping them to die by shooting unarmed enemy sailors or soldiers in the water? This is perhaps the most controversial question of all relating to submarine operations in World War II. In 1987, ABC–Circle Films released a television mini-series *War and Remembrance*, based on the novel by Herman Wouk (the sequel to *The Winds of War*). In this sequel, the crew of a U.S. submarine, after sinking a Japanese vessel, was depicted on the submarine's deck, machine-gunning survivors who were helplessly treading water. The airing of this scene brought protest and outrage from many American submarine veterans of World War II, who insisted that American submariners would never shoot unarmed and helpless enemies.[4]

This defensive reaction from a number of submariners is a good example of why documenting relatively recent historical events presents special challenges. The events have not yet been cloaked with the neutrality that starts to overtake history as it slips deeper into the past. Rather, they are still emotionally charged, and the players and participants involved in these events remain emotionally connected to them. In addition, many of the institutions with the role of documenting and interpreting the events—including World War II ships-turned-museums, like *Pampanito*—take upon themselves the roles of commemoration, honoring, and even celebration. Yet these details, these difficult questions, must be addressed if we genuinely want to learn of, and learn from, our past.

There has been much discussion about whether the officers and crew of the submarines knew that the transports were carrying POWs.[5] Whether or not senior command at Pearl Harbor knew is still debated by historians. What is known is that *Rakuyo Maru* and *Kachidoki Maru* were traveling unmarked. They were not lit up, they had no red crosses or markings on them to indicate that they were prisoner ships. Indeed, the crews of the submarines seemed to genuinely have no idea what—or who—was aboard those transports, other than valuable supplies making their way to Japan to aid the enemy's war effort. They had no inkling that the holds of two of the ships were crammed with Allied soldiers.

In the years since the war, the submariners have had time to consider such questions, and to ponder their role in events. The thrill of saving lives, bolstered by the unbounded gratitude of the rescued men and their families, has been tempered to a degree over the years by the realization that the deaths of the hundreds of POWs who were *not* rescued were the result of the submarines' own handiwork.

Pampanito torpedoman Woodrow Weaver addressed the issue in a 2002 interview: "It was tragic," he said, "that we didn't know those ships were carrying prisoners of war and the fact that so many of them died because of our actions in sinking those vessels. But the skippers out there, they shoot at anything that floated, you know, and so those ships came by—why, they were fair game as far as being a target for torpedoes. And I guess that was part of the war, you know; something that had to be faced and put up with, because— you couldn't do it any other way."[6]

Perhaps the most valuable perspective in this debate is that of the survivors themselves—the victims of *Pampanito*'s torpedoes. How did they feel about *Pampanito*'s actions? Of those who have commented on this issue, most do not hesitate to state outright that they understood why the submarines torpedoed the hellships and, it being wartime and the hellships being unmarked, that they believe the submarines were entirely justified in doing so. That the submarines returned to attempt rescue is proof enough that of their intentions and good will. Furthermore, many interpreted the subs' actions not as an act of violence toward them but as, ultimately, an act of liberation. By torpedoing the hellships, the submariners had released the POWs from their captivity. Even if they drowned in the sea, they would die as free men. This, many insist, was a much better option than remaining a prisoner of the Japanese.

But is this perspective born out of the many years' reflection on events? In other words, is this way of thinking a product of the way we try to make sense of even the most senseless events in our lives when we look back on them? For although many of the ex-POWs have claimed that they would have preferred death as free men in the waters of the South China Sea over remaining prisoners of the Japanese, it is also clear from their accounts that many, if not all of them, would have gladly accepted rescue by a Japanese vessel, even though this meant a return to captivity. In fact, when it was realized by the hellship survivors that the Japanese rescue ships circling the area were only picking up Japanese victims from the water, the POWs were not only disappointed, but angry. Their bitterness over what they perceived as Japanese indifference and inhumanity formed a deep impression and appears repeatedly in the accounts and reflections of the ex-POWs.

Related to this, of course, is the question of *Pampanito*'s own selectiveness in choosing whom to rescue. While the limitations of space and concerns regarding shipboard security may be used to help justify a submarine's refusal to take enemy soldiers or sailors on board as POWs, *Pampanito* did not just leave Japanese sinking victims in the sea to their fates, but prepared to shoot them. Many submarine veterans, in the years since the war, have been reluctant to discuss these sensitive issues, or, in true Navy fashion, to say anything that could be perceived as criticism of the CO. However, as the years continue to pass, there is more discussion, more reflection, and eventually more openness. Many veterans have confirmed that it was not at all unheard of for victims of a sunken enemy vessel to be shot while still in the water. Over the years and over successive crew reunions, *Pampanito*'s officers and men have become more and more reflective of events, as well as open and straightforward about the skipper's policies.[7]

Gordon Hopper was part of the 20-millimeter deck gun crew, and when the rafts were spotted on September 15 he was ordered topside: "the captain had said we'll make a run past . . . one of these rafts and when I give the word, we'll shoot the men off them." Richard Sherlock, acting as assistant OOD that day, confirms that taking Japanese sailors on board as POWs was not even considered: "the captain passed the word, break open the gun locker: anybody that wants to shoot Japs, come on, get a gun and come up on board. I know that's not according to the Geneva Convention, but there were a few things that weren't according to the Geneva Convention when we were fighting." Several of the rescued POWs' first memory of the sub included the rather daunting image of a huge figure poised on the bow of the sub pointing a huge shotgun at them: this was Tony Hauptman, whom Captain Summers had ordered topside to shoot the Japanese sailors believed to be on the rafts: "I got a box of buckshot and I got down on the bow of the submarine and we're coming alongside this raft—there was 12 of them on there, we thought they were Japs, so I was going to see if I could get all 12 of them in one shot with buckshot, and just before I shot one of them just happened to say 'Yank' and so I didn't shoot." One of the submarine's lookouts recalls that it took a full fifteen to twenty minutes for the decision to be made to take the men aboard.[8]

Then, of course, there are the recollections of the POWs them-selves, which clearly suggest that the Americans aboard *Pampanito* were ready to shoot. K. C. Renton, a soldier from Melbourne, Aus-tralia, described in his memoirs the precarious events preceding his rescue: "That afternoon between four and five the marvellous and wonderful thing happened—a submarine was making straight for us, but we did not know to whom it belonged. My eyes were pain-ing with oil and I could not see clearly but when it was right op-posite I saw a couple of men with machine guns pointing them at us. I didn't care because it would have been a quicker way out and believe me they looked tough but instead of lead we got a rope and was taken aboard." And several of the submarine's crew reported hearing one of the men in the water yell out to them: "You bloody Yanks, first you sink us, now you want to shoot us!"[9]

The policy was the same aboard the other subs. The patrol narra-tive of *Barb*'s skipper shows how tenuous the line between life and death could be when quick decisions had to be made in war: "As we approached the raft to determine their nationality, we wouldn't have picked up any Japs at that time, just probably would have elimi-nated them if anything." Unlike the POWs who had been picked up earlier by the first subs to reach the scene, the exhausted figures on the rafts that *Barb* encountered were too weak and too dazed to react when they saw the approaching sub, and their lack of response led the submarine crew to assume at first glance that they must be Japanese. They had to be—Allied soldiers would surely wave and shout upon spotting an American vessel. Finally, one of the POWs on the raft summoned from the depths of his being one final morsel of energy, pulled himself, shaking, to his knees, and shouted, "Hey, Yank." This one small, desperate act surely saved his life. These hapless POWs had come frighteningly close to being the victims, for a second time, of friendly fire.[10]

Standard policy or not, shooting the men in the water was not something taken lightly by all of the crew. Gordon Hopper recalls: "I can't speak for the others, but I, a 20 mm gunner, was appalled at the prospect of shooting helpless men on rafts in the middle of the South China Sea. Waiting for the captain's word, I was debating what to do, knowing that if I refused to fire or fired wildly I could be court-martialled or even shot on the spot for disobeying an order during combat." His relief was tremendous when the order never came, and instead a rescue operation began. "All of my life I have treasured the memory of helping save lives rather than terminate them."[11]

So how should *Pampanito* be remembered, be interpreted by historians? As an indiscriminate wartime killer, or as the savior of lives? It is possible that, in this incident—the rescue of the POWs—the reality of war was finally brought home to the submariners. Many were shocked, even repulsed, at seeing the condition the POWs were in when they were brought aboard. Frank Fives found himself unable to assist with first aid, because "My stomach couldn't take it. It was terrible." Submarines, like aircraft, hit their targets from a distance and had the luxury of rarely seeing the results of their actions up close: the damage done, the victims. In one patrol report, Captain Summers reflected on the beauty of an exploding ship after a torpedo hits it in the night: like watching Fourth of July fireworks, he wrote. But it is only in the past few years—some fifty years after the war—that the crew of *Pampanito* seems to be coming to grips with the fact that the human damage they witnessed that day in the South China Sea was the result of their own torpedo attacks. "We all felt pretty good about hitting our targets, but our targets did become humanized," said Gordon Hopper.[12]

Although their ranks are thinning, members of *Pampanito*'s crew continue to gather for reunions, to reminisce about the wartime experiences they shared. "Still our most treasured memory of World War II is the rescue of 73 Allies," reflects Gordon Hopper. "It's the part of the *Pampanito* experience that I'm proudest of. It was a unique thing that we were able to save lives rather than take lives. And I always felt very good about that, the fact that we saved men." Richard Sherlock also appreciated the experience of saving lives: "We had spent all the time during the war primarily killing people, but when we started to pull those people aboard . . . and saw the pathetic condition they were in and the tales they told. . . . Doing something positive and saving those fellows can't compare to anything else that happened while I was aboard." "It is one of the highlights of my life," remarked Hubert Brown of the rescue.[13]

Without a doubt, the impact of the rescue on *Pampanito*'s crew has been significant. It brought the reality of war home. "Doc" Demers confessed in his 1958 letter to Admiral Dykers: "although most of the submariners are tough and rugged, they are nothing but 'chicken hearted' when it comes to human misery." Demers's son, Larry, believes that rescuing and caring for the seventy-three POWs was truly a defining moment for his father, setting the tone for the rest of his life with a commitment to public service and the military.[14]

It was wartime. Killing is the business of war. It was their job, their duty, their obligation to country, to family. Yet on that day in September 1944, in the South China Sea, in the midst of war, *Pampanito*'s crew got to see and experience another aspect of warfare. They were made witness to the harsh reality of their own actions, while at the same time they were given a chance to make amends, to show mercy in wartime. Although *Pampanito*'s skipper Pete Summers was quick to prepare to shoot, that is not what he is remembered for. As Richard Sherlock says: "I will always have a warm feeling for Peter for no other reason than he was not about to leave one man out there so long as he could have a chance to find anyone. And he would have stayed there, I think, several more days looking for people if they hadn't ordered him back to Pearl."[15]

Notes

Series Foreword

1. Some sources, including the postwar report issued by the Joint Army-Navy Assessment Committee (JANAC), credit *Pampanito* with only five sinkings. It was not uncommon for JANAC's totals to vary from those reported by submarine skippers, as in many cases the extent of damage done to a vessel was difficult to confirm.

Preface

Epigraph sources: W. McKittrick, "My Name Is . . ."; Hopper, oral history interview, 7 November 2000.

1. Published accounts of the rescue include Blair and Blair's *Return to the River Kwai* and Michno's *USS* Pampanito: *Killer-Angel*. The motion picture *The Bridge on the River Kwai* (1957), based on the 1954 novel by Pierre Boulle, is a fictionalized account of the POWs forced to build the Burma-Thai Railroad. *Return to the River Kwai* was also made into a motion picture.

2. Renton account in W. Weaver, journal.

Chapter 1. The Sighting

1. Michno, *USS* Pampanito, 182.

2. Oakley, Patrol Report of Task Group 17.17; P. E. Summers, Report of War Patrol Number Three.

3. Hopper, oral history interview, 8 November 2002.

4. Tony and Betty Hauptman, oral history interview; Elaine Graybill, "Harrowing Experiences as POW Live On," *Bloomington-Normal (Ill.) Pantagraph*, 9 September 1984.

5. W. McKittrick, "One Man's War."

6. Oakley, Patrol Report of Task Group 17.17.

7. Bennett, oral history interview, 8 November 2002; Hopper, oral history interview, 8 November 2002; Tony and Betty Hauptman, oral history interview.

8. Oakley, Patrol Report of Task Group 17.17.

9. C. Williams, oral history interview.

10. P. E. Summers, Report to the Public Relations Officer; C. Williams, oral history interview.

11. Oakley, Patrol Report of Task Group 17.17.

12. Sherlock, oral history interview, 8 November 2002. In the twenty-four-hour clock used in the military, 2200 denotes 10 p.m.

13. Sherlock, oral history interview, 7 November 2000.

Chapter 2. USS *Pampanito*

1. Walters, oral history interview; W. Weaver, oral history interview, 8 November 2000.

2. Hopper, "*Pampanito* Recollections"; Grady, oral history interview.

3. Hopper, "*Pampanito* Recollections."

4. Bennett, oral history interview, 8 November 2000.

5. Grady, oral history interview.

6. D. Brown, journal; Hopper, "*Pampanito* Recollections."

7. Pappas, Bixler, and Stabler, oral history interview.

8. Hopper, oral history interview, 7 November 2000.

9. Hopper, "*Pampanito* Recollections"; *Pampanito*, War Diary Notes; D. Brown, journal.

10. McGuire et al., oral history interview.

11. *Pampanito*, War Diary Notes; Hopper, "*Pampanito* Recollections"; D. Brown, journal.

12. Hopper, "*Pampanito* Recollections"; Scherer, Report.

13. W. Weaver, personal account.

14. Ibid.; Hopper, "*Pampanito* Recollections."

15. L. Demers, oral history interview; M. Demers, journal.

16. P. E. Summers, Report of War Patrol Number Three.

17. Ibid.; W. Weaver, personal account.

18. *Pampanito*, War Diary Notes.

19. P. E. Summers, Report of War Patrol Number Three.

20. Ibid.

21. Ibid.

22. Ibid.; J. H. Brown, Third Endorsement to *Pampanito* Report of Third War Patrol.

Chapter 3. The Fall of Singapore

1. "Brief stories told by prisoners of war," 17 November 1944. The Australian Imperial Force was composed of five divisions of fifteen thousand men each, including the 8th Division, which was assigned to the defense of Singapore and Malaya during World War II.

2. Robert John Wall, "Taken Prisoner and Rescued: Conditions Whilst Japanese Prisoner," *Hopetown Guardian*, 8 December 1944.

3. Anderson and Barker, "Experiences of the War."

4. Anderson, "Survivor's Tale."

5. "Brief stories told by prisoners of war," 17 November 1944.

6. McKernan, *This War Never Ends,* 6.

7. Anderson and Barker, "Experiences of the War."

8. Anderson, "Survivor's Tale"; "Brief stories told by prisoners of war," 17 November 1944.

9. Anderson, "Survivor's Tale"; "Brief stories told by prisoners of war," 17 November 1944.

10. "Brief stories told by prisoners of war," 17 November 1944; Ward, account.

11. J. E. Hocking, letter to NMMA, 28 August 1987.

12. Ward, account.

13. Director of Prisoners of War and Internees, "Report on Information Obtained."

14. Ibid.

15. Tufnell, "Rescue of Allied POW's"; J. E. Hocking, letter to NMMA, 28 August 1987.

16. Tufnell, "Rescue of Allied POW's"; Anderson, "Survivor's Tale"; Ward, account.

Chapter 4. The Burma-Thai Railroad

1. Kinvig, *River Kwai Railway,* 27.

2. United States Forces, India-Burma Theater, "Report of Information Obtained in Interrogation of Prisoners of War"; McKernan, *This War Never Ends,* 12.

3. Director of Prisoners of War and Internees, "Report on Information Obtained"; Kinvig, *River Kwai Railway,* 198; Aiko Utsami, "Prisoners of War in the Pacific War: Japan's Policy," in McCormack and Nelson, *The Burma-Thailand Railway,* 75.

4. "Brief stories told by prisoners of war," 17 November 1944; United States Forces, India-Burma Theater, "Report of Information Obtained in Interrogation of Prisoners of War."

5. Tufnell, "Rescue of Allied POW's"; United States Forces, India-Burma Theater, "Report of Information Obtained in Interrogation of Prisoners of War."

6. United States Forces, India-Burma Theater, "Report of Information Obtained in Interrogation of Prisoners of War."

7. Burridge, account; Anderson, "Survivor's Tale."

8. United States Forces, India-Burma Theater, "Report of Information Obtained in Interrogation of Prisoners of War." Korea, which had been in the Japanese sphere of influence since the 1890s, was annexed into the Japanese Empire in 1910. Japan began recruiting Koreans for its military in 1938; some Koreans were forcibly seized for military or other service. Korean soldiers were regarded as being at the bottom of the Japanese military hierarchy, however, and were generally relegated to menial tasks, along with having to endure much verbal abuse. Kinvig, *River Kwai Railway*, 11; Yi Hak-Nae, "The Man between: A Korean Guard Looks Back," trans. Gavan McCormack, in McCormack and Nelson, *The Burma-Thailand Railway*, 121.

9. United States Forces, India-Burma Theater, "Report of Information Obtained in Interrogation of Prisoners of War."

10. Tufnell, "Rescue of Allied POW's"; United States Forces, India-Burma Theater, "Report of Information Obtained in Interrogation of Prisoners of War."

11. Peacock, *Prisoner on the Kwai*, 47.

12. Ibid., 51.

13. Bryan, Enclosure 4 to Memorandum to Edwin A. Plitt; Kinvig, *River Kwai Railway*, 88–89. The Geneva Convention of 1864 had included terms concerning the treatment of sick and wounded combatants, but not POWs. Subsequent international conventions, such as the Hague Conventions of 1899 and 1907, had included some vague provisions regarding the treatment, employment, and pay of POWs by the detaining power. During World War I the International Red Cross largely assumed the task of acting as a central agency for POW information, as well as organizing and sending delegates to visit POW camps. After the war, at the urging of the International Red Cross Committee, a diplomatic conference was called to adopt a special convention relating to POWs. The conference took place in Geneva in 1929 and saw the formulation of a code related specifically to the treatment of POWs, based on the experiences of and knowledge gathered from 1914 to 1918 by the Red Cross, and covering items such as notification of capture, the conditions of internment, the food and clothing provided to prisoners, their intellectual and moral needs, the sanitary and medical services in the camps, the correspondence of the prisoners, and so forth. Japan was represented at the 1929 conference and signed the convention, along with forty-six other countries, but it was never formally ratified by the Japanese government. Marc Peter, "Prisoners of War and the International Red Cross Committee," American National Red Cross, *Prisoners of War Bulletin* 1, no. 3 (August 1943): 4–5, 12; Kinvig, *River Kwai Railway*, 87–89.

14. Costello, "Survivor's Story"; "Brief stories told by prisoners of war," 17 November 1944; United States Forces, India-Burma Theater, "Report of Information

Obtained in Interrogation of Prisoners of War "Brief stories told by prisoners of war," 17 November 1944; Tufnell, "Rescue of Allied POW's."

15. "Brief stories told by prisoners of war," 17 November 1944.

16. Tufnell, "Rescue of Allied POW's."

17. United States Forces, India-Burma Theater, "Report of Information Obtained in Interrogation of Prisoners of War."

18. R. Cornford and McKittrick, oral history interview; United States Forces, India-Burma Theater, "Report of Information Obtained in Interrogation of Prisoners of War; Tufnell, "Rescue of Allied POW's."

19. United States Forces, India-Burma Theater, "Report of Information Obtained in Interrogation of Prisoners of War." Former POW Basil Peacock says that cigarettes were a highly sought after trade item by the POWs, providing "more comfort to most prisoners than anything else. Starving men, on occasion, would sell some of their food for a gasper." Cigarettes were also reportedly popular because they were reminders of home; smoking also helped assuage POWs' hunger. Peacock, *Prisoner on the Kwai,* 26; Nussbaum, *Chaplain on the River Kwai,* 83.

20. R. Cornford and McKittrick, oral history interview.

21. Ward, account; "Brief stories told by prisoners of war," 17 November 1944; United States Forces, India-Burma Theater, "Report of Information Obtained in Interrogation of Prisoners of War."

22. Tufnell, "Rescue of Allied POW's"; United States Forces, India-Burma Theater, "Report of Information Obtained in Interrogation of Prisoners of War."

23. United States Forces, India-Burma Theater, "Report of Information Obtained in Interrogation of Prisoners of War."

24. Ward, account; Kinvig, *River Kwai Railway,* 94; United States Forces, India-Burma Theater, "Report of Information Obtained in Interrogation of Prisoners of War"; Costello, "Survivor's Story"; Renton, account; W. Weaver, journal.

25. "Brief stories told by prisoners of war," 17 November 1944; United States Forces, India-Burma Theater, "Report of Information Obtained in Interrogation of Prisoners of War."

26. United States Forces, India-Burma Theater, "Report of Information Obtained in Interrogation of Prisoners of War."

27. Tufnell, "Rescue of Allied POW's"; "Brief stories told by prisoners of war," 17 November 1944.

28. United States Forces, India-Burma Theater, "Report of Information Obtained in Interrogation of Prisoners of War"; "Brief stories told by prisoners of war," 17 November 1944.

29. Farlow, account.

30. J. E. Hocking, letter to NMMA, 28 August 1987; Tufnell, "Rescue of Allied POW's."

31. R. J. Wall, "Taken Prisoner"; "Brief stories told by prisoners of war," 17 November 1944.

32. "Brief stories told by prisoners of war," 17 November 1944; War Office, Imperial Prisoners of War Committee, "Summary of Action Taken in Matters Relating to Prisoners of War in September, 1944"; F. Farmer, POW postcard.

33. Ward, account; United States Forces, India-Burma Theater, "Report of Information Obtained in Interrogation of Prisoners of War"; Anderson, "Survivor's Tale."

34. Tufnell, "Rescue of Allied POW's"; "Brief stories told by prisoners of war," 17 November 1944.

35. "Brief stories told by prisoners of war," 17 November 1944.

36. Ibid.

37. Director of Prisoners of War and Internees, "Report on Information Obtained"; United States Forces, India-Burma Theater, "Report of Information Obtained in Interrogation of Prisoners of War."

38. Chivers, account; Renton, account; W. Weaver, journal.

39. Tufnell, "Rescue of Allied POW's."

40. Ward, account; Kinvig, *River Kwai Railway,* 164.

41. Tufnell, "Rescue of Allied POW's."

42. Director of Prisoners of War and Internees, "Report on Information Obtained"; Kinvig, *River Kwai Railway,* 169; Tufnell, "Rescue of Allied POW's"; Renton, account; W. Weaver, journal.

43. Tufnell, "Rescue of Allied POW's."

Chapter 5. The Hellships

1. R. Cornford, "A Lucky Survivor."

2. Daws, "Notes for *Prisoners of the Japanese*," 43–44; "Brief stories told by prisoners of war," 17 November 1944.

3. Director of Prisoners of War and Internees, "Report on Information Obtained"; Chivers, account; Renton, account; Burridge, account.

4. "Brief stories told by prisoners of war," 17 November 1944; Chivers, account; Clifton, "Singapore to Japan."

5. "Brief stories told by prisoners of war," 17 November 1944; Chivers, account; Renton, account.

6. Chivers, account; Burridge, account; W. McKittrick, "*Pampanito*"; R. Cornford, account. *Kachidoki Maru* was a captured American vessel, formerly named *President Harrison.*

7. R. Cornford, "A Lucky Survivor"; W. McKittrick, "*Pampanito*"; R. Cornford, "A True Story"; R. Cornford, account; W. McKittrick, "One Man's War."

8. W. McKittrick, "One Man's War"; R. Cornford, "A Lucky Survivor"; K. Williams, "Ken Williams POW."

9. Ward, account.

10. J. C. Huckins, letter to NMMA, 14 July 1999.

11. W. McKittrick, "*Pampanito*" and "One Man's War."

12. "Brief stories told by prisoners of war," 17 November 1944; R. Cornford, account; Mandley, account.

13. W. McKittrick, "*Pampanito*"; J. C. Huckins, letter to NMMA, 14 July 1999.

14. Commander of the Prisoner Escort, Japanese Navy, "Regulations for Prisoners."

15. R. J. Wall, "Taken Prisoner"; "Brief stories told by prisoners of war," 17 November 1944; R. Cornford, account.

16. J. C. Huckins, letter to NMMA, 14 July 1999; Clifton, "Singapore to Japan."

17. Clifton, "Singapore to Japan."

18. Massey, account; R. Cornford, "A Lucky Survivor."

19. R. Cornford, account; R. Cornford, "A Lucky Survivor."

20. R. Cornford, "A Lucky Survivor."

21. Martin, letter to Russell Booth, 3 June 1986.

22. R. Cornford, "A Lucky Survivor."

23. Burridge, account.

24. R. Cornford and McKittrick, oral history interview; W. McKittrick, "*Pampanito*" and "One Man's War."

25. "Brief stories told by prisoners of war," 17 November 1944.

26. McArdle, letter to Russell Booth, 8 January 1986.

27. R. Cornford, "A Lucky Survivor."

28. Ibid.

29. R. J. Wall, "Taken Prisoner."

30. Burridge, account.

31. Ibid.

32. R. Cornford, "A Lucky Survivor"; R. Cornford, account; Mandley, account.

33. "Brief stories told by prisoners of war," 17 November 1944.

34. "*Pampanito*'s Tribute to *Rakuyo Maru* Survivor, Frank Farmer," 6.

35. Clifton, "Singapore to Japan."

36. Massey, account.

37. Ibid.

38. J. C. Huckins, letter to NMMA, 14 July 1999; J. C. Huckins, account in "Huckins Newsletter" 45 (January 1998).

39. Goodman, letter to Russell Booth, 23 December 1992.

40. Clifton, "Singapore to Japan."

Chapter 6. The Rescue

1. Renton, account; J. C. Huckins, account in "Huckins Newsletter" 44 (November 1997); Martin, letter to Russell Booth, 3 June 1986; Clifton, "Singapore to Japan."

2. J. C. Huckins, account in "Huckins Newsletter" 45 (January 1998); Philip, Duff, and Pope, "Experience of Survivors from a Sunken Japanese Transport"; "Brief stories told by prisoners of war," 17 November 1944; "*Pampanito's* Tribute to *Rakuyo Maru* Survivor, Frank Farmer," 6; Clifton, "Singapore to Japan."

3. Martin, letter to Russell Booth, 3 June 1986; "*Pampanito's* Tribute to *Rakuyo Maru* Survivor, Frank Farmer," 6.

4. "World War II Tragedy Recalled: Photo Jogs Memory of Ship's Sinking," *Mackay (Queensland) Daily Mercury*, 27 January 1986.

5. "Brief stories told by prisoners of war," 17 November 1944; R. Cornford, "A Lucky Survivor"; J. C. Huckins, account in "Huckins Newsletter" 45 (January 1998).

6. R. Cornford, account; Chivers, account; "Brief stories told by prisoners of war," 17 November 1944; Ward, account. Some of the men were picked up by Japanese ships. They were sent to the Kawasaki group of factories in Japan, and to Moji and Sakata POW camps. "General Information about Australian Prisoners of the Japanese."

7. R. Cornford, account; "Brief stories told by prisoners of war," 17 November 1944.

8. "*Pampanito's* Tribute to *Rakuyo Maru* Survivor, Frank Farmer," 6; R. Cornford and McKittrick, oral history interview; W. McKittrick, "*Pampanito*" and "One Man's War."

9. "Brief stories told by prisoners of war," 17 November 1944; K. Williams, "Ken Williams POW"; Chivers, account.

10. W. McKittrick, "*Pampanito*" and "My Name Is. . . ."

11. W. McKittrick, "One Man's War."

12. J. C. Huckins, account in "Huckins Newsletter" 45 (January 1998).

13. "Brief stories told by prisoners of war," 17 November 1944.

14. Ibid.

15. R. Cornford, account.

16. Mandley, account.

17. R. Cornford, account.

18. "Brief stories told by prisoners of war," 17 November 1944; W. McKittrick, "One Man's War"; R. Cornford and McKittrick, oral history interview.

19. "Brief stories told by prisoners of war," 17 November 1944.

20. R. Cornford, "A Lucky Survivor."

21. "Brief stories told by prisoners of war," 17 November 1944.

22. Ibid.

23. R. Cornford, "A Lucky Survivor."

24. W. McKittrick, "*Pampanito*"; photocopy of unidentified newspaper article and photograph captioned "Bill McKittrick today and as he was as a young man heading off to war with a friend." Supplied to SFMNPA in February 2002 by Gary Volkers, a cousin of McKittrick's.

25. "*Pampanito*'s Tribute to *Rakuyo Maru* Survivor, Frank Farmer," 6.

26. Ibid.

27. Ibid.

28. K. Williams, "Ken Williams POW."

29. McArdle, letter to Russell Booth, 8 January 1986.

30. Ibid.

31. Renton, account.

32. Longey, account.

33. "Brief stories told by prisoners of war," 17 November 1944.

34. Chivers, account.

35. "World War II Tragedy Recalled."

36. Account and photocopy of unidentified newspaper article and photograph of W. McKittrick (see note 24 above).

37. W. McKittrick, "*Pampanito*," "My Name Is . . . ," and "One Man's War"; R. Cornford and McKittrick, oral history interview.

38. R. Cornford and McKittrick, oral history interview; R. Cornford, "A Lucky Survivor"; R. Cornford, account; Bennett, oral history interview, 8 November 2002.

39. Oakley, Patrol Report of Task Group 17.17.

40. Pappas, Bixler, and Stabler, oral history interview; Towers, "Possession of cameras and taking of photographs by Naval Personnel"; P. E. Summers, Report to the Public Relations Officer.

41. R. Cornford and McKittrick, oral history interview; Mandley, letter to Russell Booth, 18 February 1987.

42. R. Cornford, "A Lucky Survivor"; R. Cornford, account.

43. Renton, account.

44. Reich, Action Report.

45. Ibid.; Hunter, letter to Robin Deley, 7 August 2003.

46. "Brief stories told by prisoners of war," 17 November 1944.

47. Ibid.

48. Pearson, letter to Russell Booth, 29 March 1989.

49. "Brief stories told by prisoners of war," 17 November 1944.

50. Fluckey, Report of Ninth War Patrol.

51. Fluckey, narrative; Fluckey, Report of Ninth War Patrol.

52. Tufnell, "Rescue of Allied POW's"; Fluckey, Report of Ninth War Patrol.

53. Fluckey, narrative.

54. Ibid.; Fluckey, Report of Ninth War Patrol.

55. Fluckey, Report of Ninth War Patrol.

56. USS *Fulton*, Action Report; Fluckey, narrative.

57. United States Navy Department, "History of Ships Named *Queenfish*"; Loughlin, Report of First War Patrol; Loughlin, Action Report, "Report of Allied Prisoner of War Survivors."

Chapter 7. The POWs aboard the Subs

1. H. Brown, oral history interview, 8 November 2000.

2. Sherlock, oral history interview, 8 November 2002; H. Brown, oral history interview, 8 November 2000.

3. P. E. Summers, Report to the Public Relations Officer; W. Weaver, oral history interviews, 8 November 2000, 8 November 2002.

4. Stimmler, oral history interview; McGuire et al., oral history interview.

5. P. E. Summers, Report to the Public Relations Officer; R. Cornford, "A Lucky Survivor."

6. P. E. Summers, Report to the Public Relations Officer; W. Weaver, oral history interview, 1996; W. Weaver, oral history interview, 8 November 2002; Weaver, personal account.

7. M. Demers, letter to Tommy Dykers, 7 April 1958.

8. H. Brown, oral history interviews, 8 November 2000, 8 November 2002.

9. Stimmler, oral history interview.

10. P. E. Summers, Report of War Patrol Number Three; M. Demers, letter to Tommy Dykers, 7 April 1958; P. E. Summers, Report to the Public Relations Officer.

11. P. E. Summers, Report to the Public Relations Officer; W. Weaver, oral history interview, 8 November 2002.

12. P. E. Summers, Report to the Public Relations Officer.

13. M. Demers, journal; Tufnell, "Rescue of Allied POW's."

14. M. Demers, letter to Tommy Dykers, 7 April 1958. RADM Thomas M. Dykers, USN (Ret.), produced, wrote, and hosted the series *The Silent Service*, which was based on actual World War II submarine patrols and was aired 1957–59.

15. L. Demers, oral history interview. Maurice Demers was serving aboard USS *Conger* (SS-477) when the episode was completed. The film company presented him with a 16-millimeter copy of the episode in a ceremony aboard the sub, with the entire *Conger* crew in attendance to honor Demers. L. Demers, oral history interview.

16. P. E. Summers, Report of War Patrol Number Three; P. E. Summers, Report to the Public Relations Officer.

17. M. Demers, letter to Tommy Dykers, 7 April 1958; P. E. Summers, Report to the Public Relations Officer.

18. Sherlock, oral history interview, 8 November 2002; P. E. Summers, Report to the Public Relations Officer.

19. P. E. Summers, Report to the Public Relations Officer; Granum, journal.

20. M. Demers, letter to Tommy Dykers, 7 April 1958.

21. R. Cornford and McKittrick, oral history interview; Oakley, Patrol Report of Task Group 17.17.

22. Sherlock, oral history interview, 8 November 2002.

23. P. E. Summers, Report to the Public Relations Officer; Sherlock, oral history interview, 8 November 2002; Certificate of Death for John Campbell.

24. P. E. Summers, Report of War Patrol Number Three; Cresswale, "A Story to Remember"; Bennett, oral history interview, 8 November 2002; Hopper, oral history interview, 8 November 2002; Carmody, "*Pampanito*'s Omen," 14.

25. Certificate of Death for John Campbell.

26. P. E. Summers, Report to the Public Relations Officer; R. Bullock, letter to Russell Booth, 3 February 1986; W. McKittrick, "*Pampanito*," R. Cornford, account; Martin, letter to Russell Booth, 3 June 1986.

27. Hopper, oral history interview, 8 November 2002; McGuire, oral history interview; Granum, journal; Costello, "Survivor's Story"; Longey, account.

28. Bourgeois, journal; D. W. Cunneen, account; Baron, journal.

29. Bourgeois, journal; D. W. Cunneen, account; Baron, journal.

30. Beard, USS *Case* War Diary; Tufnell, "Rescue of Allied POW's."

31. P. E. Summers, Report to the Public Relations Officer; P. E. Summers, Report of War Patrol Number Three; Cornford and McKittrick, oral history interview.

32. P. E. Summers, Report of War Patrol Number Three; M. Demers, letter to Tommy Dykers, 7 April 1958.

33. Philip, Duff, and Pope, "Experience of Survivors from a Sunken Japanese Transport"; Kearney, letter to John Clear, 8 March 1999.

34. Reich, Action Report; Reich, Report of War Patrol Number Two.

35. Philip, Duff, and Pope, "Experience of Survivors from a Sunken Japanese Transport."

36. Ibid.

37. Reich, Action Report.

38. Reich, Report of War Patrol Number Two.

39. Philip, Duff, and Pope, "Experience of Survivors from a Sunken Japanese Transport"; Loughlin, Report of First War Patrol.

40. Philip, Duff, and Pope, "Experience of Survivors from a Sunken Japanese Transport."

41. Ibid.; "Brief stories told by prisoners of war," 17 November 1944.

42. Philip, Duff and Pope, "Experience of Survivors from a Sunken Japanese Transport"; United States Navy Department, "History of Ships Named *Queenfish*"; Loughlin, Report of First War Patrol.

43. Philip, Duff and Pope, "Experience of Survivors from a Sunken Japanese Transport."

44. Ibid.

45. Ibid.; United States Navy Department, "History of Ships Named *Barb*."

46. Fluckey, Report of Ninth War Patrol; Philip, Duff and Pope, "Experience of Survivors from a Sunken Japanese Transport."

47. Fluckey, narrative.

48. Tufnell, "Rescue of Allied POW's"; Fluckey, narrative.

Chapter 8. Saipan

1. W. McKittrick, "One Man's War."

2. Oakley, Patrol Report of Task Group 17.17; W. McKittrick, "One Man's War.

3. Oakley, Patrol Report of Task Group 17.17; Scherer, Sherlock, and Moffett, oral history interview; Sherlock, oral history interview, 8 November 2002; R. Bullock, letter to Russell Booth, 3 February 1986.

4. M. Demers, letter to Tommy Dykers, 7 April 1958; L. Demers, oral history interview.

5. L. Demers, oral history interview.

6. Philip, Duff and Pope, "Experience of Survivors from a Sunken Japanese Transport."

7. M. Demers, letter to Tommy Dykers, 7 April 1958.

8. P. E. Summers, Report to the Chief of the Bureau of Naval Personnel, 6 October 1944.

9. Lockwood, Report to the Chief of Naval Personnel, 25 October 1944; Wakefield, Report to Medical Officer in Command, U.S. Naval Hospital, Brooklyn.

10. P. E. Summers, Report to the Commander Submarine Force, U.S. Pacific Fleet, "Recommendation for Awards to Certain Personnel," 6 October 1944, Serial (029) and Serial (030); Fenno, "Recommendation of Certain Officers and Men for Suitable Awards."

11. R. Cornford, account.

12. Hart, letter to Aldona Sendzikas, 28 November 2003.

13. Philip, Duff and Pope, "Experience of Survivors from a Sunken Japanese Transport."

14. Tufnell, "Rescue of Allied POW's"; W. McKittrick, "My Name Is . . ."

15. Tufnell, "Rescue of Allied POW's."

16. W. McKittrick, "One Man's War"; R. J. Wall, "Taken Prisoner"; D. Wall, *Heroes at Sea*, 100.

17. H. Brown, oral history interview, 8 November 2000; P. E. Summers, Report of War Patrol Number Three.

18. Reich, Action Report; Reich, Report of War Patrol Number Two.

19. Hopper, "*Pampanito* Recollections."

20. Scherer, Report; Hopper, "*Pampanito* Recollections."

21. W. Weaver, personal account; Granum, journal; M. Demers, letter to Tommy Dykers, 7 April 1958.

22. D. Cocking, letter to Betty Hauptman, 15 January 1945; Madison, oral history interview.

23. Hopper, "*Pampanito* Recollections."

Chapter 9. Home

Epigraph source: *Rakuyo Maru* survivor Corporal James Campbell, upon return to Australia, in "Brief stories told by prisoners of war," 17 November 1944.

1. R. Cornford, account; R. Cornford and McKittrick, oral history interview.

2. Tufnell, "Rescue of Allied POW's."

3. W. McKittrick, "Unseen" and "One Man's War."

4. Holmes, *Five Thousand Bowls of Rice*, 76; W. McKittrick, "Unseen" and "One Man's War."

5. W. McKittrick, "Unseen."

6. "Brief stories told by prisoners of war," 17 November 1944.

7. W. McKittrick, "Unseen" and "One Man's War."

8. "Brief stories told by prisoners of war," 17 November 1944; McKernan, *This War Never Ends*, 50.

9. W. McKittrick, "Unseen"; "Brief stories told by prisoners of war," 17 November 1944.

10. "Brief stories told by prisoners of war," 17 November 1944.

11. W. McKittrick, "Unseen"; "Brief stories told by prisoners of war," 17 November 1944.

12. McKernan, *This War Never Ends*, 52–53.

13. "Tragic Story of P.O.W. Transport Sinking," *Sydney Morning Herald*, 18 November 1944, 1. Seven of the 159 rescued POWs died while on board the submarines.

14. "Brief stories told by prisoners of war," 17 November 1944; "Japanese Horrors," *The West Australian*, 18 November 1944, 7–8; "Tragic Story of P.O.W. Transport Sinking." Prime Minister John Curtin was hospitalized for two months after suffering a heart attack in early November 1944; during this time, Deputy Prime Minister Forde assumed Curtin's official duties.

15. "Brief stories told by prisoners of war," 17 November 1944.

16. "*The Times* Demands Retribution," *Sydney Morning Herald*, 20 November 1944, 1; "Australia Protests to Japan," *Melbourne Argus*, 22 November 1944, 3; "Protest to Japan," *Sydney Morning Herald*, 22 November 1944, 4; "Survivors from Hell Ship," *Sydney Morning Herald*, 8 December 1944, 3; "More Rescues from Prison Ship 'Remote,'" *Sydney Morning Herald*, 16 December 1944, 4.

17. McKernan, *This War Never Ends*, 16–17, 19, 28–30.

18. Coombes, letter to "Bill," 20 November 1944; T. Farmer, oral history interview; R. Cornford and McKittrick, oral history interview; W. McKittrick, "Unseen."

19. R. J. Wall, "Taken Prisoner."

20. "Relatives Seek News from Returned POWs," *Sydney Morning Herald*, 25 January 1945, 4.

21. "Australian POW from Jap Vessel," *Melbourne Argus*, 8 December 1944, 3; "Survivors from Hell Ship"; "Option for Rescued POWs," *Melbourne Argus*, 2 February 1945, 6.

22. W. McKittrick, "Unseen."

23. R. Cornford and McKittrick, oral history interview.

24. Director of Prisoners of War and Internees, "Report on Information Obtained"; "More News Sought of POWs," *Sydney Morning Herald*, 20 December 1944, 1.

25. R. Cornford, account; W. McKittrick, "Unseen."

26. W. McKittrick, "One Man's War."

27. Ibid.; W. McKittrick, "Unseen."

28. W. McKittrick, "Unseen."

29. Ibid.; R. Cornford, account.

30. "Brief stories told by prisoners of war," 17 November 1944; "World War II Tragedy Recalled: Photo Jogs Memory of Ship's Sinking," *Mackay (Queensland) Daily Mercury*, 27 January 1986.

31. Adjutant-General, Australian Military Forces, "Reception, Treatment and Disposal of AMF Ex Prisoners of War on Arrival in Australia."

32. Mawby, letter to NMMA, 15 December 1987.

33. Adjutant-General, Australian Military Forces, "Letter to Next of Kin of Repatriated Prisoners of War."

34. Elaine Graybill, "Harrowing Experiences as POW Live On," *Bloomington-Normal (Ill.) Pantagraph*, 9 September 1984; Jesse family, letter to Peck, Deley and Hastings, 6 September 2003; R. Cornford, account.

35. S. McKittrick, oral history interview.

Chapter 10. Looking Back

1. Hopper, "*Pampanito* Recollections."

2. Ibid.; Scherer, Sherlock, and Moffett, oral history interview.

3. Hopper, "*Pampanito* Recollections"; Hopper, oral history interview, 7 November 2000; W. Weaver, oral history interview, 8 November 2000.

4. Scherer, Sherlock, and Moffett, oral history interview.

5. Dingman, *Ghost of War*, 176.

6. Hopper, oral history interview, 7 November 2007.

7. Walters, oral history interview.

8. S. McKittrick, oral history interview; R. Cornford and McKittrick, oral history interview.

9. S. McKittrick, oral history interview.

10. Pickett, e-mail to Robin Deley, 25 June 2003.

11. T. Farmer, e-mail to *Pampanito* staff, 14 September 2001.

12. Hosoya, letter to Thomas Richardson, 5 August 2001.

13. Cray, letter to Robert Bennett, 6 December 1944; Bennett, oral history interview, 8 November 2002.

14. W. Weaver, personal account; Kip Cooper, "Dramatic WWII Sub Action Recalled in Meeting Here," *San Diego Tribune*, 20 May 1968; W. Weaver, oral history interview, 8 November 2002.

15. McArdle, letter to SFMNPA, 7 August 2003; Tony and Betty Hauptman, oral history interview.

16. Arcement, letter to Russell Booth, 28 February 1988; K. Williams, letter to Russell Booth, 6 February 1988.

17. L. Summers, letter to Russell Booth, 16 September 1993; T. Farmer, oral history interview; "*Pampanito*'s Tribute to *Rakuyo Maru* Survivor, Frank Farmer," 6.

18. "*Pampanito*'s Fiftieth Anniversary 1943–1993," *Sea Letter*, Winter 1993, 6–7; R. Cornford and McKittrick, oral history interview; Hopper, oral history interview, 8 November 2002.

19. S. McKittrick, oral history interview.

20. L. Demers, oral history interview.

21. F. Farmer, letter to NMMA, 26 January 1990; F. Farmer, letter to Bob Hawke, 4 July 1989.

22. Plaque presented to *Pampanito* on 25 April 2002 by Scott Thiele, grandson of Ken Williams; Thiele, e-mail to Aldona Sendzikas, 28 May 2002; Thiele, e-mail to Racheal Perry, 26 June 2003.

23. R. Cornford and McKittrick, oral history interview; Collins, letter to Russell Booth, 25 August 1986.

Epilogue

Epigraph source: Hopper, "*Pampanito* Recollections."

1. P. E. Summers, Report of War Patrol Number Three.

2. McGuire, oral history interview.

3. Unrestricted submarine warfare (USW) had been outlawed by the 1930 London Naval Treaty. Admiral Charles Lockwood defended his submarine fleet's use of USW in World War II by pointing out that it was being waged by the German Navy in the Atlantic; and since it was impossible to determine if a Japanese ship was a merchant vessel or a naval auxiliary vessel, it was justifiable to sink any ship flying the enemy flag. Dingman, *Ghost of War*, 153, 157.

4. On 26 January 1943, USS *Wahoo* (SS-238) reportedly spent an hour shooting Japanese survivors of a torpedoed troopship in the water. C. Blair, *Silent Victory*, 383–86.

5. Greg Michno deals with this question in *Pampanito: Killer-Angel* and *Death on the Hellships*. Michno is convinced that the COs of *Sealion* and *Pampanito* were unaware that there were POWs aboard the transport ships they attacked, although he believes FRUPAC may have known.

6. W. Weaver, oral history interview, 8 November 2002.

7. McGuire et al., oral history interview.

8. Hopper, oral history interview, 8 November 2002; Sherlock, oral history interview, 8 November 2002; Tony and Betty Hauptman, oral history interview; McGuire, oral history interview.

9. Renton, account; W. McKittrick, "One Man's War."

10. Fluckey, narrative. According to Gavan Daws, Japanese soldiers' duty to the Emperor was to die rather than be captured. As POWs, they were considered dead as Japanese soldiers; accordingly, the Japanese government did not inquire of the Allies regarding Japanese POWs the Allies might be holding. "The Allies, on their side, never had any serious intention of taking Japanese prisoners, at least beyond a handful for interrogation. They intended not to capture Japanese but kill them. From the start, and especially after the war turned the Allies' way, for every one Japanese they took prisoner they killed hundreds." Daws, "Notes for *Prisoners of the Japanese*," 11–13.

11. Hopper, "*Pampanito* Recollections"; Hopper, oral history interview, 7 November 2000.

12. Quoted in Michno, USS "*Pampanito*," 236; Hopper, oral history interview, 7 November 2000.

13. Hopper, e-mail to Gary Volkers, 19 April 2002; Hopper, oral history interview, 8 November 2002; Sherlock, oral history interview, 7 November 2000; H. Brown, oral history interview, 8 November 2002.

14. M. Demers, letter to Tommy Dykers, 7 April 1958; L. Demers, oral history interview.

15. Sherlock, oral history interview, 8 November 2002.

Bibliography

Primary Sources

Adjutant-General, Australian Military Forces, 2nd Echelon LHQ, Melbourne. "Letter to Next of Kin of Repatriated Prisoners of War." 21 May 1945 (AWM54, 779/1/12). Australian War Memorial Archives, Canberra, Australian Capital Territory [hereafter referred to as AWM].

Adjutant-General, Australian Military Forces, HQ, Victoria Barracks, Melbourne. "Reception, Treatment and Disposal of AMF Ex Prisoners of War on Arrival in Australia." SM5167, 9 June 1945 and SM7862, 10 September 1945 (AWM54, 77/14/1). AWM.

Anderson, C. "Survivor's Tale." USS *Pampanito*/San Francisco Maritime National Park Association Archives [hereafter referred to as SFMNPA].

———. "What Price Freedom?" SFMNPA.

Anderson, C., and H. J. Barker. "Experiences of the War as Written by Two of the Survivors." SFMNPA.

Anonymous *Barb* crew member. E-mails to Aldona Sendzikas. 20 October 2003 and 31 October 2003. In author's possession.

Arcement, Norman. Letters to Russell Booth. 28 February, 12 July 1988. SFMNPA.

Bailey, Clifford. Letter to Russell Booth. 20 October 1987. SFMNPA.

Bancroft, Arthur. Letter to Russell Booth. 15 June 1987. SFMNPA.

Barnett, Wilf. Letters to Russell Booth. June 1993, no date. SFMNPA.

Baron, Leonard. Journal. SFMNPA.

Beard, J. W., Navigator, USS *Case* (DD-370). War Diary for September 1944. Serial 0146. 1 October 1944 (RG38, World War II Diaries, Box 699, 370/45/34/1). National Archives and Records Administration, College Park [hereafter referred to as NARA].

Benison, Peter. Letter to Russell Booth. 29 November 1993. SFMNPA.

Bennett, Robert. Oral history interviews. 8 November 2000, 8 November 2002. SFMNPA.

Betts, Ed. C., Senior ETOUSA Representative, Combined British-American Repatriation Committee. Memorandum to The Provost Marshal General, War Department, Washington, D.C. With attachment: Technical Memorandum No.13, "The Prisoner of War Comes Home." The British Directorate of Army Psychiatry (May 1944). 28 June 1944 (RG389, Entry 452, Box 1388). NARA.

Blair, Joan, and Clay Blair Jr. Letter to interview subjects. No date (probably 1979). SFMNPA.

Booth, Russell. Letter to Keith Taylor. 4 November 1985. SFMNPA.

Bourgeois, Roger. Journal. SFMNPA.

Bowring, Harry. Oral history interview. 8 November 2000. SFMNPA.

"Brief stories told by prisoners of war rescued by U.S.A. submarines, from a Japanese transport, torpedoed on 12th September 1944, in the South China Sea. Together with a Statement by the Prime Minister of Australia, The Rt. Hon. John Curtin," 17 November 1944 (AWM54, 779/10/3). AWM.

"British and Australian Prisoner-of-War Survivors—Rescue of. Names and Next of Kin of Survivors." SFMNPA.

Brown, Duncan. Journal. SFMNPA.

Brown, Hubert. Oral history interviews. 8 November 2000, 8 November 2002. SFMNPA.

Brown, J. H., Jr., for Commander Submarine Force, Pacific Fleet. Third Endorsement to *Pampanito* Report of Third War Patrol. FF12-10/A16-3(15). 12 October 1944. SFMNPA.

Bryan, B. M., Assistant The Provost Marshal General. Enclosure 4 to Memorandum to Edwin A. Plitt, Chief, Special War Problems, Division, Department of State. 3 April 1945 (RG389, Entry 452, Box 1388). NARA.

Bullock, Hazel. Letter to Russell Booth. 17 March 1993. SFMNPA.

Bullock, Reg. Letter to Robert Bennett. No date. SFMNPA.

———. Letters to Russell Booth. 3 February 1986, 12 September 1990. SFMNPA.

Bullock, Reg, and Hazel Bullock. Letter to Russell Booth. 20 February 1991. SFMNPA.

Burridge, Raymond. Account. SFMNPA.

———. Letter to Russell Booth. 17 August 1987. SFMNPA.

Cannalte, David R. Press release re: Arthur Bancroft. 19 October 1983. USS Bowfin Submarine Museum and Park Archives [hereafter referred to as USSBSMP].

Certificate of Death for John Campbell. NMS-Form N (1940). 16 September 1944. SFMNPA.

Chappell, E. L., Commander Submarine Division Two Eight One. First Endorsement to CO *Pampanito* Conf. Ltr. SS383/A16. Serial (023) of 28 September 1944, FB5-281/A16. 3 October 1944. SFMNPA.

Chivers, Harry. Account. SFMNPA.

Citation for Bronze Star Medal for Anthony Carl Hauptman, Chief Gunner's Mate, USN. No date. SFMNPA.

Clifton, Ralph. Letters to Russell Booth. 12 March [no year], no date. SFMNPA.

———. "Singapore to Japan." SFMNPA.

Cocking, Doris. Letter to Betty Hauptman. 15 January 1945. SFMNPA.

Cocking, Jim. Letter to Pampanito staff. 22 August 2001. SFMNPA.

Collins, A. B. R. Letter to Russell Booth. 25 August 1986. SFMNPA.

Collins, Robert A. Letter to D. G. Kaye. 10 March 1986. SFMNPA.

———. Letter to Russell Booth. 25 August 1986. SFMNPA.

Commander in Chief, U.S. Pacific Fleet. Report to Commander in Chief, U.S. Fleet. Serial 000869. 4 October 1944 (RG38, WWII War Diaries, Box 25: CINCPAC September 1944–Vol. 1 September 1–14, 1944, 370/45/20/2-3.) NARA.

Commander of the Prisoner Escort, Japanese Navy. "Regulations for Prisoners." No date. (Harry Pence Papers, 1893–1976. MSS 144, Box 12, Folder 13.) University of California at San Diego, Manderville Special Collections Library [hereafter referred to as UCSD].

Coombes, Frank. Letter to "Bill." 20 November 1944. SFMNPA.

Cornford, Joan. Letter to Russell, Daria, and Hannah Booth. 14 February 1994. SFMNPA.

Cornford, Roy. Account. SFMNPA.

———. Letters to Russell Booth. 11 March, 3 November 1986, 22 March, 16 September 1993. SFMNPA.

———. "A Lucky Survivor." SFMNPA.

———. "A True Story." SFMNPA.

Cornford, Roy, and Joan Cornford. Letters to Russell and Daria Booth. 1995 and no date [probably 1994]. SFMNPA.

———. Letters to Russell Booth. No date [probably 1994], 20 April [no year]. SFMNPA.

Cornford, Roy, and William McKittrick. Oral history interview. 1993. Tape 24, 93-34-016, 017, 018, 019, and 87-34-005. SFMNPA.

Costello, Stanley. "Survivor's Story." SFMNPA.

Courtney, Scott. E-mail to SFMNPA staff. 7 September 2003. SFMNPA.

Cray, Bill. Letter to Robert Bennett. 6 December 1944. SFMNPA.

Cresswale, Douglas. "A Story to Remember." SFMNPA.

Cunneen, Donald William. Account. SFMNPA.

Cunneen, Kath. Letter to Robin Deley. No date [probably 2003]. SFMNPA.

Currier, Andy. Journal. SFMNPA.

Curtis, Roger B. Letters to Russell Booth. 9 March, 11 May, 19 May 1987. SFMNPA.

Davis, H. Letter to Russell Booth. 6 June 1993. SFMNPA.

Daws, Gavan. Notes for *Prisoners of the Japanese*: 43–44. University of Hawai'i at Manoa, Hamilton Library, Pacific Collection.

Demers, Lawrence. E-mail to Thomas Richardson. 12 August 2000. SFMNPA.

———. E-mail to Thomas Richardson and Aldona Sendzikas. 10 November 2000. SFMNPA.

———. Oral history interview. 23 September 2003. SFMNPA.

Demers, Maurice L. Journal. SFMNPA.

———. Letter to Tommy Dykers. 7 April 1958. SFMNPA.

Director of Prisoners of War and Internees. "Report on Information Obtained from Recovered Australian PW ex '*Rakuyo Maru*.'" 10 November 1944 (AWM54, 1010/9/109). AWM.

Downes, W. M., Commander Task Group 17.7, U.S. Submarine Advanced Base, Saipan. War Diary. 27 August to 30 September 1944 (RG38, 370-45-30-3, World War II War Diaries, Box 521, Saipan, Advanced Submarine Base). NARA.

Duncan, A. Letters to Russell Booth. 1 February 1994, 23 February 1994, and no date. SFMNPA.

Edwards, Pauline. Letter to *Pampanito* staff. 14 September 2003. SFMNPA.

Farlow, Cliff. Account. SFMNPA.

———. Letter to National Maritime Museum Association. 15 July 1985. SFMNPA.

———. Letters to Russell Booth. 8 October 1985, 30 August 1988. SFMNPA.

———. Letter to Tim Hastings. 25 August 2003. SFMNPA.

Farmer, Frank. Letter to Bob Hawke. 4 July 1989. SFMNPA.

———. Letter to National Maritime Museum Association. 26 January 1990. SFMNPA.

———. POW postcard. No date. SFMNPA.

———. Telegram to *Pampanito*. 14 September 1989. SFMNPA.

Farmer, Frank, and Mary Farmer. Letter to *Pampanito* Crew. April 1989. SFMNPA.

———. Letter to Russell and Daria Booth. 13 December 1994. SFMNPA.

———. Letters to Russell Booth. 17 October 1988, Friday 29th (probably 1993). SFMNPA.

Farmer, Mary. Letter to Russell and Daria Booth. 26 January 1996. SFMNPA.

Farmer, Tim. E-mail to Christian Bach. 20 December 2002. SFMNPA.

———. E-mail to *Pampanito* staff. 14 September 2001. SFMNPA.

———. Oral history interview. 23 September 2003. SFMNPA.

Farrands, Bob. Letter to D. G. Kaye. 24 February 1986. SFMNPA.

Fenno, F. W., Jr., Commanding Officer, USS *Pampanito* (SS-383). Report to The Commander Submarines, U.S. Pacific Fleet, "Recommendation of Certain Officers and Enlisted Men for Suitable Awards." SS383/P15, Serial (033). 29 October 1944. SFMNPA.

Flinn, D. A. Letter to National Maritime Museum Association. 23 February 1986. SFMNPA.

Fluckey, Eugene B., Commanding Officer, USS *Barb* (SS-220). Report of Ninth War Patrol. SS220/A16, Serial 0015. 3 October 1944 (RG38, M1752). NARA.

———, Commanding Officer, USS *Barb* (SS-220). Transcript of recorded narrative of

8th–11th war patrols, recorded 21 March 1945. Film No. 354 and 354-1. Transcribed 7 April 1945. SFMNPA.

Fulton (AS-11). Action Report: "Rescue of Allied POW's." Serial None. 30 September 1944 (RG38, WWII Action and Operational Reports, Box 994, USS *Fulton*). NARA.

———. War Diary Notes. September 1944 (RG38, 370/46/02/5, World War II War Diaries, Box 875, USS *Fulton*). NARA.

Gainger, Edith. Letter to Robin Deley. No date (postmarked 6 August 2003). SFMNPA.

Gelsthorpe, F. R. Letter to National Maritime Museum Association. 30 June 1994. SFMNPA.

Goodman, Jack. Letter to Russell Booth. 23 December 1992. SFMNPA.

———. Letter to SFMNPA. No date (postmarked 1992). SFMNPA.

Grady, William. Oral history interview. 8 November 2000. SFMNPA.

Granum, P. A. Journal. SFMNPA.

Greene, John H. Journal. SFMNPA.

Halfhide, E. C. Letter to Russell Booth. 19 February 1987 and 4 August 1993. SFMNPA.

Handwritten list of names and addresses of thirty-eight survivors rescued by *Pampanito*, belonging to H. Brown. SFMNPA.

Hart, Andrew W. Letter to Aldona Sendzikas. 28 November 2003. In author's possession.

Hauptman, Tony, and Betty Hauptman. Oral history interview. No date. SFMNPA.

Hawkins, O. D. Letter to Clarence Smith. 17 March 1994. SFMNPA.

Hayes, W. L., War Department Representative, Imperial Prisoners of War Committee and Sub-Committees. Report to the Provost Marshal General, War Department, Washington, D.C. 24 January 1945 and 8 March 1945 (RG389, Entry 452, Box 1389, File 334). NARA.

Herrick, Parmely W., Acting Assistant Chief, Special War Problems Division. Memo to Howard F. Bresee, Director, American Prisoner of War Information Bureau, Washington, D.C. 23 July 1945. With attachment: "Summary of Prisoner of War Ship Sinkings (Far East) 1944" (RG389, Entry 460A, Box 2276). NARA.

Hocking, John Edward. Letter to National Maritime Museum Association. 28 August 1987. SFMNPA.

Hocking, Joyce. Letter to Racheal Perry. 18 July 2003. SFMNPA.

Hopper, Gordon. E-mail to Gary Volkers. 19 April 2002. SFMNPA.

———. Letter to Jennifer Ann Cole. 28 February 2003. SFMNPA.

———. Letter to Russell Booth. 6 November 1994. SFMNPA.

———. Oral history interviews. 7 November 2000, 8 November 2002. SFMNPA.

———. "*Pampanito* Recollections—The Boat, the Crew, the Experiences." SFMNPA.

Hopper, Gordon, Roger Walters, Robert Bennett, and Roy Cornford. Oral history interview. 1993. Tape 19, 93-34-001, 002, 003. SFMNPA.

Hosoya, Suke-Tumo. Letter to Thomas Richardson. 5 August 2001. SFMNPA.

Huckins, J. E. Letter to Russell Booth. 28 August 1987. SFMNPA.

Huckins, James C. Account. "Huckins Newsletter" 44 (November 1997), 45 (January 1998), and 46 (March 1998). SFMNPA.

———. Letter to National Maritime Museum Association. 14 July 1999. SFMNPA.

Hunter, Norman C. Letter to Robin Deley. 7 August 2003. SFMNPA.

Ingram, George. Oral history interview. 8 November 2000. SFMNPA.

Jackson, Lt. Col., Commanding Officer, 102 Aust. Con. Depot. "Report on Ps.O.W. (8th Div.) Draft which Arrived at 102 Aust. Con. Depot on 24 March 1945." 12 April 1945. With attachment: "Medical Report on Ex. Japanese P.O.W.s." S.M.O. 102 Aust. Con. Depot. 11 April 1945 (AWM54, 779/6/2). AWM.

Japanese Orange Translations. Translations of Intercepted Enemy Radio Traffic, Contact and Sighting. 23 September 1944 to 7 September 1944 (RG38, Box 271, 370/01/10/5). NARA.

———. Translations of Intercepted Enemy Radio Traffic, Allied Attack On, 23 June 1945 (RG38, Box 228, 370-01-07-06). NARA.

Jesse family. E-mail to Fred Peck, Robin Deley, and Tim Hastings. 6 September 2003. SFMNPA.

Kearney, Laurie. Letter to John Clear. 8 March 1999. SFMNPA.

"L. Kearney. Rescued. 15–9–1944." USS *Sealion* letterhead paper with signatures of twenty-one *Sealion* crew members. SFMNPA.

Lockwood, C. A., Jr., Commander Submarine Force, Pacific Fleet. "Report of Thirteenth Coordinated Attack Group Consisting of the USS *Sealion* (SS315), the USS *Pampanito* (SS383) and the USS *Growler* (SS215)." FF12-10/A16-3(15), Serial 02457. 6 November 1944. SFMNPA.

———. Report to the Chief of Naval Personnel, "Appointment of Demers, Maurice L., PhM1c, USN to Warrant Pharmacist—Recommendation for." FF12-10/P17-2/MM, Serial 02341. 25 October 1944. SFMNPA.

Longey, Claude. Account. SFMNPA.

———. Letter to Russell Booth. 4 April 1986. SFMNPA.

Loughlin, C. E., Commanding Officer, USS *Queenfish* (SS-393). Action Report, "Report of Allied Prisoner of War Survivors; Treatment and Disposition." SS393/A9-8/P2, Serial 021. 2 October 1944 (RG38, 370/46/02/5, World War II Action and Operations Reports, Box 1359, USS *Queenfish*, Serial 021, 2 October 1944). NARA.

———. Action Report, "Sinking of Japanese Ship *Awa Maru*, Report of." SS393/A9, Serial (07). 8 April 1945. With attachments: "Interrogation of Japanese survivor from *Awa Maru*"; C. A. Lockwood, Jr., "First Endorsement to CO conf. Ltr. SS393/A9 ser. 07 of 8 April 1945," 17 April 1945; C. H. McMorris, "Second Endorsement on CO, USS *Queenfish* ltr, SS393/A9, ser 07 of 8 April 1945, 24 April 1945 (RG38,

370/46/02/05, World War II Action and Operations Reports, Box 1359, USS *Queenfish*, Serial 07, 8 April 1945). NARA.

———. Report of First War Patrol. SS393/A4-3, Serial (023). 3 October 1944 (RG38, M1752). NARA.

Madison, Walter. Oral history interview, 23 September 2003. SFMNPA.

Mandley, W. A. W. Account. SFMNPA.

———. Letters to Russell Booth. 18 February, 12 May, 28 May 1987. SFMNPA.

Manning, Leo. Letter to Russell Booth. 5 April 1989. SFMNPA.

———. Letter to SFMNPA. 4 July 2003. SFMNPA.

Martin, H. D. Letter to D. G. Kaye. 20 December 1985. SFMNPA.

———. Letters to Russell Booth. 6 March, 3 June 1986. SFMNPA.

Massey, N. H. Account. SFMNPA.

———. "Diary Notes—June-November 1945." SFMNPA.

———. Letters to Russell Booth. 2 November, 3 November, 5 November 1987, 22 March 1989. SFMNPA.

Mawby, Raymond. Letters to National Maritime Museum Association. 1 August 1987, 15 December 1987, and no date. SFMNPA.

McArdle, Don. Letter to Russell Booth. 8 January 1986. SFMNPA.

———. Letter to SFMNPA. Postmarked 7 August 2003. SFMNPA.

McGuire, Charles. Oral history interview. 8 November 2002. SFMNPA.

McGuire, Charlie, George Moffett, Paul Pappas, Johnny Green, Herman Bixler. Oral history interview. 1993. Tape 21, 93-34-007, 008, 009. SFMNPA.

McKechnie, Charles. Letter to Russell Booth. 29 January 1986. SFMNPA.

McKechnie, Lorna. Letter to Russell Booth. 14 July 1986. SFMNPA.

McKittrick, Sybil. Oral history interview. 6 November 2005. SFMNPA.

McKittrick, William. Letters to Russell Booth. 20 August 1986 [1987?], 25 February 1987, 3 November 1993, and no date. SFMNPA.

———. "My Name Is . . ." SFMNPA.

———. "One Man's War." SFMNPA.

———. "*Pampanito*." SFMNPA.

———. "Unseen, Unheralded and Unsung." SFMNPA.

McKittrick, William, and Sybil McKittrick. Letter to Russell Booth. No date [probably 1993]. SFMNPA.

Michno, Greg. Letter to Thomas Richardson. 28 June 1999. SFMNPA.

Miller, Don. Letter to Aldona Sendzikas. 25 November 2003. In author's possession.

———. Letter to Aldona Sendzikas and Robin Deley. 22 October 2003. SFMNPA.

Moffett, George. Oral history interview. 23 September 2003. SFMNPA.

Morgan, H. B. Letters to Russell Booth. No date [postmarked 22 April 1987], and no date. SFMNPA.

Morris, B. Letter to Russell Booth. 25 April 1987. SFMNPA.

"Not planning to do any celebrating." Unidentified newspaper article, no date. SFM-NPA.

Oakley, T. B., Jr., Commander Task Group 17.17. Patrol Report of Task Group 17.17. 20 September 1944. SFMNPA.

Obituary for Paul E. Summers. Oklahoma City, OK, 1993. SFMNPA.

Order of Service, Memorial Service on the 50th Anniversary for the Australian Prisoners of War Who Died in the Sinking of the Japanese Prison Ship *Rakuyo Maru* 12 September 1944. HMAS *Sydney*. 12 September 1994. SFMNPA.

Pampanito (SS-383). War Diary Notes. SFMNPA.

Pappas, Paul, Herman Bixler, and Owen Stabler. Oral history interview. No date. SF-MNPA.

Pearce, E. S. Memorandum for Captain H. L. Pence, USN (Retired): "Rates of Pay, Japanese Armed Forces." Op-16-FE. 27 April 1945 (Harry Pence Papers, 1893–1976. MSS 144, Box 9, Folder 3.) UCSD.

Pearson, Ernest A. Letter to Russell Booth. 29 March 1989. SFMNPA.

Pease, Alec A. Letter to Brian Richardson. 7 October 1988. SFMNPA.

Philip, A. J., T. F. Duff, and W. N. Pope, Medical Officers, USS *Fulton* (AS-11). Report to The Chief of the Bureau of Medicine and Surgery, "Experience of Survivors from a Sunken Japanese Transport Recovered from Life Rafts in the South China Sea, Reports Concerning." AS11/P2-5. 30 September 1944. SFMNPA.

Pickett, Harry. E-mail to *Pampanito* staff. 25 June 2003. SFMNPA.

———. E-mail to Robin Deley, 25 June 2003. SFMNPA.

———. Letter to Russell Booth. 12 January 1986. SFMNPA.

Quilty, Neryl. E-mail to *Pampanito* staff. 13 September 2003. SFMNPA.

———. Letter to Aldona Sendzikas. 21 December 2005. In author's possession.

Reich, E. T., Commanding Officer, USS *Sealion* (SS-315). Action Report: "Rescue of Allied POWs, Report of." Serial 08-44. 24 September 1944. (RG38, WWII Action and Operational Reports, Box 1424, 370/45/13/1.) NARA.

———. Report of War Patrol Number Two. SS315/A16-3/WFO, Serial (010-44). 30 September 1944. (RG38, M1752.) NARA.

Renton, K. C. Account. SFMNPA.

"The Repatriated Prisoner of War from the Medical Aspect." Appendix 'A' to LHR SM5167 of 9 June 1945, "Reception and Treatment of Australian Military, ex Prisoners of War Far East" (AWM54, 779/9/20). AWM.

Returned Servicemen's League (Victoria). Letter to D. G. Kaye. 7 April 1986. SFM-NPA.

Richardson, Brian. Letter to *Pampanito* staff. 21 November 2002. SFMNPA.

Ross, J. M. Letter to Russell Booth. No date. SFMNPA.

Scherer, Donald A., Commanding Officer, USS *Pampanito* (SS-383). Report to Office of the Secretary of the Navy, with Ship's History attached (Enclosure (A)). SS383/219. 20 October 1945. SFMNPA.

Scherer, Donald A., Richard Sherlock, and George Moffett. Oral history interview. 1993. Tape 22, 93-34-010, 011, 012. SFMNPA.

Shatford, E. J. Letters to Russell Booth. 14 December 1987 and no date. SFMNPA.

Sherlock, Richard. Oral history interviews. 7 November 2000, 8 November 2002. SF-MNPA.

Sherlock, Richard, Ted Swain, Woodrow Weaver, and Elmer Smith. Oral history interview. 1993. Tape 23, 93-34-013, 014, 015. SFMNPA.

Spinall, J. Letter to Russell Booth. 23 June 1993. SFMNPA.

"Statement of Recovered PW and Civilian Relating to His or Her Self." 'A' Interrogation No. 1, Appendix 'A' to Adv. LHQ Adm. Instruction No. 62. 21 August 1945 (AWM54, 779/9/13, Admin. Instructions Nos. 1–7). AWM.

Stimmler, Spencer. Oral history interview. 7 November 2000. SFMNPA.

Summers, Laverne. Letters to Russell Booth. 16 September 1993 and 1993. SFMNPA.

Summers, P. E., Commanding Officer, USS *Pampanito* (SS-383). Report of War Patrol Number Three. SS383/A16. 28 September 1944. SFMNPA.

———. Report to the Chief of the Bureau of Naval Personnel, "Appointment of De-mers, Maurice L., PhM1c, USN to Warrant Pharmacist—Recommendation for." SS383/P17-2, Serial (028). 6 October 1944. SFMNPA.

———. Report to the Commander Submarine Force, U.S. Pacific Fleet, "Recommendation for Awards to Certain Personnel, USS *Pampanito* (SS383), Third War Patrol." SS383/P15, Serial (029). 6 October 1944. SFMNPA.

———. Report to the Commander Submarines, U.S. Pacific Fleet, "Recommendation for Awards to Certain Personnel, USS *Pampanito* (SS383), Third War Patrol." SS383/P15, Serial (030). 6 October 1944. SFMNPA.

———. Report to the Public Relations Officer, Staff, Commander in Chief, U.S. Pacific Fleet. With attachment: "Subject: British and Australian Prisoner of War Survivors—Rescue of." Enclosure (A), SS383/A16, Serial (024). 28 September 1944. USSBSMP.

Swinburne, E. R., Commander Task Group 17.16. Coordinated Patrol Report. 4 August–3 October 1944 (RG38, 370/44/20/7, World War II Action Reports, TG 17.16, Box 98). NARA.

———, Senior Member, The Board of Awards, Submarine Force, Pacific Fleet. Report to the Commander, Submarine Force, Pacific Fleet, "Rescue Operations—Recommendation for Awards to Certain Personnel, USS *Pampanito* in connection therewith." QB/Awards, Serial 0377. 21 December 1944. SFMNPA.

Thiele, Scott. E-mail to Aldona Sendzikas. 28 May 2002. SFMNPA.

———. E-mail to Christian Bach. 20 March 2002. SFMNPA.

———. E-mail to *Pampanito*. 15 September 2003. SFMNPA.

———. E-mails to Racheal Perry. 26 June, 2 September 2003. SFMNPA.

Towers, J. H., Deputy CinCPac and CinCPOA, for Commander in Chief, U.S. Pacific Fleet. Pacific Fleet Letter No. 38L-44: "Possession of cameras and taking of photographs by Naval Personnel." CinCPac File A2-11/A7-5. 5 July 1944 (RG-181-58-3154, Box 5479, "Pacific Fleet Letters [Restricted].") National Archives and Records Administration, Pacific Sierra Region.

Tufnell, D. N. C., British Intelligence Liaison Officer, U.S. Pacific Fleet. "Rescue of Allied POW's, Report of." 3 October 1944 (AWM54, 1010/9/109). AWM.

United States Forces, India-Burma Theater. "Report of Information Obtained in Interrogation of Prisoners of War and Civilian Internees Evacuated from Camps in Southeast Asia During the Period 23 August to 15 October, 1945." (SEAC POW Report.) 20 November 1945 (RG389, Entry 460A, Box 2155). NARA.

United States Navy Department, Office of the Chief of Naval Operations, Naval History Division (OP-09B9), Ship's Histories Section. "History of Ships Named *Barb*." USSBSMP.

———. "History of Ships Named *Queenfish*." USSBSMP.

United States War Claims Commission. Circular Letter No. 72-52: "52-220: Claims Under War Claims Act of 1948." Pers-G25a-1b, L6-1. 7 May 1952 (RG38, Entry: POW-Desk, Box 31, File A27). NARA.

Wakefield, E. K., for the Commandant, Twelfth Naval District, Report to Medical Officer in Command, U.S. Naval Hospital, Brooklyn, New York. "Pharmacist Maurice L. Demers, USN—Award—Forwarding of." ND12-60-cs, (SC) P15, Serial 03257. 5 June 1945. SFMNPA.

Walker, C. F. Letter to Russell Booth. 15 June 1987. SFMNPA.

Wall, Gwen. Letter to D. G. Kaye. No date (probably 1985 or 1986). SFMNPA.

Wall, Rod. E-mail to Aldona Sendzikas. 10 May 2001. SFMNPA.

———. E-mail to *Pampanito* staff. 25 April 2001. SFMNPA.

Walters, Roger. Oral history interview. 7 November 2000. SFMNPA.

Ward, George. Account. SFMNPA.

———. "Survivors Picked Up by USS *Pampanito* Sept. 15, 1944." SFMNPA.

War Office, Imperial Prisoners of War Committee. "Summary of Action Taken in Matters Relating to Prisoners of War in September, 1944." Summary No. 40, War Office File No. 0103/3305 (RG389, Entry 452, Box 1389, File 334). NARA.

Weaver, Everett P. Letter to Robin Deley. 8 October 2003. SFMNPA.

Weaver, Woodrow. Journal. SFMNPA.

———. Letter to Aldona Sendzikas. 15 November 2002. In author's possession.

———. Oral history interview. 1996. Tape 18, 96-8MM-002. SFMNPA.

———. Oral history interviews. 8 November 2000, 8 November 2002. SFMNPA.

———. Personal account. Sent to Aldona Sendzikas with letter, 15 November 2002. SFMNPA.

Whitehead, R. I. Letters to Russell Booth. No date (received June 2002), no date. SFMNPA.

Williams, Clarence. Oral history interview. 8 November 2000. SFMNPA.

Williams, Ken. "Ken Williams POW—written in 1944 on return to Adelaide."
  SFMNPA.

———. Letters to Russell Booth. 6 February 1988 and no date. SFMNPA.

Wilson, Hugh F. Letters to Russell Booth. 13 February 1987, 24 July 1989. SFMNPA.

Winter, Helen. Letter to D. G. Kaye. 3 February 1986. SFMNPA.

Wyatt, John. Letter to SFMNPA. 14 July 2003. SFMNPA.

Yeomans, E. E. Letter to P. E. Summers. October 1944. SFMNPA.

Newspapers

Anaheim Bulletin, 11 August 1976.

Bloomington-Normal (Ill.) Pantagraph, 9 September 1984.

Hopetown Guardian, 8 December 1944.

Mackay (Queensland) Daily Mercury, 27 January 1986–1988.

Melbourne Argus, 18 November 1944–24 March 1945.

San Diego Tribune, 20 May 1968.

Sydney Morning Herald, 1 November 1944–19 June 1945.

West Australian, 18 November 1944.

Secondary Sources

American National Red Cross for the Relatives of American Prisoners of War and Civilian Internees. *Prisoners of War Bulletin* (Washington, D.C.) 1, no. 2 (July 1943), 1, no. 3 (August 1943), 1, no. 5 (October 1943), and 2, no. 2 (February 1944).

American Red Cross. "Relief to Prisoners of War: Answering Eleven Frequent Questions about Aid to War Prisoners." Washington, D.C. February 1943.

"*Barb*." *The Dictionary of American Naval Fighting Ships*, 1: 92. Washington, D.C.: Naval History Division, Department of the Navy, 1959.

Blair, Clay, Jr. *Silent Victory: The U.S. Submarine War against Japan*. Philadelphia and New York: J. B. Lippincott, 1975.

Blair, Joan, and Clay Blair Jr. *Return from the River Kwai*. New York: Simon and Schuster, 1979.

Carmody, C. Mike. "*Pampanito's* Omen." *Polaris*, June 2002, 14–15.

"*Case*." *The Dictionary of American Naval Fighting Ships*, 2: 46. Washington, D.C.: Naval History Division, Department of the Navy, 1963.

Dingman, Roger. *Ghost of War: The Sinking of the* Awa Maru *and Japanese-American Relations, 1945–1995*. Annapolis: Naval Institute Press, 1997.

Duncan, P. L., J. H. Greenwood, T. L. B. Johnson, K. G. Mosher, and S. E. J. Robertson. "Morbidity of Prisoners of War." The P.O.W. Association of Australia. June 1985.

"*Fulton*." *The Dictionary of American Naval Fighting Ships*, 2: 456–57. Washington, D.C.: Naval History Division, Department of the Navy, 1963.

"General Information about Australian Prisoners of the Japanese." Australian War Memorial Encyclopedia. http://awm.gov.au/encyclopedia/pow/general_info.htm.

Hart, Andrew W. *Connections: A Life, A Family, and Good Friends.* Lansing, Mich.: Self-published, 2003.

Holmes, Linda Goetz. *Five Thousand Bowls of Rice: A Prisoner of War Comes Home.* St. Leonards, N.S.W.: Allen and Unwin, 1993.

Kinvig, Clifford. *River Kwai Railway: The Story of the Burma-Siam Railroad.* London: Brassey's, 1992.

McCormack, Gavan, and Hank Nelson, eds. *The Burma-Thailand Railway.* Chiang Mai, Thailand: Silkworm Books, 1993.

McKernan, Michael. *This War Never Ends: The Pain and Separation of Return.* St. Lucia, Qld.: University of Queensland Press, 2001.

Michno, Gregory F. *Death on the Hellships: Prisoners at Sea in the Pacific War.* Annapolis: Naval Institute Press, 2001.

———. *USS* Pampanito: *Killer-Angel.* Norman: University of Oklahoma Press, 2000.

Nussbaum, Chaim. *Chaplain on the River Kwai: Story of a Prisoner of War.* New York: Shapolsky, 1988.

"*Pampanito.*" *The Dictionary of American Naval Fighting Ships*, 5: 206–7. Washington, D.C.: Naval History Division, Department of the Navy, 1970.

"*Pampanito's* Fiftieth Anniversary 1943–1993." *Sea Letter*, Winter 1993, 6–7.

"*Pampanito's* Tribute to *Rakuyo Maru* Survivor, Frank Farmer." *Vetaffairs*, October 1996, 6.

Peacock, Basil. *Prisoner on the Kwai.* Edinburgh and London: William Blackwood and Sons, 1966.

Peters, Betty. "The Life Experiences of Partners of ex-POWs of the Japanese." *Journal of the Australian War Memorial* 28. April 1996. http://www.awm.gov.au/journal/j28/j28-petr.htm.

"*Queenfish.*" *The Dictionary of American Naval Fighting Ships*, 5: 412–13. Washington, D.C.: Naval History Division, Department of the Navy, 1970.

"The Sandakan Underground." *Borehole Bulletin*, January 1984, 13–15.

"*Sealion.*" *The Dictionary of American Naval Fighting Ships*, 6: 416–18. Washington, D.C.: Naval History Division, Department of the Navy, 1976.

"Submarines to the Rescue." *White Ensign* 42, no. 4 (Summer 1988): 39.

"Thailand Report." *Borehole Bulletin*, October 1985, 12–15.

Tuohy, William. *The Bravest Man: The Story of Richard O'Kane and U.S. Submarines in the Pacific War.* Phoenix Mill, U.K.: Sutton, 2001.

Wall, Don. *Heroes at Sea.* Mona Vale, N.S.W.: Self-published, 1991.

Index

Adelaide, South Australia, 68

AIF. *See* Australian Defence Force

Alcoa Polaris, 177–78

Anderson, C. (Andy), 39, 41–42, 46, 51, 67

Arcement, Norman (Norm), 206

Australian Consulate General, San Francisco, 207

Australian Defence Force, 211

Australian Imperial Force (AIF), 43, 225n1; "A" Force, 43; Anderson Force, 44, 78; 8th Division, 34, 188, 225n1; Green Force, 44; Java Force, 44; Ramsay Force, 44

Balao class, x, 17

Balintang Channel, 122, 143–44

Bangkok, Thailand, 47, 48, 71, 73, 76

Barb (SS-220), 7, 30; arrives at Saipan, 156–57, 169; departs Saipan, 169; rendezvous with *Case*, 154, 156; rescue of POWs, 125–29, 151; sighted by POWs, 125; after WW II, 200–201

—POWs on board: cleaning of, 154–55; clothing provided to, 155; diseases found in, 154–55; feeding of, 155; sleeping arrangements of, 154

Barker, H. J., 36–38, 40

Baron, Leonard, 147

Bartholomew, Charles, 139, 140

"Base camps," 50

Battle flag, *Pampanito. See under Pampanito*

Battle of the Bismarck Sea, The, 181

Bennett, Gordon, 188

Bennett, Robert (Bob), 6, 20–21, 115, 141, 144; after WW II, 204, 209

"Ben's Busters," 1–2, 29–32, 83

Blair, Clay, Jr., 223n1

Blair, Joan, 223n1

Blamey, Thomas, 182

Booth, Russell, 206–7

Boulle, Pierre, 223n1

Boulter, James, 194–95

Bourgeois, Roger, 147

Bridge on the River Kwai, The (film), 223n1

Brisbane, Queensland, 179, 180

Brisbane (D-41), 204

Brisbane River, 179

Brown, Duncan, 21, 23, 25

Brown, Hubert, 60, 130, 134, 136, 172, 221

Bukit Tinah Road, Singapore, 37–38, 43

Bullock, Reg, 73, 113–14, 145, 159, 195, *208*

Burma-Thai Railroad, 82, 191; Allied bombing of, 71, 74, 191; completion of, 71; construction of, xv, 5, 48, 51, 52–53, 155; death toll, 49; decision to build, 47–48; route, 47–48; time schedule for construction, 49; transportation of POWs to site, 43–45
Burridge, Raymond (Ray), 50, 85–86, 88–90

Campbell, James, 91, 100, 101, 105, 108, 124–25, 176
Campbell, John (Jock), 143–44
Cape Douglas, 177
Carmody, C. Mike, 144
Caroline Islands, 177
Case (DD-370), 147, 149, 151, 153–54
Changi POW camp, 41; conditions at, 41; labor assigned to POWs at, 42; morale of POWs at, 42; pay for POWs at, 42; rations provided to POWs at, 41–42; recreation for POWs, 42; rumors circulating at, 42–43
Chappell, L. H., 172
Chicago, Ill., 177
Chivers, Harry, 70, 76, 113, 147
Clifton, Ralph, 82, 92–93, 95–96, 98
Cocking, Alfred John (Jack), 174, 204
Cocking, Ron, 204–5, *205*
Collins, Robert, 212
COMSUBPAC. *See* Lockwood, Charles A., Jr.
Conger (SS-477), 232n15
"Convoy College," 29
Coombes, Frank, 189
Cornford, Roy: aboard *Pampanito*, 115, 118–19, 133, 145; aboard *Rakuyo Maru*, 74, 77, 78, 81–82, 83–84, 88, 90; on Saipan, 148, 176–77; in South China Sea, 100, 101, 106, 108; after WW II, 197, 204, 208–9, *210*
Costello, Stanley, 55

Cray, Bill, 204
Cresswale, Douglas, 143
Cunneen, Donald William (Bill), 34, 60, 65, 146, 147
Curran, Max, 86, 88
Curtin, John, 186–87

Darwin, Northern Territory, 68; Japanese bombing of, 40
Davis, Jeff, 174
Davis, Landon L., 166
Daws, Gavan, 238n10
Death on the Hellships (Michno), 238n5
Deguarra, Michael, 91, 112–13
Demers, Kevin, 209–10
Demers, Lawrence (Larry), 139, 209–10, 221
Demers, Maurice ("Doc"), 5–6, 161, 174, 221; diary, 138; and POWs aboard sub, 130–31, 132, 134, 136–144, 149, 159–160, *163*; promoted to warrant pharmacist, 162–64; receives Navy and Marine Corps Medal, 164; transfers aboard *Pampanito*, 28; after WW II, 209, 211, 232n15
Diseases diagnosed in rescued POWs, 170, 181
Dixon, Harold, 151–53
Donnelly, William, 154–55
Dykers, Thomas M. (Tommy), 138, 221, 232n14. See also *Silent Service, The*

"Ed's Eradicators," 30
8th Division, Australian. *See under* Australian Imperial Force
18th Division, 36
Eniwetok (Marshall Islands), 178

Far East POW Association, 207
Farlow, Cliff, 64
Farmer, Frank, 5, *35*, 66, 92, 99, 103, 109–10, *162*, *183*, 189; telegrams, annual, 207, 210;

after WW II, 202–3, 204, 206–7, *208*, 209–10

Farmer, Mary, 66, 211

Farmer, Tim, 202–3, 206

Fenno, Frank W., Jr. (Mike), 24, 174

Fives, Frank, 2, 166, 220

Flinn, David, 147

Flynn, Jack, 171

Fluckey, Eugene B., 125–29, 156–57, 219

Forde, Francis, 185–86, 187–88, 190

Formosa Straits, 78

4th Royal Norfolk Regiment, 36

Fremantle, Western Australia, 34, 173–75, 206

Fulton, Howard, 30, 167

Fulton (AS-11), 148, 151, 156, 158, 159, 160

Gainger, Ray, 206

Gato class, 17

Geneva Convention, 42, 54–55, 57, 61, 218, 226n13

Gloucester, Duke of, 192

Goodman, Jack, 95

Gordon Highlanders' Regiment, 143

Grady, William, 19, 21

Granum, Peder, 141

Great Lakes, Ill., 20

Greene, John H. (Johnny), 132, 146

Grommet, Clifford, 167

Growler (SS-315), x, 1, 10–13, 29, 31; attack on HI-72, 83

Guadalcanal, 177, 178, 179

Guam, 24, 177

Guavina (SS-362), 175

Hague Convention, 226n13

Hainan, 2, 14, 29, 138, 173

Hart, Andrew, 169–70

Hart, Reginald, 170

Hauptman, Betty, 205–6

Hauptman, Tony, 4, 7, 23, 31, 167, 174, 218; after WW II, 205–6

Hawke, Bob, 211

Hellships, 73, 155; bodies, disposal of on board, 82; conditions on board, 44, 79, 82; deaths on board, 82; guards on board, 81; illnesses on board, 81, 82; morale of POWs on board, 82; rations for POWs on board, 44, 81, 82; regulations regarding behavior of POWs on board, 81; toilet facilities on board, 80–81

HI-72 (convoy): attacked by wolf pack, 1–2, 11, *12–13*, 31–32, 83, 92, 125, 214, 238n5; departs Singapore, 31, 77–78; POWs loaded aboard, 77–78; underway, 81; wreckage of, 127

Hirado, 1–2

Hocking, John, 43, 45, 64

Honshū, 26

Hopetown, Victoria, 34, 65, 189

Hopper, Gordon, xiii, 19, 20, 21, 22, 24–25, 198, 199; in Fremantle, 173, 174; and rescue of POWs, 4, 6, 145, 214, 218, 220, 221; after WW II, 201, 209, 210

Hosoya, Suke-Hiko, 203

Hospitals, POW camp, 50, 63; medical supplies available at, 63–64

Huckins, John, 82, 93–94, 97, 98, 100, 104

Hunter, Norman, 123

Hunter's Point, Calif., 175, 198, 200

Ingleburn Military Camp, 192–93

Intelligence collected from rescued POWs, 178, 181–82, 190–91

Intelligence Liaison Officer, British. *See* Tufnell, D.N.C.

Jackson, Charles B., Jr., 19, 23

JANAC. *See* Joint Army-Navy Assessment Committee

Japan, invasion of, 198–99
"Japan Force," 73
Jesse, Frank, 196–97
Jesse, Pam, 197
Johnson, McMillan, 8
Joint Army-Navy Assessment Committee
    (JANAC), 223n1

Kachidoki Maru, 77, 78, 83, 186, 215, 228n6;
    Allied survivors of, 104; conditions
    on board, 79–80, 82–83; recreation on
    board, 83; sinking of, x, 2, 32, 92–95, 203
Kanchanaburi POW camp, 45, 50, 72, 89;
    conditions in, 45–46
Kawasaki, 230n6
Kearney, Laurie, 150
Kokoda Trail, 181
Korea, 226n8
Kwai River, 54. *See also Bridge on the River
    Kwai, The*
Kwai Valley, 53
Kyūshū, Japan, 26

Leonard Wood (AP-25), 36
Linnane, Pat, 106
Lockwood, Charles A., Jr., 10, 32, 163–64,
    200, 214, 237n3
Longey, Claude, 112, 206
Loughlin, Charles E., 152, 153
Luzon, Philippines, 125

Madison, Walter, 174
Majuro, Marshall Islands, 169
Malaya, 34, 35, 45, 48, 182, 191, 194, 225n1;
    fall of, 36
Mandley, W.A.W. (William), 80, 90–91,
    106, 119
Mare Island, Calif., 200
Marianas Islands, 24, 147
Martin, Harold (Curly), 99, 103, 109–10,
    183; aboard *Pampanito*, 145

Massey, Norman, 83, 93
Mawby, Raymond, 196
McArdle, Don, 107–8, 110–11, 196
McGuire, Charles (Charlie), 145
McKittrick, Sybil, 197, 201–2, 210
McKittrick, William (Bill, Mac), xiii, 77,
    189; on Guadalcanal, 178; at Ingle-
    burn, 193–94; meets Sybil, 197; aboard
    Monadnock, 179; aboard *Pampanito*,
    118–19, 145; aboard *Rakuyo Maru*, 78,
    79, 80, 86, 88; on Saipan, 158–59; in
    South China Sea, 102, 103–4, 109, 114;
    at Stuartholme, 184; after WW II, 197,
    201–2, 208–10, 212
Melbourne, Victoria, 34, 191, 192, 219
Michno, Greg, 223n1, 238n5
Midway Island, 1, 26–28, 29; Battle of, 47
"Mobile camps," 49–50; conditions in, 50
Moffett, George, 166
Moji, 230n6
Monadnock (CM-9), 179, *180*
Moulmein, Burma, 44, 48, 66
Mount Vernon (AP-22), 36

Nagatoma, Lieutenant Colonel, 51
National Maritime Museum Association.
    See San Francisco Maritime National
    Park Association
Natives: interactions with POWs, 59, 61,
    227n19; as laborers on Burma-Thai
    Railroad, 48; as laborers at Singapore
    Harbor, 77
New Farm Wharf, Brisbane, 179–80
New London, Conn., 20–21, 28
New York City, 177
Nimitz, Chester W., 164

Oakley, T. B. (Ben), 29
Ocean Beach Hotel, Western Australia, 173
Officers' camp, 50
Okinawa, 198

105-Kilo Camp, 65, 68
Orser, Lynn, 174

Pampanito (SS-383), *25*; arrives at Saipan,
    148–49, 158–59; attack on HI-72, 1–2,
    11, *12–13*, 31–32, 83, 92, 125, 214, 238n5;
    battle flag, xv–*xvi*; commissioning of,
    19–20; conditions on board, 17–18,
    20–21; conversion to radar picket, 199;
    departs Saipan, 161, 172; depth charged,
    1, 11, 19, 23, 24–25, 29, 32; history of,
    x–xi; launching of, 17; museum, xiii–
    xiv, xvi, 200–203, 207–9, 212, 213, 215;
    overhaul at Hunter's Point, 198; rafts,
    sighting of, 2–4, 8–9, *12–13*, 14–15, *111*;
    rendezvous with *Case*, 147–48; rescue
    of POWs, 5–10, *12–13*, 15, 59, 109–20,
    116, *117*, *118*, *120*, *121*, *122*, *130*, *131*; rest
    and recreation, crew, 19, 27–28, 172,
    173–75; reunions, crew, 201, 218, *210*,
    221; sighted by POWs, 109–10, 112–14,
    124; wolf pack with *Growler* and *Sealion*,
    1–2, *12–13*, 29–32, 83; after WW II, 200,
    201–3
—POWs on board, 55, 60, 61, 64, 70,
    79, *142*, *160*, *161*, *162*, *163*, *164*, *165*, *166*;
    cleaning of, 130, 132, 139–40; cloth-
    ing provided to, 140, 183–84; death of
    John Campbell, 143–44; diseases found
    in, 132–34, 136–38; feeding of, 136, 141,
    142–43; sleeping arrangements of, 132–33,
    134, *135*
—war patrols: first patrol, 24–26; second
    patrol, 26–27; third patrol, 1–15; fourth
    patrol, 173; fifth patrol, 175; sixth patrol,
    175
"*Pampanito* Story, The." See *Silent Service,
    The*
Panama, 17, 21–22, 23
Pappas, Paul, 22, 115–16, 117, 118, 144, 159;
    after WW II, 209

Parche (SS-384), 19
Peacock, Basil, 53–54, 227n19
Pearl Harbor, xi, 10, 21, 149, 151, 162, 170,
    173, 175, 198–99, 215, 222; attack on, 34;
    POWs transported to, 177; submarine
    base, 23, 24, 26, 172, 199
Pearson, Jack, 124
Perry, Charles, 146
Perth, Western Australia, 173, 201
Pharmacist's mate, *Barb*. See Donnelly,
    William
Pharmacist's mate, *Pampanito*. See Demers,
    Maurice
Pharmacist's mate, *Queenfish*. See Dixon,
    Harold
Pharmacist's mate, *Sealion*. See Williams, P. J.
Pharmacist's mates, 160–61
Phnom Penh, Cambodia, 73
Pickett, Harry, 206
Picuda (SS-382), 17
Plunger (SS-179), 19
Portsmouth, New Hampshire, x, 16, 17,
    19–21
POW camps, 44; "Blitz Parades" in, 57;
    bodies, disposal of in, 64, 70; holidays,
    celebration of in, 67, 72; death rate
    in, 64; drinking water in, 60; escape
    attempts from, 57–59; guards in, 51–52,
    65, 67; illnesses at, 50–51, 55–57, 62–63,
    64, 69, 70; living and working condi-
    tions in, 52, 55–56, 62, 65; mail allowed
    in, 65–66, 67, 188; monsoon season in,
    69–70; morale of POWs in, 65, 67, 72;
    pay for POWs in, 61; rations provided to
    POWs in, 51, 55, 59–61, 69–70, 72; rec-
    reation for POWs in, 55, 66–67; rumors
    circulating in, 68 52, 65. See also Changi;
    Kanchanaburi; Moji; 105-Kilo Camp;
    River Valley; Saigon; Sakata; Singapore;
    Thanbyuzayat; Wampo
P.O.W. (journal), 188

POW officers, 58, 61, 68; on board hell-ships, 81, 87, 95; medical officers among, 63; work assigned to in camps, 57

POWs: deaths of aboard submarines, 122–23, 129, 143–44, 150, 152–53, 235n13; Japanese, 238n10; leave granted, 190; aboard *Monadnock, 180*; rescued by *Barb*, 125–29, 151; rescued by Japanese ships, 98, 187, 217, 230n6; rescued by *Pampanito*, 5–10, *12–13*, 15, 59, 109–20, *116, 117, 118, 120, 121,* 122, 130, *131*; rescued by *Queen-fish*, 123–24, 128, 151; rescued by *Sealion*, 120–23; reunions with rescuers, 204–10; trade with natives, 227n19; transferred aboard *Fulton, 167, 168*;

President Harrison. See *Kachidoki Maru*

Prisoner of war camps. *See* POW camps

Prisoners of war. *See* POWs

Prisoners of War Relatives Association, 188, 189; meeting of, 190

Propaganda, Japanese, 68–69, 71

Proteus (AS-19), 26, 28

Queenfish (SS-393), 7, 30, 125, 126; arrives at Saipan, 156, 169; departs Saipan, 169; rendezvous with *Case*, 153, 156; rescue of POWs, 123–24, 128, 151; sighted by POWs, 123; after WW II, 201

—POWs on board, 124, 128; cleaning of, 153; clothing provided to, 153; deaths, 129, 152–53; diseases found in, 152; feeding of, 153; sleeping arrangements of, 152

Queen Mary, 177

R-10 (SS-87), 19

"Railway of Death." *See* Burma-Thai Railroad

Rakuyo Maru, 5, 73, 77, 186, 215; Allied survivors of, 43, 44, 52, 96, 97, 176, 190, 212; conditions on board, 79–81; rations for POWs on board, 80; sinking of, 85–91, 101, 146

Ramage, Lawson P. (Red), 19

Rangoon, Burma, 47

Red Cross, 178, 182, 192, 226n13; parcels for POWs, 42, 65, 188; symbol, 78, 215

Reich, E. T., 151, 238n5

Renton, K. C., xix, 61, 70, 72, 75, 112, 219

"Rest camps," 50

Return to the River Kwai (Blair), 223n1

Reunions, *Pampanito* crew. *See under Pampanito*

Reunions, POWs with rescuers. *See under* POWs

River Valley POW camp, 43, 73

Royal Hawaiian Hotel, Waikiki, 26, 172

Rutter, David C., 212

S-16 (SS-121), 17

Saigon, Vietnam, 73, 74, 89; living conditions for POWs at, 75

Saipan, xi, 10, 15, 24, 29, 122-23, 129, 132, 140, 141, 157, 176–77, 191; POWs arrive at, 148–49, 151, 154, 156, 160, 169; Tanapag Harbor, 148, 151, 156–57; U.S. Army 148th General Hospital, 151, 154, 161, 169–71, 176

Sakata, 230n6

San Diego, Calif., 204

San Francisco, Calif., xiii, 68, 177, 198, 199–200, 202, 207, 211

San Francisco Maritime National Park Association, 200, 211–12

Scherer, Donald A., 175, 198, 199

Sealion (SS-215), x, 1–2, 5, 7, 9, 10–15, 28, 29, 31, 172, 203, 212; arrives at Saipan, 149, 151, 160; attack on HI-72, 83, 125, 238n5; rendezvous with *Case*, 147; rescue of POWs, 120–23; sighted by POWs, 122–23; after WW II, 201

—POWs on board: cleaning of, 149–50; clothing provided to, 150–51; deaths, 122–23, 150; diseases found in, 150; feeding of, 150

Sharks, 7, 108–9

Sherlock, Richard, 2, 8, 9, 10, 130, 218, 221, 222

Shikoku, 26

Siam, Gulf of, 175

Silent Service, The, 138, 232n14, 232n15. *See also* Dykers, Thomas M.

Singapore, 31, 34–36, 41, 43, 47, 73, 93, 188, 225n1; fall of, xv, 5, 34, 36–40, 155, 187, 212; harbor, 77; Japanese guards at, 76–77; Korean guards at, 78; living conditions of POWs in, 76; transport of POWs from Saigon to, 75–76

Smith, Clarence, 167

Smith, Pat, 193

Smith, Sydney, 188

Smith, W. G., 87, 101, 123–24, 153

Softball games, crew. *See under Pampanito*: rest and recreation, crew

South China Sea, 2, 83, 96, 97, 98, 101, 108, 125, 151, 173, 183, 204, 214, 220, 221

Spearfish (SS-190), 19

Stantke, Victor, 182

Stark, Edith Monk, 178

Stewart, Reginald (Reg), 34

Stimmler, Spencer (Spence), 132, 136

Stingray (SS-186), 20

Stockslader, E. W., 30

Stuartholme convent, 180–84

Subic Bay, Philippines, 175

Submarine Combat Insignia awarded to *Pampanito* crew, 172, 200

Submarine Division 202, 28

Submarine Division 281, 172

Summers, Paul E. ("Pete"), 2–10, 20, 22, 25, 29–32, 92, 115–16, 118, 211, 214, 218, 220, 222, 238n5; assumes duties as skipper, 23–24, 174; on death of John Campbell, 143; on Demers, 136, 161–63; and POWs, 132, 137, 139, 140, 145, 148, 158; promotion and award recommendations for crew, 162–69; replaced by Mike Fenno, 172–73; replaced by Donald Scherer, 175; Stuartholme, visit to, 184; track chart narrative, third patrol, 11–15; after WW II, 207

Swain, T. N. (Ted), 139, 140, 168

Swinburne, Edwin (Ed), 30, 126, 156–57

Switzerland, 187

Sydney, New South Wales, 68, 190, 192; Japanese midget submarine attack on, 57

Tanapag Harbor. *See under* Saipan

Tanglin barracks, Singapore, 39

Task Group 17.6, 125, 126

Tavoy, Burma, 44

Taylor, Thomas, 147

Thanbyuzayat, Burma, 44–45, 48, 49, 50

Thiele, Scott, 212

Times (London), 187

Trout (SS-202), 173

Tufnell, D.N.C., 170–71

Tunny (SS-282), 125

U-boat, German, 9, 28, 77, 110, 214

Unrestricted submarine warfare (USW), 237n3

U.S. Army 148th General Hospital. *See under* Saipan

U.S. Naval Hospital, Brooklyn, 164

USS Pampanito: *Killer-Angel* (Michno), 223n1, 238n5

USW. *See* unrestricted submarine warfare

V-J Day, 199

Varley, Arthur L., 43

Volleyball games, crew. *See under Pampanito*: rest and recreation, crew

Wahoo (SS-238), 238n4
Wakefield (AP-21), 36
Waldo, Paul, 148
Wall, Robert John (Jack), 34–36, 65, 81, 88, 189
Walters, Roger, 17–18
Wampo, Thailand, 46, 50–51
War and Remembrance (Wouk), 215
Ward, George, 43, 60, 61, 66, 78–79, 101
Weaver, Woodrow, 18, 21, 27–28, 29, 199; and POWs, xviii, 61, 72, 131–32, 133, 137; after WW II, 204–5, 216, *205*
West Point (AP-23), 36, 39

Wilcox, Lynn, 148
Wiles, F. E., 147
Williams, Clarence, 7–8
Williams, Ken, 102–3, 110, *183*; after WW II, 206, 212
Williams, P. J., 149–50
Wilson, Leslie, 182
Wilson, Winifred (Lady Wilson), 182
Winds of War, The (Wouk) 215
Wouk, Herman, 215

Yap Island, 24
Ye, Burma, 48

Zuiho Maru, x

Aldona Sendzikas is an associate professor at the University of Western Ontario in London, Canada, where she teaches U.S. and military history, American studies, and museum studies. She is also the former curator and education manager for the restored World War II submarine USS *Pampanito* in San Francisco.